Advanced Introduction to International Humanitarian Law

Elgar Advanced Introductions are stimulating and thoughtful introductions to major fields in the social sciences and law, expertly written by the world's leading scholars. Designed to be accessible yet rigorous, they offer concise and lucid surveys of the substantive and policy issues associated with discrete subject areas.

The aims of the series are two-fold: to pinpoint essential principles of a particular field, and to offer insights that stimulate critical thinking. By distilling the vast and often technical corpus of information on the subject into a concise and meaningful form, the books serve as accessible introductions for undergraduate and graduate students coming to the subject for the first time. Importantly, they also develop well-informed, nuanced critiques of the field that will challenge and extend the understanding of advanced students, scholars and policy-makers.

Titles in the series include:

International Political Economy
Benjamin J. Cohen

The Austrian School of Economics
Randall G. Holcombe

Cultural Economics
Ruth Towse

Law and Development
Michael J. Trebilcock and Mariana Mota Prado

International Humanitarian Law
Robert Kolb

International Conflict and Security Law
Nigel D. White

Comparative Constitutional Law
Mark Tushnet

International Human Rights Law
Dinah L. Shelton

Entrepreneurship
Robert D. Hisrich

Advanced Introduction to

International Humanitarian Law

ROBERT KOLB

*Professor of Public International Law,
University of Geneva, Switzerland*

Elgar Advanced Introductions

Edward Elgar
Cheltenham, UK • Northampton, MA, USA

Published by
Edward Elgar Publishing Limited
The Lypiatts
15 Lansdown Road
Cheltenham
Glos GL50 2JA
UK

Edward Elgar Publishing, Inc.
William Pratt House
9 Dewey Court
Northampton
Massachusetts 01060
USA

A catalogue record for this book
is available from the British Library

Library of Congress Control Number: 2014947022

ISBN 978 1 78347 751 7 (cased)
ISBN 978 1 78347 753 1 (paperback)
ISBN 978 1 78347 752 4 (eBook)

Typeset by Servis Filmsetting Ltd, Stockport, Cheshire

Contents

Preface   viii
Abbreviations   x

**1 The main epochs of modern international humanitarian law
    and their related legal constructions**   1
    1.1 Purpose of the chapter   1
    1.2 Two phases of development   1
    1.3 Classical international humanitarian law, 1864–1949   2
    1.4 Modern international humanitarian law
         (1949–present)   12
    1.5 Reasons for the Additional Protocols of 1977   15
    1.6 International humanitarian law: a system attributive of
         powers or a system prohibitive of action?   17

**2 International armed conflict and non-international armed
    conflict**   22
    2.1 Basic types of armed conflict   22
    2.2 Classical laws of war   23
    2.3 Reasons for regulating non-international armed
         conflicts   26
    2.4 The general state of international humanitarian law
         relating to non-international armed conflict   28
    2.5 Content of international humanitarian law applicable to
         non-international armed conflict   33

**3 The sources of international humanitarian law and their
    subject matter specificity**   49
    3.1 Definition of the term "sources"   49
    3.2 The significance of treaties in international
         humanitarian law   49
    3.3 Important treaties of international humanitarian law   54
    3.4 The importance of customary international law   65

3.5 The content of customary international law with regard
to international humanitarian law   70

4 The main principles of international humanitarian law   **75**
4.1 The role of general principles in international law   75
4.2 The role of general principles of law in international
humanitarian law   76
4.3 Examples of general principles of law in international
humanitarian law   78

5 Applicability issues: finding a way out of the quagmire   **93**
5.1 The problem stated   93
5.2 The material applicability of international armed
conflict   94
5.3 The material applicability of non-international armed
conflict   104
5.4 Mixed armed conflicts   116
5.5 The way out of the quagmire   120

6 Combatants and civilians: a sometimes difficult divide   **124**
6.1 General aspects   124
6.2 Who enjoys the privilege/status of the combatant?   126
6.3 The reform through Additional Protocol I   134
6.4 Civilians directly participating in hostilities   142
6.5 International humanitarian law, "War on Terror" and
drones   147

7 Targeting: a context-related legal set of rules   **156**
7.1 The prohibition of attack on civilian objects   156
7.2 Precautions in attack: article 57 of AP I   165
7.3 Proportionality   172
7.4 Excursus: bombardments for humanitarian reasons
and article 52, § 2, of AP I   176

**8 Implementation of international humanitarian law: the
Achilles heel of the system**   **187**
8.1 General features of the implementation system   187
8.2 Prevention   189
8.3 Control   190
8.4 Suppression   194
8.5 Possible reforms   196

9 Conclusion: the challenges ahead **198**

Select bibliography 200
Index 203

Preface

When I was proposed to write this small book by Edward Elgar Publishing, I hesitated for a long time. I considered that having already written two manuals on international humanitarian law (IHL), one in French the other in English, there was hardly space, before significant further time elapsed, to write a third one without repeating myself. However, the friendly personnel of Elgar discreetly but firmly insisted on their proposal, and I finally reflected afresh on it. The solution I found was to write a piece covering new ground, under the quadruple flag to be mentioned in the next paragraph.

This book aims at providing an advanced, challenging, short and selective introduction to IHL. The word "advanced" is meant to connote the idea that the reader has acquired basic knowledge of the subject matter elsewhere and can now focus on specific aspects of this branch of the law. The word "challenging" is intended to convey the idea of an exploration, including difficult, controversial and sometimes unusual questions, as part and parcel of the following pages. Conversely, I will refrain from covering basic knowledge on IHL and will replace it by dwelling on some questions not devoid of arduousness. The reader who feels the necessity to refresh basic notions of IHL could do so with another introductory book of the present author, namely R. Kolb and R. Hyde, *An Introduction to the International Law of Armed Conflicts* (Oxford/Portland, 2008). I must stress again: this is not an introduction for the beginner in the field of IHL. The present book will also be "short". The intention is to remain within the compass of 150 manuscript pages. Reducing, manifold and sometimes difficult sets of facts and norms in scope and complexion, is a rewarding enterprise. It forces the writer to go to the essence of things and to propose fresh perspectives on the subject matter. Indeed, the present author, while writing these introductory lines, does not yet know exactly what will be the content of the different chapters outlined above. The present book also does not purport to cover all the areas comprising the branch of IHL, but rather to shed light on certain crucial aspects for its proper functioning. In this sense, it is not only concise but also selective. The discussion is a web exposing the law as it stands, through its written and unwritten rules, and also the uncertainties, gaps, controversies and practical problems which have arisen in all those crucial aspects. This double approach allows us to seize IHL as a living tool, as an ever-adapting means to an ever-remaining need for protection during times of armed conflict.

Abbreviations

AJIL	American Journal of International Law
BYIL	British Yearbook of International Law
CIL	customary international law
DPH	direct participation in hostilities
ECHR	European Convention on Human Rights
ECtHR	European Court of Human Rights
EJIL	European Journal of International Law
GPL	general principles of law
GYIL	German Yearbook of International Law
HRL	human rights law
IAC	international armed conflict
ICC	International Criminal Court
ICJ	International Court of Justice
ICRC	International Committee of the Red Cross
ICTR	International Criminal Tribunal for Rwanda
ICTY	International Criminal Tribunal for the former Yugoslavia
IDT	internal disturbances and tensions
IHL	international humanitarian law
ILC	International Law Commission
ILM	International Legal Materials
ILR	International Law Reports
NGOs	non-governmental organizations
NIAC	non-international armed conflict
PCA	Permanent Court of Arbitration
PCIJ	Permanent Court of International Justice
RCADI	Recueil des cours de l'Académie de droit international de La Haye, Hague Recueil
RGDIP	Revue générale de droit international public
RIAA	Reports on International Arbitral Awards
RICR	Revue internationale de la Croix Rouge
ROE	Rules of Engagement
RSDIE	Revue suisse de droit international et européen
UN	United Nations

UNGA   United Nations General Assembly
UNSC   UN Security Council
US   United States

1 The main epochs of modern international humanitarian law and their related legal constructions[1]

1.1 Purpose of the chapter

The purpose of this chapter is to provide the reader with a sense and feeling for the social and legal environment in which international humanitarian law (IHL) has unfolded since the time of the first Geneva Convention of 1864. This date opens the era of IHL studied today, as opposed to historical studies on the laws of war in antiquity, in the Middle Ages or in other than European cultures of the past. It is trite knowledge that no legal norm operates aloof from and in isolation of a certain social setting, a dominant ideological outlook and a certain way of considering the law itself. All these factors constitute an environment into which the law is cast. This environment does not represent the law; it is at best a material source aiding in its understanding. As such, it may be a good starting point for our exploration, since it will indicate to us what were the pivotal points of IHL during the last one and a half centuries, how these pillars have evolved and also why they have changed.

1.2 Two phases of development

In a very rough categorization, there are two main phases in the development of modern IHL. First, the phase spanning 1864 to 1949, which can be called the phase of classical IHL, or better the laws of war; second, the phase from 1949 to today, which can be called

---

1 See also R. Kolb, "The Main Epochs of Modern International Humanitarian Law since 1864 and their Related Dominant Legal Constructions", in K. Mujezinovic-Larsen, C. Guldahl Cooper and G. Nystuen (eds), *Searching for a "Principle of Humanity" in International Law*, Cambridge, 2013, pp. 23ff.

the phase of modern IHL.[2] Each of these bodies of law has its own characteristics and functioned in a system with its own coordinates. The reasons for the demise of the classical system and the passage to the modern are linked to the concomitant passage of so-called classical international law to so-called modern international law. The change was essentially due to the experience of inhumanity and utter persecution by the totalitarian regimes before and during World War II. It was therefore felt that a tighter law, centred on the protection of the human person, should replace the old law, centred on military purposes and largely based on powers and competencies given to the belligerents.

1.3 Classical international humanitarian law, 1864–1949

Classical IHL (or better "laws of war", since the humanitarian side of the law was mainly stressed after 1949) was based on certain assumptions. We will review them in the following lines. Before doing that, it may be advisable to recall that the features to be mentioned do not exclude the presence of contravening trends and realities. Thus, if stress is laid on the "military" focus of classical laws of war, this by no means pretends to exclude a humanitarian interest in some of its norms, as shown by the first Geneva Convention of 1864, the Convention on Hospital Ships of 1904, the revised Geneva Convention for the Injured or Sick Military Personnel of 1906 or the two Geneva Conventions of 1929 on the Injured or Sick Military Personnel and on Prisoners of War. Some military focus is still inherent in those very "humanitarian" conventions, since it will have been noted that the humanitarianism only extends to military personnel. There is no Geneva Convention for the protection of civilians at that time. But there remains the basic fact that these conventions are essentially of a humanitarian nature, even while militarily coloured. In addition, even in the core military law, in other words, the so-called Hague Law on means and methods of warfare, a humanitarian note is manifest. If, for example, the law prohibits the use of expanding or exploding bullets, or generally of weapons causing "unnecessary suffering", the aim of such provisions is to protect the military personnel from certain

---

2 This echoes the distinction between classical and modern international law, the shifting points in the latter context being 1919 and 1945, with the League of Nations and later the UN. See W. Friedmann, *The Changing Structure of International Law*, London, 1964.

evils. It can hardly be said that the reason for the law is other than humanitarian. In short, the law of armed conflicts has to do with the smoothing of the harsh consequences of warfare; and this smoothing always has a humanitarian side, since it will result in a limitation of destruction and suffering. But there remain different layers and parameters in humanitarianism. It can have a more indirect or a more dominating presence; it can be the main reference point of the system or appear only incidentally as the ultimate aim of the rules; it can be an implicit rule or a directly applicable principle of the law. Bearing this in mind, we may now review the pivotal aspects of the classical law.

1.3.1   Military character of the classical law

The classical laws of war focused on the military branch, in other words, on the rights and duties of the military personnel during warfare. It was thus at that time mainly "Hague Law", in other words, law related to the means and methods of warfare. Hence, the law developed questions such as prohibited weapons, prohibited methods (such as perfidy or treacherous killing, misuse of protective emblems, and so on), belligerent reprisals or administrative duties of the occupying power in the occupied territory. Even the humanitarian rules were seen under the lens of subjective rights and duties closely linked to the battlefield. Thus, for example, under certain factual conditions, the combatants had to search for the injured and sick, and to secure care for them by handing them over to sanitary services of the army (see, for example, article 6 of the 1864 Convention); there was consequently a subjective duty on each belligerent to possess such sanitary services and organize them in advance, and so on. While the civilian was largely ignored by the system of the laws of war, the military bend of the law would remain dominant. The foregoing also means that the laws of war were at that time mainly the law of the military branch. They did not have the broad reach they have today, where they feature prominently even in the mass media. They were mainly laws for a professional branch, and they remained largely confined to that branch and to some specialized lawyers.

1.3.2   Incomplete character of the classical law

Classical laws of war were replete with gaps. The regulation was minimal, and concomitantly the sovereignty of the belligerents was largely preserved. In the nineteenth century, and still at the beginning of the twentieth century, which was the heyday of the sovereign State and of its independence,[3] it was considered that only the most necessary limitations on warfare could be imposed on States and would be acceptable to them. In the case of war, supreme State interests of survival were at stake. It was therefore considered impossible and useless to try to impose a series of tight and precise rules: supreme necessity may know laws, but these must be flexible and reduced to a minimum. There was, moreover, another layer of thought contributing to this same minimizing result: civilizational optimism. The conception was that it sufficed to pose the main principles in the international conventions, and that the States would spontaneously carry out these obligations and codify the details in their internal law. The argument was that lengthy and detailed international conventions were of no avail and had no usefulness.[4] Either the States were ill-disposed, in which case they would flout the rules, be they detailed or non-detailed; or else the States were well-disposed, in which case a short text stating the essence was much more useful than a complex one that was difficult to understand and intelligible only to specialized lawyers. However, the results of this reasoning are to some extent odd. The short and sketchy rules in the Hague Regulations of 1907 (the main applicable convention in World War I) left glaring uncertainties and problems of interpretation. Thus, even good-willed States and their military branches faced objective problems of understanding and lack of authoritative guidance. The result was that they understandably interpreted the absence of constraining rules as a licence to act according to their own interests of the moment. This fact backfired on the laws of war. An example of this shortcoming can be found in the treatment of the civilian population of occupied territories.[5] The Hague Regulations of 1907 contain only some scattered rules in the relevant section, articles 42–56. The rules concerning civilians appear in articles 43 (maintenance of public order and upholding of civilian life), 44 (prohibition against forcing inhabitants to furnish military information to the enemy), 45 (prohibition against forcing inhabitants to swear allegiance to a hostile power), 46 (respect for family

---

3 As expressed by the very famous *Lotus* case of the PCIJ, ser. A, no. 9, pp. 18–19.

4 P. Fauchille and N. Politis, *Manuel de la Croix-Rouge*, Paris, 1908, p. 157: "Le droit hospitalier international [in other words, IHL] porte avec lui sa sanction; car le connaître, c'est le respecter. Aussi bien, pour en assurer la scrupuleuse application, il suffit que chacun soit informé de ses règles et de l'esprit utilitaire qui les inspire".

5 See the discussion and the comparison with the Geneva Convention in O. M. Uhler, *Der völkerrechtliche Schutz der Bevölkerung eines besetzten Gebietes gegen Massnahmen der Okkupationsmacht*, Zurich, 1950, pp. 81 ff.

rights, lives of persons, private property, religious convictions) and 47 (prohibition against pillage). These rules do not contain indications concerning the taking of hostages as a reaction to hostile acts, or concerning deportation of civilians out of the occupied territories. Can one therefore argue that these practices are not prohibited; the first, for example, as a result of belligerent reprisals, the second as a measure of administration of a territory? Or must one try to refer to some general rule and attempt to subsume the practices in question under it? Thus, for example, the respect for family lives may by interpretation imply a prohibition on deportation, since family life could not unfold and thus be "respected" outside the home environment of an occupied territory. As one may gather, room for argument was left on many points, and this room would operate in practice often as a perception of weakness of the applicable laws of war.

1.3.3   Absence of the civilian in the classical law

As has already been mentioned in the context of the focus on "military law", the old laws of war had a conspicuous absence, namely the civilian. The protection of civilians is today the core – or at least one of the cores – of IHL. Indeed, the greatest number of victims of warfare are now civilians. Why, then, was the law so different in its focus in the nineteenth century and at the beginning of the twentieth century? There were different causes for this state of affairs. First, there was the optimistic belief that land warfare, concerned with the relationships of professional armies, would barely impinge on the lives of civilians, and, where it unintentionally did impinge, this impingement would be inevitable (for example, besieged towns, blockade of coasts, and so on). There is here a reverberation of the classical conception of war as a relation not of hostility between peoples, but of a public contest fought by professionals. Here is the battlefield pitching the professionals one against the other; there are the civilians remaining aloof from the war. Solferino (1859), the great seminal battle giving rise to the new laws of war, concerned only injured and sick military personnel, and civilians providing relief. In the military conceptions of the time, it seemed so obvious that military forces would not attack civilians, and so clear that civilians would abstain from warfare (except in *levée en masse*), that it was considered unnecessary to venture into such a question. The twentieth century would profoundly shift these parameters, through its strong tendency towards "total war". Everyone was now caught in the web of the war effort of the State.

Second, the concept of sovereignty remained somewhat exacting, and with it the conception of the internal affairs of a State. Dealings of a State with foreign individuals could not easily be made the object of international regulations, and even less of international control. They were considered essentially a matter of domestic jurisdiction of the State where those persons claimed nationality and/or of the territorial State. Third, there was still the weight of tradition, which had viewed the so-called "innocents" (in other words, *non nocentes*, not participating in warfare) along the old casuistic lines, namely the elderly, women, children, priests, the insane, and so on. For centuries, the law attached protection to such concrete persons, not to a general category of civilians. It took some time to overcome this casuistic thinking and to erect the law on a general principle, the protection of the civilian as such. The absence of the civilian was, however, to some extent tempered by a concomitant expansion of the notion of prisoners of war, which was applied to a series of civilian captive persons,[6] unlike the law as it stands today. This absence of the civilian started to have dramatic consequences in the context of the bombardments in the 1930s and later in the internment/deportations of World War II. Indeed, the International Committee of the Red Cross (ICRC) attempted to introduce a convention for the protection of civilians, but it did not succeed.[7]

1.3.4 Predominance of the principle of military necessity

The classical laws of war were not a fully-fledged codification of the rules applicable in warfare. Indeed, codification was in its earliest stage. For a certain time, the 1864 Convention, with its ten short articles, remained almost the only law dealing with this matter. It was accompanied soon after by the Petersburg Declaration of 1868 regarding the prohibition of infantry explosive projectiles. The attempt to extend the 1864 regime to naval warfare by a set of supplementary articles of 1868 failed to enter into force due to lack of required ratification. It was only in 1899, through the Hague Convention II (later Hague Convention IV of 1907) that some rules of land warfare were adopted.[8] As we have seen above, the codification efforts of 1899 to

---

6 See still in 1935 G. Balladore-Pallieri, *La guerra*, Padova, 1935, p. 136.

7 See the Draft Convention on the Condition and Protection of Civilians of Enemy Nationality (1934); D. Schindler and J. Toman, *The Laws of Armed Conflicts*, Leiden/Boston, 2004, pp. 445ff.

8 These rules were often commented on by German authors. See R. Laun, *Die Haager Landkriegsordnung*, 4th edn, Hannover, 1948; C. Meurer, *Das Kriegsrecht der Haager Konferenz*, Munich, 1907; K. Strupp, *Das internationale Landkriegsrecht*, Frankfurt, 1914.

1907 did not alter the general picture of a law containing some rules but a great many unregulated areas. Two countervailing principles were intended to cover these unregulated areas. The first was the Martens Clause:

> Until a more complete code of the laws of war has been issued, the High Contracting Parties deem it expedient to declare that, in cases not included in the Regulations adopted by them, the inhabitants and the belligerents remain under the protection and the rule of the principles of the law of nations, as they result from the usages established among civilized peoples, from the laws of humanity, and the dictates of public conscience. (Preamble, Hague Convention IV, 1907)

This clause was, at that time, essentially drafted with the inhabitants of occupied territories in mind; it was, however, formulated with a general reach. Its gist was to exclude a mechanical application of the rule of residual freedom, whereby all behaviour not expressly prohibited should be considered allowed. However, this clause remained largely non-influential before World War II.[9]

Much more influential was the second principle, namely military necessity (which will be analysed substantively in Chapter 4). In the absence of a specific rule, a situation that occurred frequently, the principle of military necessity became the pivot of the system of the laws of war. This concept was nourished by two contrasting rules, one centrifugal, the other centripetal. On the one side, all action that is *necessary* to overpower the enemy must be permitted since it would be pointless to attempt to prohibit it. On the other side, only action which is indeed *necessary* to that end is permitted, which means that every action not necessary to that effect remains incompatible with the laws of war and must be considered a superfluous, inhumane and prohibited action.[10] Thus, on the one hand the principle operated as a general permissive rule; and at the same time, it operated as a general prohibitive rule. Necessity is the pivot of the classical laws of war: it permits and prohibits at the same time; that is, it indicates the extent of what is allowed in warfare. Moreover, the principle had a distinguished pedigree. It could be found in almost all the classical

---

9 G. Best, *War and Law since 1945*, Oxford, 1994, p. 250.
10 See for example, E. Lueder, "Krieg und Kriegsrecht im Allgemeinen", in *F. v. Holtzendorff, Handbuch des Völkerrechts*, vol. IV, Hamburg, 1889, pp. 186ff, 254, 265, 276, 388ff, 389 and 391.

authors, such as Grotius,[11] Wolff,[12] Vattel,[13] Rousseau;[14] furthermore, it appears more or less subliminally in many other passages of classic writers.[15] The principle of necessity (expansive and restrictive) has the advantage of masking to a significant extent the absence of precise legal rules. It offers a guideline, appearing reasonably precise *faute de mieux* for deciding what is lawful and what is unlawful in warfare. Its concomitant disadvantage is the large degree of subjective and speculative appreciation it allows. Each belligerent will tend to consider many things to be necessary in order to conduct correct and successful warfare. Indeed, is not all that a belligerent does to some extent necessary, at least from a subjective perspective, since otherwise it would not be done at all? Who wants to waste energy, time and material in warfare? The perspective of the opposite belligerent will obviously be very different in such situations. Their appreciation of what is necessary will differ considerably with regard to adverse acts, even if what is necessary might not differ when their own acts are in question. In short, the mere principle of necessity does not lead to a sufficient restraint in warfare and invites constant quibbling about the limits of what is or is not allowed. In the long run, therefore, it cannot replace a more detailed codification of the laws of war. Indeed, the criterion was abandoned in the wake of modern humanitarian law, where it no longer plays the pivotal role described above.

1.3.5   Predominant weight of municipal law and few efforts devoted to international implementation mechanisms

The nineteenth century was the heyday of State sovereignty. International law was often perceived as a sort of annex of constitutional law applying to external relations. It was construed as a law based on agreements concluded under the lead of municipal constitutional law. The bulk of legal developments were expected to take place under

---

11   In Grotius, only the positive side of the rule is stressed, the negative remains somewhat implicit (and hence there are some controversies about the exact scope of the Grotian exposé): *De jure belli ac pacis* (1625), Book III, chapter I, § 2: "In war things which are necessary to attain the end are permissible" (which incidentally is not a phrase of the text but of the index).

12   C. Wolff, *Jus gentium methodo scientifica pertractatum* (1749), chapter VII, §§ 781ff.

13   E. de Vattel, *Le Droit des gens ou principes de la loi naturelle* (1758), Book III, chapters VIII and IX, §§ 136ff.

14   *Du contrat social* (1762), Book I, chapter IV: "[L]a guerre ne donne aucun droit qui ne soit nécessaire à sa fin".

15   See for example, J. W. Textor, *Synopsis juris gentium* (1680), chapter XVIII, Carnegie edition, translation, 1916, p. 191.

municipal law, if only because of its greater republican legitimacy and because of the much more developed means for implementation and sanction of the law. This is one further reason why no idea of a comprehensive codification at the international level was pursued at this stage. Rather, the European States that dominated international society of the day, sought to produce some short and generic international texts which would be spelled out in the municipal laws of the various States. Thus, the Oxford Manual of 1880, a private codification of the laws of war, stated in its Preamble that the rules it contained were proposed as a basis for national legislation. In the United States and in many European States, an intense process of national legislation on military issues was under way.[16] The most important result of this approach is that the laws of war were not unitary but split. In a particular armed conflict, it would be the convergence of reciprocal rules contained in the municipal legislation of the warring States that would set the most important pace as to what was applicable. In other words, the area of overlap between national legislation produced an important domain of common rules to be applied. Truly international rules, unitary for all States by reason of being contained in treaties, were very few in number. Consequently, particular laws have a much greater impact than general rules (or common law).

1.3.6 Subjective triggers for the applicability of the law – increasing the gaps in application

Regarding the applicability of the law, the pre-1949 laws of war were based on a subjective trigger rather than an objective trigger.[17] The classical laws of war were considered to apply to "war". But war was not just a factual state of affairs, observable out there; it was rather a legal concept, or at least a qualitative term. A state of war between States was held to exist essentially when it was declared (this being a unilateral legal act, expressing a will), or when there was an ascertainable subjective *animus belligerendi* of at least one State to the violent contest. This explains the extraordinary importance of the declaration of war in the nineteenth century.[18] Legal doctrine later tried to expand

---

16 See for example, P. Pradier-Fodéré, *Traité de droit international public européen et américain*, vol. VII, Paris, 1906, pp. 8off, 111ff, 123ff, 131–2; 172–3, 184, 200–201, 231–5.

17 On this whole question, see R. R. Baxter, "The Definition of War", in *Revue égyptienne de droit international*, vol. 16, 1960, pp. 4, 13.

18 The Congress of Paris of 1856 (after the Crimean War) recognized that the declaration of war is necessary and thus required, except in the case of invasion and spontaneous self-defence: see C. Calvo, *Le droit international théorique et pratique*, vol. IV, 5th edn, Paris, 1896, p. 47.

the concept of war to armed contests between States where, even absent an ascertainable subjective will to consider oneself at war, the belligerent operations were of such a magnitude as to be compatible only with a state of war.[19] But this effort at expansion remained contested and uncertain. Hence, "war" was conceived by the legal system not as a simple fact, but as a legal act (*acte juridique, negozio giuridico, Rechtsgeschäft*), in other words, an expression of will producing legal consequences according to the expressed will. Moreover, this legal act was unilateral: one State could force upon another a state of war by its unilateral expression of will. The further result is that a State could bring about this state of war or refrain from doing so, according to its own free will and agenda. A state of war can be produced (or not) according to a discretionary will: if a state of war is produced, the laws of war will apply; if it is not, the laws of war will not apply. The ultimate result is thus that the laws of war will apply (or not) according to a subjective and unfettered will. This is the subjective trigger. The reasons not to recognize a state of war (but to qualify hostilities, for example, as armed reprisals or police action) were manifold: the intention to avoid the application of the laws of war, with their different constraints; the intention to avoid engaging the Parliament under municipal law regulations applicable only to a state of war; and the political reason to avoid giving a particular operation the magnitude of a war, justifying it on some narrower basis and so on. The subjective trigger in the application of the laws of war represented a grave gap in the system. The application of the laws of war could not be objectively secured for the benefit of the protected persons. They remained at their core voluntary or elective, in other words, discretionary. This was a significant weakness. To the foregoing, it may be added that a "civil war" (in today's IHL vocabulary a "non-international armed conflict", the concept of civil war not being a legal term of art) was subjected to the same subjective trigger. Indeed, a civil war could impinge heavily on the rights of neutral States. Therefore, it was accepted that through a "recognition of belligerency" by a State (again a unilateral legal act embodying an expression of will) the two parties in a civil war could be treated as belligerents and placed on the same footing, meaning the laws of war, especially neutrality, would apply to both.[20] The relevant recognition could emanate from the local government or from third States. A civil war could thus be transformed, from the legal point of view, into a fully-fledged "war" between the recognizing State and the

---

19 L. Kotzsch, *The Concept of War in Contemporary History and International Law*, Geneva, 1956.
20 E. C. Stowell, *International Law*, New York, 1931, p. 401.

recognized entities. It has to be noted that the law applicable was in such a case the whole body of the laws of war. There was no distinction between international armed conflict (IAC) and non-international armed conflict (NIAC) before 1949. An inter-State war (if recognized as war) triggered the application of the laws of war; a civil war (if and to the extent there was a recognition of belligerency) triggered the application of the same rules of the laws of war to both parties. Civil war was thereby completely internationalized. It has to be added that in the case of recognition of belligerency, the application of the laws of war remained bilateral. The application would be limited to the dealings among the recognizing State and the warring parties. Conversely, the laws of war would not apply among the belligerents and a third State not having issued a recognition of belligerency. The law, therefore, was split into a series of bilateral regimes. We will see in Chapter 5 that the trigger for modern IHL is objective: when certain facts occur on the ground, the application of IHL is triggered independent of the will of a belligerent. We will also see that States may still not recognize a state of armed conflict (especially in NIAC), and we will consider what ways exist for exiting this quagmire.

1.3.7   The inter-war period: doubts on the possibility of a law of war

In a series of concordant articles,[21] several authors considered that it had been a mistake to concentrate on the laws of war instead of putting the means of avoiding war altogether at the centre of interest (*jus contra bellum* instead of illusory *jus in bello*). Moreover, they considered that it was impossible to regulate the war by so-called rules on warfare, violence of this type being intrinsically unsuitable to legal restrictions, especially in the context of modern total wars. These new total wars, engaging all components of a society in the war effort, were, in their view, unavoidably lawless. Thus one could realistically only attempt to prohibit such occurrences, not try to regulate them. The focus of legal attention, in the wake of the League of Nations, thus turned to the avoidance of war. The laws of war were neglected, classified as being illusory, bygone naïvetés, child's play. This purportedly realistic, but indeed short-sighted, attitude, was criticized with good arguments;[22] however, it was largely

---

21 See Anonymous, "The League of Nations and the Laws of War", *BYIL*, vol. 1, 1920–1921, pp. 109ff.

22 See in particular A. de la Pradelle, "Négligera-t-on longtemps encore l'étude des lois de la guerre?", *Revue de droit international (Paris)*, vol. 12, 1933, pp. 511ff; J. Kunz, "Plus de lois de la guerre?",

dominant during the inter-war period. It hampered any adaptation and progress in the laws of war, especially with regard to weapons, aerial warfare and civilian protection. The essential conventions adopted in this time-span were the Geneva Gas Protocol of 1925 and the two Geneva Conventions of 1929 on the Injured or Sick Military Personnel and on Prisoners of War. All other questions were left unanswered. This neglect of the laws of war did not serve the cause of belligerent constraints during World War II. In particular, the complete lack of adequate rules for the protection of civilians – as well as the absence of proper rules for aerial warfare – was to have a heavy impact. Supervening events thus showed that so-called "realism" is sometimes unrealistic, and that the policy of putting one's own head in the sand is not a successful path with regard to the persistent existence of armed conflict, notwithstanding all efforts to maintain the peace. If the phenomenon persists, it needs some legal regulation, as do all social phenomena, even if they are fraught with a degree of violence.

1.4 Modern international humanitarian law (1949–present)

Modern IHL is based on a set of different structural parameters, and has also substantially evolved. There are two essential changes from the old to the new law.

First, the main colouring and complexion of this body of law has changed. The laws of war predating the Geneva Conventions of 1949 were essentially based on a military paradigm: what could the armed forces do, what were the allowable means and methods of warfare, what were their duties to their fellows once wounded or sick (later also including prisoners)? IHL, as inaugurated by the Geneva Conventions, places at the centre of the new law the principle of humanity and the idea of "protected persons". The point is not to oust the "means and methods" limb of the old law, but to produce a new layer and to make that new layer the centre of the system. The new layer revolves around the protection of actual or potential "victims of war". From this flows the new concept of "humanization" of the law of armed conflicts, still

---

RGDIP, vol. 41, 1934, pp. 22ff, the perplexity of both authors emerging clearly through the use in both cases of question marks. See also A. de la Pradelle, *La reconstruction du droit de la guerre*, Paris/Brussels, 1936.

used in recent times.[23] This change was an answer to the egregious violations of the most basic humanitarian concerns by the Axis powers during World War II. This "humanization" of IHL has continued to expand in many directions since 1949. The most important novelty is the growing influence of international human rights law (HRL). With the adoption of the two United Nations (UN) human rights covenants of 1966 (on civil and political rights, as well as on economic, social and cultural rights[24]), a new branch of international law entered the realm of positive law at the universal level. In due course, these instruments would be applied to situations of belligerency, such as the Palestinian occupied territories after 1967. The branch of HRL thenceforward supplemented IHL. It was progressively interpreted to apply extraterritorially and also to cover times of armed conflict. Today, it is in particular through new functions of the army, namely the "maintenance of order", that HRL comes into close and sometimes symbiotic relationship with IHL. The modern missions of an army, such as the mission of the French troops in Mali (2013), are more often than not a complex mixture of "conduct of hostilities" and "maintenance of order" (or police functions), for which a common IHL/HRL approach is necessary. This in turn augments the "human centred" approach of IHL, since HRL is at least as much related to "protected persons" as is modern IHL.

Second, many gaps of the old laws of war system have been remedied. The new regulations contained in the Geneva Conventions were detailed and long. The four Geneva Conventions of 1949 contain 429 articles in total (64, 63, 143 and159 respectively) and more than 57 articles in the annexes. This makes a total of almost 500 articles, to be compared with the 60 articles of the Hague Regulations. But quantitative comparison is not enough. The provisions of the Geneva Conventions are almost all much longer than the ones in the Hague Regulations. They often contain many paragraphs and are formulated in much greater detail. A certain distrust with regard to the belligerents and their usual self-serving assertions comes to the fore, as well as a concomitant will to give as exact normative guidance as possible. This also means that regulation now becomes essentially international. Municipal law is expected to implement provisions adopted on the international plane, not to develop IHL in the first place. The

---

23 T. Meron, "The Humanization of Humanitarian Law", *AJIL*, vol. 94, 2000, pp. 239ff.

24 See the succinct overview by W. Kälin and J. Künzli, *The Law of International Human Rights Protection*, Oxford, 2009, pp. 39–42. As to the relationship with IHL, see *ibid.*, pp. 178ff.

result is an IHL of a much more unitary nature than the old laws of war. In addition, the "absence of the civilian" is remedied. Geneva Convention IV is devoted exclusively to the protection of civilians; symbolically, it is the longest of the four Geneva Conventions, a sort of moral acknowledgement of the tremendous suffering of civilians during World War II. In due course, as time went on, civilians would also be protected by the growing arm of HRL. Military necessity is now downgraded. As we shall see in Chapter 4, it can only be invoked as a reason not to apply a specific rule of IHL, if that rule itself makes provision for the military necessity exception. For example, article 23, letter g, of the Hague Regulations of 1907, reads: "[It is prohibited] to destroy or seize the enemy's property, unless such destruction or seizure be imperatively demanded by the necessities of war". If that necessity clause was not part and parcel of the normative content, necessity could not be invoked in order to justify the destruction of such property. Military necessity therefore loses it pivotal role in the system. Specific provisions take its place and absorb it. This is a significant progress in the strengthening of IHL and in securing legal certainty. By the same token, the subjective trigger for the application of the law is abandoned for an objective trigger. The law applies automatically when a certain fact exists, namely either an "armed conflict" (as a matter of actual fighting), or a state of "war", or an occupation of territory without hostilities (see common article 2 of the Geneva Conventions), or finally an "armed conflict not international in character" (common article 3 of the Geneva Conventions). The existence of the fact can be discussed in some circumstances, but the application of the law ceased to be discretionary. Thus, for example, when hostilities exist, IHL must be applied; the qualification or etiquette put on those hostilities (is it war?) has no significance anymore. In still other words, the central trigger of the modern system, namely "armed conflict", is configured as a legal fact and not as a legal act. The legal consequences flow from a situation on the spot and not from an act of will. It will be noticed that a new law for NIACs was also devised through common article 3 to the Geneva Conventions. It was based on the will to close another gap in the classical laws of war, by securing a minimum of objectively applicable humanity even in cases of "civil war". Lastly, we may mention the effort of the Geneva Conventions system to avoid any contracting out, which would open new unwelcome gaps in the application of this body of law with its paramount humanitarian concerns. Thus, we read in common articles 6/6/6/7 of Geneva Conventions I–IV: "No special agreement [between the belligerents] shall adversely affect the situation of the [protected persons], as defined by the present Convention, nor restrict the rights which it confers upon them". States parties to the Geneva Conventions may thus not derogate from the protections of the Conventions by concluding special agreements *inter se*, which would otherwise prevail under the principles of *lex posterior* and *lex specialis*. This is a form of international *jus cogens*, slightly distinct from the one mentioned in article 53 of the Vienna Convention on the Law of Treaties (1969). Articles 7/7/7/8 of Geneva Conventions I–IV then go on to make clear that protected persons themselves cannot renounce their rights (as happened, for example, with prisoners of war in Germany during World War II, used for exhausting work in German industries): "[Protected persons] may in no circumstances renounce in part or in entirety the rights secured to them by the present Convention. . .". Again, mistrust with regard to the belligerents is palpable here, as too is a will to avoid opening gaps in the application of the law. This socio-legal environment is in marked opposition to the optimistic and State-confident approach of the old laws of war period.

1.5   Reasons for the Additional Protocols of 1977

In the 1970s, it was felt necessary to adapt the Geneva Conventions. This led to the adoption of the two Additional Protocols to the Geneva Conventions, in 1977. Adaptations of the law were necessary especially in the following contexts:[25]

1. *Non-international armed conflicts.* Most armed conflicts after 1949 had been civil wars (with or without some form of foreign military intervention). Article 3 common to the Geneva Conventions proved to be too sketchy to provide adequate protection for all these multifaceted and numerous civil wars. Thus, Additional Protocol II of 1977 (AP II), devoted only to NIACs, was adopted.
2. *Definition of combatants.* In the many struggles of colonized peoples for liberation, but also in other warfare situations (for example, Vietnam) asymmetric guerrilla warfare had become

---

25 On the context of adoption of the two Additional Protocols, see Y. Sandoz, C. Swinarski and B. Zimmermann (eds), *Commentary on the Additional Protocols of 8 June 1977 to the Geneva Conventions of 12 August 1949*, Geneva, 1987, pp. xxixff; G. H. Aldrich, "Some Reflections on the Origins of the 1977 Geneva Protocols", in C. Swinarski (ed.), *Studies and Essays on the International Humanitarian Law and Red Cross Principles, Essays in Honour of J. Pictet*, Geneva/ The Hague, 1984, pp. 129ff.

a frequent occurrence. The Geneva Conventions[26] did not allow guerrilla fighters to be considered regular combatants: the conditions were too exacting and could only be fulfilled when the rebels controlled a part of the territory. This inequality in status (guerrilla fighters could not be regular combatants, claim prisoner of war status or combatant privileges) led to discrimination and inequality in the application of IHL. Articles 43–44 of Additional Protocol I of 1977 (AP I), somewhat relaxed the criteria for regular combatant status. However, the Protocol attempted to avoid an excessive refashioning of the relevant criteria, since this would have paved the way for terrorist action and put the principle of distinction between civilians and combatants under too heavy strain. The question as to whether AP I succeeded in striking a proper balance has remained controversial. We will discuss this question later, in Chapter 6.

3. *Law relating to conduct of warfare.* The laws relating to means and methods of warfare had not been reformed since 1907. The Vietnam War in particular had shown that some new efforts were necessary to better protect the civilian population, especially in cases of aerial bombardments. This led to the adoption of the highly important articles 48ff of AP I, protecting civilians in the phase of hostilities (principle of distinction, targeting, collateral damages, precautions in attack, and so on). Geneva Convention IV concerns the protection of civilians only outside the context of hostilities, when these civilians are "in the hands"[27] of the adverse party; AP I added to that a protection during hostilities.

4. *Human Rights Law.* Since 1949, HRL had constantly evolved. In 1977, it was felt necessary to extend to persons protected under the Geneva Conventions some fundamental protections flowing from the growing arm of HRL. Thus, article 75 of AP I and articles 4–6 of AP II were adopted. These are quite detailed provisions, whose human rights pedigree can hardly be overlooked.

---

26 See article 13, Geneva Convention I, article 13, Geneva Convention II, article 4, Geneva Convention III.

27 See article 4, § 1, Geneva Convention IV.

1.6   International humanitarian law: a system attributive of powers or a system prohibitive of action?

A last point needs to be made on the nature of the system of IHL: is it attributive of rights for belligerent action, or is it prohibitive of belligerent behaviour? Is it centred on rights or obligations (prohibitions)? Does it confer the rights and powers which the belligerent can claim – or does it prohibit certain action, leaving the non-prohibited action legally unaffected? In the past, under the classical laws of war, the prohibitive stance was clearly privileged. Has modern IHL changed the position? A first aspect of clarification is necessary: the point of the question posed is not to deny that "rights" are conferred by IHL, notably on protected persons. To wit, article 13 of Geneva Convention III confers a right on the prisoner of war to be respected and protected in his physical integrity; this implies a corresponding duty on the detaining power. The point here is rather to focus on the general system with regard to the powers of belligerents and to find out whether IHL purports to define what they may do in warfare or whether IHL purports to determine what belligerent parties may not do in warfare. The answer to this question must be made with some degree of nuance.

First, the general approach of IHL is indisputably negative or prohibitive: IHL mainly defines the prohibited means and methods, or conduct, of warfare, in other words, the actions or omissions that are regarded as excessive and therefore prohibited. There would be no point in IHL trying to tell belligerents all that they may do; the list of permissive action would be endless. Moreover, the legal result of any omission on the list of accepted conduct could have the result of prohibiting that action. This would produce a too far-reaching domain of prohibition since the general rule must remain that what is necessary to overpower the enemy must in general terms be regarded as lawful. The belligerent States being sovereign, there is no legal need to utter what they are entitled to do. Their power to act is inherent in their sovereignty and does not need to be further buttressed. What is necessary is to extract from that general power to act, flowing from sovereignty, a certain number of conducts in view of the common interest of the belligerents and the community at large. In other words, a "permission-approach" would be legally redundant: powers would be attributed twice, once by the general principle of sovereignty, and then also by a series of specific rules of IHL. Legally, difficult questions of the relation of one notion to the other could arise: would IHL be a self-contained regime, where only the attributed powers could be exercised, the powers flowing from sovereignty being derogated from by virtue of a *lex specialis* approach? Or would general international law, including sovereignty, remain in the background as a fall-back regime, so that any gaps in the attributive rules of IHL could be filled by recourse to the general principle of sovereignty and the powers it confers? The reader will recognize a discussion much debated in the context of the so-called fragmentation of international law.[28] By choosing the prohibitive side of the coin, IHL avoids this type of difficulty. The rules it poses are not seconding sovereignty, but are to be analysed as classical limitations on sovereignty. The sharing of work is thus optimized: sovereignty confers all the powers of belligerent action; IHL limits these powers by prohibiting certain action. The two sets of rules pull in opposite directions and adjust one to the sphere of the other.

Second, the attribution-of-rights approach would also produce some other legal difficulties. Indeed, if IHL conferred a "right" of belligerent action, this would mean that belligerent A would have a legal entitlement to realize a conduct X, with the concomitant duty of the other belligerent B to suffer this very action. Notice that there is no right of the opposing party to thwart the exercise of a right by the bearer of that right. But in our context, this would produce an odd result, which moreover does not correspond to reality. No belligerent feels itself bound to passively accept the regular belligerent action of the adverse party. Quite on the contrary, everything possible and lawful is done, and may be done, in order to oppose this conduct, to minimize its effects or even to neutralize it.[29] Hence, neither sovereignty nor IHL confer "rights" of belligerency, in the strict sense, on the belligerent parties. These bodies of law confer simple powers or faculties of action to the parties; these legal positions are deprived of the correlative duty to accept and suffer the action imposed on the other party. This position can easily be squared with the general approach of prohibitive rules: no rights are conferred, but obligations are imposed. In legal theory, while there can be no rights without concomitant duties, there can be obligations without defined concomitant rights. If I say that A

---

28 See for example, M. Prost, *The Concept of Unity in Public International Law*, Oxford/Portland, 2012.

29 An equivalent problem arises for the concepts of counter-measures or of self-defence under international law: see for example, L. A. Sicilianos, *Les réactions décentralisées à l'illicite, Des contre-mesures à la légitime défense*, Paris, 1990, pp. 44ff.

has a subjective right to X, I must define the bearer of a concomitant obligation to give to A his due. But if I say that A has an obligation to act, I must not confer at the same time a subjective right on somebody else. Thus, I can perfectly impose on the public administration a duty to take action when certain conditions are met, without concomitantly conferring upon anybody a subjective right to such action. Contrary to what has been said, this "no attributed rights" approach must not lead to a sphere of factual freedom in warfare, in other words, to postulating the absence of norms. This position was taken, for example, by G. Balladore-Pallieri,[30] in a book on the laws of war of greatest intellectual profoundness. The argument of this brilliant author was in essence that since the adverse party is not bound to suffer the belligerent action (and thus no right of action is conferred), the result is that the laws of war are based on the absence of norms. This "vacuum" leads to a sphere of freedom of action for the belligerents based on the lack of any normative constraint. The Italian author thus opposes a *legal* freedom to act (by the legal residual rule "everything which is not prohibited is permitted") to a *factual* freedom to act (by the complete absence of legal constraints), the practical result in both cases being essentially the same. However, the freedom of action of the belligerent does not rest on a wholesale absence of rules (apart from the prohibitive ones). Rather, it is rooted in the general principle of sovereignty, providing the State with a *legal* basis of action. The only point is that this sovereignty does not confer "rights" to belligerent actions, but mutual unilateral powers or faculties.

Third, there are certain general norms of IHL whose reach is so overwhelming that the prohibitive range of IHL is considerably increased. These norms may therefore paradoxically be seen as limits, or even as a reversal, of the general prohibitive approach we have been discussing above; alternatively they may also be regarded as pushing the prohibitive approach to its apogee.

One of these norms is the Martens Clause, which has been considered to be part of modern positive IHL.[31] A modern version of this clause, reads: "In cases not covered by this Protocol or by other international agreements, civilians and combatants remain under the protection and authority of the principles of international law derived from

---

30 G. Balladore-Pallieri, *La guerra*, Padova, 1935, pp. 163–4.
31 US Military Tribunal at Nuremberg, *Krupp* case (1948), *Annual Digest of Public International Law Cases* (now *ILR*), vol. 15, 1948, p. 622.

established custom, from the principles of humanity and from the dictates of public conscience" (article 1, § 2, of AP I). There is some debate as to the precise scope of this clause. There is, however, no doubt that it limits the residual freedom of action of States even when there is no explicit prohibition in the body of IHL. At a minimum, the clause is taken to mean that if a conduct is not expressly prohibited by IHL, it is not thereby meant to be automatically lawful. A belligerent must first check whether this action would be compatible with the requirements of humanity and public conscience, and an appeal is made to him to reject the conduct if it does not comply with these notions. Thereby, the clause rebuts any mechanical application of the principle, inherent in prohibitive bodies of law, namely that "what is not prohibited is allowed". In short terms, if something is inhumane and incompatible with public conscience it is not allowed simply because there is no specific prohibitory rule. The problem with this clause is twofold. Firstly, the belligerents do not take it sufficiently seriously. Secondly, it gives rise to a high degree of subjective appreciation, since there may be discussion as to what is compatible with humanity and what is not. The discussion may also bear on the extent to which the humanitarian ideals and public conscience requirements must have already been received in the body of international law to be applicable here. The formulation of the clause is in this regard ambiguous.

A second provision having such a general reach is the one relating to "humane treatment" of protected persons, a provision to be found in all four Geneva Conventions of 1949 (articles 12/12/13/27 of Geneva Conventions I–IV). The requirements of the Martens Clause are to a large extent specifically codified here, but applicable in this context only to "protected persons". The humane treatment clause is followed by a great number of special provisions relating to the treatment of protected persons. Now, to the extent that a specific conduct is not prohibited by one of these particular provisions, a particular conduct does not automatically become lawful. It must first be measured by the requirement of humanity, which operates as a general clause. This legal situation justifies the conclusion that the prohibitive approach still has a certain reach in the so-called "Hague Law" (relating to the means and methods of warfare) but that it has been largely restricted, if not abandoned, in the "Geneva Law" (relating to the protection and humane treatment of persons *hors de combat*). However, even in the so-called Hague Law there are general principles limiting the impact of the prohibitive approach. Thus, in the law of weapons, there are some limiting general principles and a series of specific prohibitions for particular weapons. If a particular weapon is not prohibited by a specific norm (say in a treaty), it is not thereby automatically lawful to use that weapon. It must first be tested if that weapon causes what is called "unnecessary suffering" as compared with the military advantage of its use.[32] If the suffering appears excessive, the weapon is prohibited. For example, exploding bullets used in man-to-man fighting have been prohibited since the Petersburg Declaration of 1868. There is manifestly no military advantage in using such bullets (contrary, for example, to expanding bullets, which may provide some advantages in certain contexts, since they do not ricochet). Thus, even if the prohibition in the Declaration of 1868, as modified by subsequent State practice,[33] did not exist, such bullets would be prohibited under the general principle of "unnecessary suffering". In short, the body of IHL knows of some general principles whose role is to reverse (or to bring to fullest power) the "prohibitive" approach, in order to secure better protection for persons against the sufferings and evils of war.

We may end our discussion of this issue here. It has shown that if the general approach of IHL is soundly prohibitive in nature, there are many nuances to be added in order to give a full account of the complex functioning of this body of international law.

---

32 See for example, W. H. Boothby, *Weapons and the Law of Armed Conflict*, Oxford, 2009, pp. 55ff. The ICJ has recognized that this principle is part of positive international law: see the *Nuclear Weapons* (UNGA) advisory opinion, ICJ, *Reports*, 1996-I., p. 257, § 78.

33 State practice has, in particular, abandoned the 400 grams of weight criterion, which is outdated. In 1868, it was meant to distinguish infantry-bullets from artillery-ammunition, explosive bullets being prohibited only for the former and not for the latter. At that time, the 400 grams expressed the existent threshold of infantry-bullets and artillery-bullets. Technical changes have since rendered the 400 grams-weight an irrelevant criterion. It was thus abandoned. See J. M. Henckaerts and L. Doswald-Beck, *Customary International Humanitarian Law*, vol. I, Cambridge, 2005, pp. 273ff.

2 International armed conflict and non-international armed conflict

2.1 Basic types of armed conflict

Today, there are two basic types of armed conflicts, to which a certain number of identical and a certain number of differentiated rules apply.[1] One type is IAC (armed conflict between States), the other is NIAC (armed conflicts between governmental forces and insurgents or between armed groups).[2] There are fewer rules applicable to NIACs than to IACs. More precisely, the basic law applicable to NIACs, namely common article 3 of the Geneva Conventions, defines the scope of application of the rules it contains as being linked to armed conflicts "not of an international character". This is a negative definition, which could seem to operate as a residual clause: all armed conflicts that are not international in nature (inter-State) must therefore perforce be covered by article 3. No gaps are left. AP II, supplementing and developing common article 3, does, however, limit its own scope of application to armed conflicts between the armed forces of a State party on the one side and dissident armed forces or other armed groups on the other side, if the latter exercise some degree of control over part of the State territory (article 1, § 1). AP II thus sets the scene for classical government/rebels armed conflicts, which are normally of a certain intensity. Moreover, common article 3 contains the restriction "occurring in the territory of one of the High Contracting Parties". The meaning of that restriction is disputed.[3] What if the United States (US) conducts an armed conflict

---

1 The detail is much more complex: see the excellent overview in M. Milanovic and V. Hadzi-Vidanovic, "A Taxonomy of Armed Conflict", in N. D. White and C. Henderson (eds), *Research Handbook on International Conflict and Security Law: Jus ad Bellum, Jus in Bello and Jus post Bellum*, Cheltenham, 2013, pp. 256ff.

2 On NIAC, see generally L. Moir, *The Law of Internal Armed Conflict*, Cambridge, 2002; R. Abi-Saab, *Droit humanitaire et conflits internes*, Geneva/Paris, 1986.

3 See for example, N. Lubell, *Extraterritorial Use of Force Against Non-State Actors*, Oxford, 2010, pp. 100ff.

against Taliban forces in Afghanistan or Pakistan? This cannot be an IAC, since it is not inter-State; a State here confronts armed groups. But can it be NIAC in the sense of article 3, since it occurs outside the territory of the US? The correct answer is that the territorial limitation inserted in common article 3 was meant to reserve the situation of States not parties to the Geneva Conventions: only armed conflicts taking place on the territory of a State party to the Geneva Conventions should be covered by article 3.[4] This is a matter of treaty law: *pacta tertiis nec nocent nec prosunt*. Thus, if an armed conflict between a government and an armed group takes place across a State boundary, it must be ascertained that the two or more territories involved belong to States that have ratified the Geneva Conventions or have acceded to them. Otherwise, the armed conflict does not "occur on the territory of one of the High Contracting Parties" and common article 3, as conventional law, does not apply (the position under customary international law (CIL) remaining, however, unaltered). The US Supreme Court was thus correct in affirming that common article 3 applied to belligerent action between the US and armed groups in Afghanistan (*Hamdan v. Rumsfeld*, 2006[5]). In this way, an unprincipled regulatory gap is avoided: the aim of the drafters of the Geneva Conventions was to have minimum rules applicable to as many NIACs as possible, and not to open up gaps in protection without any substantive reason.[6]

2.2   Classical laws of war

In the past, under the classical laws of law, the position was somewhat easier, but not altogether deprived of legal subtleties. The basic rule was that international law *did not contain* rules on NIAC. Therefore, the belligerents remained free to act as they saw fit, possibly under the sole injunction of the Martens Clause, if it were interpreted to apply to a NIAC (which was, however, a minority position). The freedom to act was here construed as a true freedom of fact, not a freedom of law: it flowed from the absence of legal rules, not from the grant by a legal rule or by sovereignty. The whole conduct did not have to be

---

4   This is correctly stressed by M. Sassoli, "Use and Abuse of the Laws of War in the 'War on Terrorism'", *Law and Inequality: A Journal of Theory and Practice*, vol. 22, 2004, pp. 200–201.

5   Judgment of 29 June 2006, No. 05–184.

6   See D. Jinks, "September 11 and the Laws of War", *Yale Journal of International Law*, vol. 28, 2003, pp. 40–41.

justified as against other States, since it fell squarely within the realm of domestic affairs. The main reason for such an abstention of regulation was the then current conception of domestic affairs. A NIAC is an armed conflict erupting on the territory of a State and normally confined to this territory. The belligerent relationship runs between a government and a series of persons normally possessing the nationality of that State. Up to the time of World War II, the way a State treated its own nationals was regarded as a question falling under its domestic jurisdiction and not under international law. Consequently, a NIAC was a belligerent relationship falling under the sole jurisdiction of domestic law, international law having to refrain from any intrusive regulation. However, since internal armed conflicts had more often than not a certain intensity (for example, the US War of Secession, the Russian Civil War at the beginning of the 1920s or the Spanish Civil War, 1936–1939), there were some devices for international action. Two of these fall to be mentioned.

1.   The first was the *right of humanitarian initiative* of the ICRC.[7] It represented a customary right of the ICRC, enshrined in its Statutes (for example, article 5, § 2, of the Statutes of 1921). The content of the right is that the ICRC may at all times propose an action of humanitarian nature for the relief of persons during an armed conflict or internal disturbances, and that this proposal cannot be seen as an unlawful intervention in internal affairs. However, the ICRC cannot enforce its proposal. Its action will become lawfully possible only if the required government accepts the proposal. The device of the humanitarian initiative was successful in a series of internal armed conflicts, where the action of the ICRC for the benefit of prisoners, for the evacuation of civilians, and for the protection of sanitary services, and so on, has been crucial. This has been the case, for example, in the armed conflict in Upper Silesia (1921) or in the Spanish Civil War.[8] Through its right of humanitarian intervention, the ICRC could also induce the parties to conclude special agreements *inter se*, in which they would recognize the applicability of some rules of the laws of war in their conflict, or go beyond such rules,

---

7   Y. Sandoz, "Le droit d'initiative du Comité international de la Croix-Rouge", *GYIL*, vol. 22, 1979, pp. 352ff; F. Bugnion, *Le Comité international de la Croix-Rouge et la protection des victimes de la guerre*, Geneva, 1994, pp. 455ff (there is an English translation of this book, but the French is the original and will be referred to in the following pages).

8   See F. Bugnion, *Le Comité international de la Croix-Rouge et la protection des victimes de la guerre*, Geneva, 1994, pp. 302ff, 307ff.

for example by exchanging prisoners. This happened frequently in the Spanish Civil War.[9]

2. The second is the legal concept of *recognition of belligerency*.[10] A civil war could affect the interests of third States. In particular, third States could be tempted to apply the laws of neutrality to both belligerent parties when the rebels controlled a part of the territory of the State affected by the civil war. They could then claim the respect of their neutral rights from both belligerents, notably concerning their commerce at sea. The government entangled in the civil war could exceptionally also want to recognize the rebels as belligerents, though it rarely had a political interest in upgrading their position. However, if these rebels controlled a part of the national territory, the local government could divest itself of the responsibility for the internationally unlawful acts occurring under the zone of jurisdiction of the rebels only to the extent it had recognized them as belligerents. The recognition of belligerency was a unilateral legal act by which the recognizing State conferred a legal personality on the rebels. The recognition was constitutive, not declaratory: the rebels did not possess such a personality before the recognition; the recognition had the effect of creating the personality and the rights flowing there from. That personality was only relative, not absolute. It was conferred only for the mutual legal relationships of the recognizing State and the recognized entity, here the rebels. Other States were not bound by the unilateral acts of another State. Hence, an entity could exist as an international legal person for one State, while it could continue to be non-existent for the other. The unilateral nature of the act implied that any third State could impose on the local government a treatment of the rebels as an international legal person, with rights and duties, and thus apply the laws of neutrality. Recognition of belligerency was therefore a limitation on the principle of non-intervention in internal affairs, accorded by CIL. The legal consequence of such recognition of belligerency was that the armed conflict between the State forces and the rebels was treated as a "war" and the laws of war were applied to it. In other words, the result was that the armed conflict ceased

---

9 M. Junod, *Le troisième combattant*, Lausanne, 1947, pp. 75ff; P. Marquéz, *La Croix-Rouge pendant la guerre d'Espagne*, Paris, 2000.

10 See R. Kolb, "Le droit international public et le concept de guerre civile depuis 1945", *Relations internationales*, No. 105, 2001, pp. 9ff; L. Moir, *The Law of Internal Armed Conflict*, Cambridge, 2002, pp. 3ff.

to be a simple civil war, to which international law did not apply, ushering it into a category of war to which all the rules of the laws of war applied, including neutrality. Hence, a civil war could be regulated by the laws of war only if it was qualified in totality as an "international armed conflict", in other words, as "war". There was nothing in between the absence of legal regulation of civil war and the fully-fledged legal regime for war between States. An armed conflict could be only the one or the other. The trigger for passing from the one to the other, from legal limbo to legal regulation, was a discretionary act of will by a State. There was no objective application of the laws of war flowing from the existence of a mere situation of fact, in other words, the existence of armed hostilities. It is not surprising that as a form of allowed intervention in internal affairs, recognition of belligerency was dependent on a set of strict conditions: (1) the control of part of the national territory by the rebels, with the establishment therein of a *de facto* government; (2) the conduct of hostilities by disciplined and organized rebel troops, under a responsible command and conforming themselves to the laws of war.[11] In the practice of the nineteenth century, recognitions of belligerency were frequent.[12]

2.3   Reasons for regulating non-international armed conflicts

Why should IHL attempt to regulate internal conflicts? Could the whole question not be left to the conjunctive action of municipal law and international HRL? These are two distinct questions to which two separate answers must be proposed.

The reasons for regulating NIACs are manifold. Some reasons explain why such regulation should exist, while others rather help to create a favourable environment for such regulation. First, there is an obvious humanitarian concern. Civil wars during the inter-war period had significantly gained in force and destructiveness. Humanitarian suffering had been intense: the Russian and Spanish Civil Wars were in everyone's memories during the drafting of the

---

11 See the Resolution of the Institute of International Law on the rights and duties of foreign powers with respect to insurrections (1900), www.idi-iil.org.
12 See the meticulous study by H. Wehberg, "La guerre civile et le droit international", *RCADI*, vol. 63, 1938-I, pp. 1ff.

Geneva Conventions of 1949. Should not a humanitarian minimum be devised for such conflicts as well, in order not to leave a glaring protection gap? This humanitarian need was a decisive argument in 1949. Second, experience had shown that in the twentieth century world, a NIAC rarely remained confined to government and national rebels, fighting on the national territory. Foreign forces often intervened to sustain the government or the rebels. This had happened in the Russian and the Spanish Civil Wars. In the latter, famously, Italy, Germany and Russia intervened massively. These interventions did not make of these civil wars IACs, thus covered by the laws of war. The rules of attribution in case of "effective" or "overall" control, as we have them today, were not yet developed or applicable.[13] But the foreign interventions showed that the matter could (and perhaps had to be) considered of international concern, justifying some international legal regulation. Third, experience also tended to show that NIACs have an impact on international peace and security. It is not infrequent that hostilities spill over into neighbouring States. Thus, hostilities may escalate. This element may not be directly relevant to *jus in bello* issues (it is linked rather with maintenance of peace and *jus ad bellum*), but it again accounts for a shift in the perception of NIAC. The question not being merely of domestic concern, there are reasons for international regulation. Fourth, modern international law paved the way for the protection of human rights. The UN Charter is the first international agreement to set the pace in this direction.[14] If the concern of how a government treats its own people in peacetime induces a regulation in international law, it is understandable to also be concerned for the protection of persons during times of armed conflict. This analogy was only foreshadowed at the time of the Geneva Conventions. But it would gain momentum, as the arm of HRL would progressively grow.

The answers to the second question – could the whole question not be left to municipal law or HRL? – lie on two planes. First, municipal law could not be considered sufficient, for the same reasons as it could not be considered satisfactory in the human rights context, and also for reasons beyond that. Municipal law does not guarantee

---

13 See for example, the thorough discussion in M. Milanovic, "State Responsibility for Genocide", *EJIL*, vol. 17, 2006, pp. 575ff; or the strongly emotional and opposite assessment in A. Cassese, "The Nicaragua and Tadic Tests Revisited in the Light of the ICJ Judgment on Genocide in Bosnia", *EJIL*, vol. 18, 2007, pp. 649ff.

14 H. Lauterpacht, "The International Protection of Human Rights", *RCADI*, vol. 70, 1947-I, pp. 5ff; R. Brunet, *La garantie internationale des droits de l'homme*, Geneva, 1947.

a minimum standard of objective treatment. It can fall below "civilization", as the Nuremberg Laws in Germany graphically showed. Moreover, municipal laws will vary. There can be no objective standard based on such a diversity of rules, some more protective than others. Moreover, and specifically in the context of armed conflict, municipal law presents two salient defects. The first aspect is that this legal order generally does not function correctly anymore: the social order has to a greater or lesser extent crumbled in armed conflict, and the legal institutions do not function adequately. The second aspect is that the State organs dominate the municipal legal order. In other words, municipal law sides with the government, and is controlled by the ruling forces in the State; the rebels, rising against these forces, are considered as simple criminals. There can be no expectation that such a legal order could suffice to regulate a NIAC placed in this context. This law will not be "neutral", nor will it be used as such or considered as such. Second, international HRL is also not sufficient. In the first place, when common article 3 of the Geneva Conventions was drafted, international HRL was still in its infancy. It could not be relied upon for protection. This situation only gradually changed in the immediately following years. It has been finally altered only when the body of international HRL came to full maturity, in other words, from the 1980s onwards. In the second place, while international HRL may play a distinctive role in the protection of persons in the context of armed conflict, it does not suffice to regulate the subject matter in a fully adequate way. International HRL is mainly predicated upon relationships situated in times of peace. This is not to say that it cannot be applied in times of armed conflict – and it is in effect so applied. However, there are certain rules on the conduct of hostilities, on the use of weapons, on targeting, on methods of warfare, which suppose regulation by a specialized branch of law. This branch can be only an IHL constructed for NIAC.

2.4 The general state of international humanitarian law relating to non-international armed conflict

For a long time it could be said that IHL relating to NIAC was reduced to a minimum; today, it must perhaps mainly be said that IHL relating to NIAC is in an unbalanced and chaotic state, not ensuring sufficient legal certainty. The reasons for this "minimality", "unbalancedness" and "chaoticness" are explored below.

2.4.1   Minimality

States, the legislators in international law and, in particular, in IHL, are extremely reluctant to accept the existence and development of NIAC law. States have always considered insurrection as a most delicate matter, in which the survival of their institutional structure and their legal order is at stake. They utterly dislike having to follow international rules and to be bound to accept international supervision in the application of these rules when it comes to a fight against what these States consider as criminal elements (the fashionable word today would be "terrorists") on their territory. States have thus always attempted to reduce international NIAC regulation to a minimum. Many States, either because they were entangled in a civil war (for example, Greece in 1949), or because they feared to be caught in such conflicts in the future (for example, France), or because they were fiercely attached to a sovereignty lately obtained (for example, Third World States), continuously fought to reduce the scope and impact of IHL for NIAC. Hence, the following statement of the Indian delegate at the Geneva Conference of 1977:

> "[T]he application of draft Protocol II to internal disturbances and other such situations would be tantamount to interference with the sovereign rights and duties of States. The definition of non-international conflicts was still too vague and no convincing arguments had been put forward to justify the need for draft Protocol II. . .".[15]

Hence, also, the non-intervention reminder in article 3 of AP II. As a result, the ICRC draft AP II (devoted to NIACs) was torn down: from the roughly 60 substantive articles contained in the draft, only approximately 20 found their way into a severely shortened AP II. Moreover, the provisions of AP II, echoing analogous provisions contained in AP I, were all reduced to a much sketchier wording, leaving a significantly greater reign to discretionary arguments. Compare, to this effect, articles 48ff of AP I with articles 13ff of AP II.[16]

---

15 *Official Records of the Diplomatic Conference on the Reaffirmation and Development of International Humanitarian Law Applicable in Armed Conflicts, Geneva (1974–1977)*, vol. VIII, p. 224.

16 See K. J. Partsch, "Regeln des humanitären Völkerrechts in nicht internationalen bewaffneten Konflikten – Umfang und Grenzen", in H. Schöttler and B. Hoffmann (eds), *Die Genfer Zusatzprotokolle, Kommentare und Analysen*, Bonn, 1993, p. 126.

2.4.2 Unbalancedness

The second problem is the fact that IHL for NIAC suffers from a certain imbalance, going to the heart of the principle of "equality of belligerents".[17] In an IAC, the basic rule is of the equality of belligerents: each belligerent, representing a State, is placed on a footing of equality and has to apply the same rules, notwithstanding the justice or injustice, the legality or illegality of its recourse to force.[18] The aggressor State and the State acting in self-defence are obliged to respect the same rules of warfare. Their discrimination under *jus ad bello* (for example, by sanctions against the aggressor) is not translated into discrimination under *jus in bello* (for example, by a faculty to assert more belligerent rights for the State acting with a recognized legal cause of resort to force).[19] There are three reasons for this separation rule. First, there is a humanitarian reason, since it is not acceptable that the minimum protections offered by IHL should be dropped for the sole reason that, say, the targeted civilians are on the "wrong side" in an armed conflict they have generally not chosen to conduct. Second, there is a practical reason, since IHL could not work if it was not based on some degree of reciprocity (no State would accept that the adverse party takes liberties with the law of armed conflicts without reciprocating, thus inaugurating a spiralling down). Third, there is a structural reason, since there is no organ in the international community endowed with the function to make, in each case, the determination of which State is the one using force legally and which State is the one using force illegally. The result of this state of affairs is that each belligerent interprets the issue for itself, and manifestly each will consider itself to be the party using force lawfully.[20] It will then take liberties with the application of IHL, and again there will be a spiralling down with concomitant breakdown of IHL. In NIAC today, this principle of equality does not apply with the same degree of force.[21]

---

17 See on this notion, the seminal work by H. Meyrowitz, *Le principe de l'égalité des belligérants devant le droit de la guerre*, Paris, 1970.

18 See for example, C. Schmitt, *Die Wendung zum diskriminierenden Kriegsbegriff*, Munich, 1938. Notably, such a constraint does not exist in NIAC.

19 On the issue, see for example, M. Sassoli, "Ius ad bellum and Ius in bello – The Separation between the Legality of the Use of Force and Humanitarian Rules to be Respected in Warfare: Crucial or Outdated?", in M. Schmitt and J. Pejic (eds), *International Law and Armed Conflict* (*Essays in Honor of Y. Dinstein*), Leiden/Boston, 2007, pp. 242ff. See also M. Sassoli, A. Bouvier and A. Quintin, *How Does Law Protect in War?*, vol. I, 3rd edn, Geneva, 2011, pp. 114ff.

20 Compare Christ's Word in Luke 6:41–42, or Matthew 7:3–5.

21 See F. Bugnion, "Jus ad bellum, Jus in bello and Non-International Armed Conflicts", *Yearbook of International Humanitarian Law*, vol. 6, 2003, pp. 167ff.

It fades away, and this in turn explains a fundamental weakness of IHL in NIAC. Certainly, there is an expectation that both belligerent sides must apply the relevant IHL rules reciprocally. This flows from article 1, § 1 of AP II and from the very conception of a conventional obligation.[22] But for all other purposes, the belligerents are not on an equal footing. Only the State's armed forces are entitled to use force; the rebels will be qualified by applicable municipal law as simple criminals, remaining to a full extent under the sway and the jurisdiction of the local penal courts. Notice that there is no analogous provision in municipal law as for IAC. In the latter, the foreign armed forces are not qualified as criminals. They are not generally under the jurisdiction of the adverse State. The foregoing also entails that the fighters on the side of the rebels have no combatant status. They enjoy no rights as combatants under IHL which their home State would be bound to respect. In particular, they are deprived of the so-called "combatant privilege", which consists of the right and duty to commit belligerent action and a concomitant immunity against any criminal prosecution for such acts, when conforming to IHL.[23] This, in turn, leads to an unwelcome result. The rebel fighter has no incentive to respect IHL. If he or she does, he or she will not gain any privilege; if he or she does not, the legal position remains the same: he or she remains subject to the wheels of municipal criminal law. But there is more: the fighter will have all incentives not to be captured. He or she will therefore resist to the upmost, without calculating any losses. If one adds to this state of affairs other relevant aspects, such as the ideological hatred quite common in NIAC, or else the fact that many rebel movements are today entangled in international crime and have no particular interest in respecting IHL (their fight is not so much for political ends than for private ends, for example, through abductions and trafficking), or lastly the fact that many rebel movements use analphabetic fighters and have no training whatsoever in warfare as well as poor discipline, it then becomes clear that the position of IHL in NIAC is considerably more difficult than it is in IAC. It is not a surprise to see that Syria (2011 to present)[24] is the theatre of massive violations

---

22 It may, however, be noted that this does not obviously explain the legal basis of the obligation of the rebels, since the Protocol will have been ratified only by the State. See L. Moir, *The Law of Internal Armed Conflict*, Cambridge, 2002, pp. 52ff, 96ff; and M. Sassoli, "Taking Armed Groups Seriously: Ways to Improve their Compliance with IHL", *Journal of International Humanitarian Legal Studies*, vol. 1, 2010, pp. 10ff.

23 G. Aïvo, *Le statut de combattant dans les conflits armés non internationaux*, Brussels, 2013.

24 See for example, W. van der Wolf and C. Tofan (eds), *Law and War in Syria: A Legal Account of the Current Crisis in Syria*, Nijmengen, 2013.

of IHL applicable in NIAC, while conversely the NATO warfare in Libya (2011), an IAC, was characterized by the highest specialization and most careful targeting.[25] However, no generalization is possible: the armed conflict in Mali (2013), with the intervention of the French forces, was again significantly respectful of the IHL rules, albeit it was a NIAC. This can be explained by the impact of the disciplined and trained French armed forces in that conflict.[26]

2.4.3   Chaoticness

This last factor flows from the state of legal regulation. As has already been said, IHL in NIAC is replete with gaps in the written law. These gaps are the result of the minimum approach described above. Not only is there a complete absence of legal regulation on a series of important points, such as perfidy or reprisals in NIAC. There are, moreover, many sketchy and skinny rules, not sufficiently detailed to warrant a comfortable application. Here the question arises to what extent such gaps in proper formulation can be filled by having recourse to the law of IAC, for example, by interpreting articles 13ff of AP II by analogy to the similar provisions contained in articles 48ff of AP I. Manifestly, the drafters of the two Protocols made a difference between both articles. Can we now undo this difference by pouring AP I formulations into AP II?[27] There are some bodies which do not hesitate to steer such a course: for example, the European Court of Human Rights (ECtHR) in the *Issaieva and Others v. Russia* case (2005).[28] According to the Court, the protection of the right to life under article 2 of the European Convention on Human Rights (ECHR) implies a proper preparation of attacks likely to affect civilians. These duties of precaution were found in article 57 of AP I (a provision not

---

25 See G. Bartolini, "L'operazione 'Unified Protector' e la condotta delle ostilità in Libia", *Rivista di diritto internazionale*, vol. 95, 2012, pp. 1012ff; C. De Cock, "Operation Unified Protector and the Protection of Civilians in Libya", *Yearbook of International Humanitarian Law*, vol. 14, 2011, pp. 213ff; F. Gaub, *The North Atlantic Treaty Organization and Libya: Reviewing Operation Unified Protector*, Carlisle (US Army War College), 2013.

26 See different contributions in *Rivista di diritto internazionale*, vol. 96, 2013.

27 On analogies in this context, see A. Carillo-Suarez, "Hors de Logique: Contemporary Issues in International Humanitarian Law as Applied to Internal Armed Conflict", *American University International Law Review*, vol. 15, 1999, pp. 1ff. The argument for abating the distinction between IAC and NIAC is also maintained: see for example, E. Crawford, "Unequal before the Law: The Case for the Elimination of the Distinction between International and Non-International Armed Conflicts", *Leiden Journal of International Law*, vol. 20, 2007, pp. 441ff.

28 Judgment of 24 February 2005. See G. Gaggioli, *L'influence mutuelle entre les droits de l'homme et le droit international humanitaire à la lumière du droit à la vie*, Paris, 2013, pp. 360–61.

even mentioned *expressis verbis* in the judgment) and then applied to a NIAC.

When the written law presents so many gaps and uncertainties, it is mainly through CIL that a body of law develops. This has been the case for the law of NIAC. It is mainly through practice, in particular the one of the International Criminal Tribunal for the former Yugoslavia (ICTY) and the International Criminal Tribunal for Rwanda (ICTR), that many rules applicable to IAC were found to also apply to NIAC – sometimes more by an *ipse dixit* than by any sound demonstration.[29] The Customary Law Study of the ICRC tried to sum up the position, at least for the rules contained in the two Protocols.[30] However, customary law constantly continues to evolve. As we will see in the next chapter, it is uncommon for IHL to be based too heavily on unwritten law. Rather, it is normally rooted in conventional, in other words, written law, and there are good reasons for this. The net result of this state of affairs is a great deal of legal uncertainty, which is highly unwelcome in IHL. This legal uncertainty nourishes what has here been called a certain degree of "chaoticness" in the law of NIAC. As there will not be any official codification of this law any time soon, we will have to accommodate the current state of affairs as much as is possible.[31]

2.5   Content of international humanitarian law applicable to non-international armed conflict

It is beyond the scope of the narrow compass of this introductory book to try to provide a general analysis of the content of applicable IHL in

---

29 The reasoning of the ICTY has sometimes seemed to be directed by the famous maxim expressed in § 119 of the *Tadic* Appeals Chamber Judgment of 1995, according to which "[w]hat is inhumane and consequently proscribed, in international wars, cannot but be inhumane and inadmissible in civil strife". The ICTY has acted more than once on that principle, by presuming that a regulation should be transferred from IAC to NIAC, even without a careful analysis of State practice. Thus, for example, in the *Blagojevic and Jokic* case (Trial Chamber, 2005), § 599, the Tribunal affirmed that the rule against separation of families is not repeated in article 17, AP II, but that it finds no reason "why this general principle should not be applicable also to non-international armed conflict".

30 J. M. Henckaerts and L. Doswald-Beck, *Customary International Humanitarian Law*, vol. I, Cambridge, 2005.

31 There is, however, a private codification: Institute of Humanitarian Law, *The Manual on the Law of Non-International Armed Conflict, With Commentary*, Sanremo, 2006.

NIAC. However, some general remarks may be made, supplemented by certain specific points.

2.5.1 Similarities to international humanitarian law in international armed conflict

First, under the "humanization of IHL" limb already noted, the tendency of the last 20 years has been constantly to extend the reach of IHL in NIAC so as to bring it closer to the legal position of the IHL in IAC. An emblematic phrase in this context is the one famously used by the ICTY in the *Tadic* case of 1995: "What is inhumane and consequently proscribed, in international wars, cannot but be inhumane and inadmissible in civil strife".[32] The ICTY then went on to live up to that maxim in its case-law, in declaring more often than not that a certain war crimes offence and the concomitant duty under IHL were also applicable in NIAC – even in somewhat sophisticated matters, such as command responsibility.[33] Already in 1995, in the quoted *Tadic* judgment, the Appeals Chamber innovated in declaring that there existed "war crimes" (grave violations of IHL) in NIAC.[34] The practice of States is less clear with regard to such a progressive merger of IHL relating to IAC and NIAC. However, it appears that many rules in the military manuals are drafted without distinction regarding the type of armed conflict. It indeed appears questionable whether an army like the French one will function according to markedly different rules in Libya and in Mali.[35] This would to some extent be incompatible with the unity of their training. It is therefore not a great surprise that the quoted Customary Law Study of the ICRC found that most rules of the Additional Protocols of 1977 are applicable in both conflicts; even if that does not necessarily imply that the detail of these common rules will be the same. In any case, the principle behind the detailed rules, and thus the gist of the matter, will apparently be common. Examples: Rule 11 of the Study, relating to the prohibition of indiscriminate attacks;[36] Rule 22 relating to the duty of the parties to the conflict to take all feasible precautions to protect the civilian population and civilian objects against the effects of

---

32 ICTY (Appeals Chamber, 1995), § 119.

33 See for example, the *Hadzihasanovic* case (Trial Chamber, 15 March 2006), § 65.

34 At §§ 96ff, 128ff.

35 But this covers only one type of NIAC – could the same be said for military actions against rebels on French territory?

36 J. M. Henckaerts and L. Doswald-Beck, *Customary International Humanitarian Law*, vol. I, Cambridge, 2005, p. 37.

attack;[37] Rule 25 relating to respect and protection in all circumstances of medical personnel exclusively assigned to medical duties;[38] Rules 38ff concerning the respect of cultural property;[39] Rule 53 relating to the use of starvation of the civilian population as a method of warfare;[40] Rule 74 prohibiting the use of chemical weapons;[41] Rule 90 relating to the prohibition of torture, cruel or inhumane treatment;[42] and so on. Sometimes, a rule is presented as possibly or arguably extending to NIAC, as in the case of Rule 24: "Each party to the conflict must, to the extent feasible, remove civilian persons and objects under its control from the vicinity of military objectives".[43] The same is true for Rule 82, relating to the duty to record, so far as possible, the placement of landmines.[44] As a result of such extension, the reach of IHL protection in NIAC has significantly increased. If there remain many violations of the law, this increase in scope at least allows the stigmatization of some conduct and reaction by criminal prosecution. In Switzerland in February 2014, there were 14 pending criminal cases concerning in great part the commission of war crimes in NIAC abroad.

2.5.2   Applicable to both parties to the conflict

Second, it must be noted that an extension of IHL in NIAC is neither always welcome nor necessarily to be hailed as a progress. It must be keenly borne in mind that IHL in NIAC shall apply to both parties to the conflict, the governmental forces, but also the rebel forces. The latter need not have a territorial control for IHL in NIAC to apply to them under common article 3 of the Geneva Conventions. The rules devised to apply to NIAC must therefore be practically applicable by both parties, lest IHL be discarded by armed groups who consider that it does not reflect their possibilities and military necessities.[45] It may be correct to devise rules on detention with a certain degree of exigency; or to hold that *habeas corpus* fair trial rights have to be respected for detained persons. It may be clearly the case that the

---

37 *Ibid.*, p. 68.

38 *Ibid.*, p. 79.

39 *Ibid.*, pp. 127ff.

40 *Ibid.*, p. 186.

41 *Ibid.*, p. 259.

42 *Ibid.*, p. 315.

43 *Ibid.*, p. 74.

44 *Ibid.*, p. 283.

45 See M. Sassòli, "Taking Armed Groups Seriously: Ways to Improve their Compliance with IHL", *Journal of International Humanitarian Legal Studies*, vol. 1, 2010, pp. 15ff.

State can (and must, even in wartime) ensure such rights through its institutions. It is not clear that every armed group, not controlling a part of the territory, has the same logistic or practical possibilities.[46] At the end of the day, the mentioned duties may thus boil down either to an indirect prohibition on detaining persons, or to a duty to attempt to hand them over as quickly as possible to a third State willing to accept them on its territory. The government of the territory caught in a NIAC would have to give its assent. Some of the duties under articles 13ff of AP II practically suppose a territorial basis of the rebels – but article 1, § 1, of that Protocol indeed requires such a basis as a material condition of its applicability. Conversely, not all extensions of IHL in NIAC are problematic. If modern IHL progressively extends prohibitions as to weapons law from IAC to NIAC, no particular problem in the context of implementation by armed groups arises. The obligation stated is purely negative – not positive – and requires no particular factual possibilities: it is limited to not using a class of weapons. Moreover, armed groups that possess sophisticated weapons are generally of a high degree of organization and control a part of the national territory. This increases the degree to which they appear as a quasi-State and can assume more exacting obligations. The point made here is that a progressive merger of IHL in NIAC to IHL in IAC according to the generous formula of the *Tadic* Tribunal quoted above is not to be seen as a univocal and undoubted betterment of a previously unsatisfactory or even barbaric law, in need of messianic liberation. IHL has its own needs and its own inner equilibrium. A strengthening of IHL in NIAC is welcome and the ICTY has done important pioneering work. However, and this is the gist of the matter, every situation should be analysed critically on its own merits, without recourse to excessively bold ideological preconceptions.

2.5.3   Areas of law exclusive to international armed conflict

Third, there are areas where IHL in IAC and IHL in NIAC cannot come together because of profound differences of a legal, political and systematic nature. In other words, there are areas of IHL which for a long time will remain limited to the law of IAC and not extend to the law of NIAC. This is the case for the following areas:

---

46 See J. Somer, "Jungle Justice: Passing Sentence on the Equality of Belligerents in Non-International Armed Conflict", *International Review of the Red Cross*, vol. 89, 2007, pp. 655ff.

1. Firstly, the notion of *combatant* (and the related privileged of the combatant) will remain limited to IAC. In NIAC, States do not accept that members of the insurgent movement be granted an international status entitling them to commit acts of belligerent violence for which they could not be prosecuted. Thus, in NIAC there are strictly speaking only civilians "directly participating in hostilities" and targetable according to the rules of direct participation (see Chapter 6). The members of the State armed forces and the members of the armed groups, having engaged in a "continuous combat function", may be called "fighters" as opposed to civilians, in order to keep manifest the dividing line for the application of the principle of distinction. The civilians only sporadically engaging directly in hostilities will then be qualified as such, in other words, civilians occasionally participating in hostilities. The result of that regulation is that "fighters" can be targeted throughout their armed engagement, even while sleeping, whereas civilians directly participating in hostilities can only be targeted on a sporadic basis during the phase of active engagement. When captured, no fighter or civilian directly participating in hostilities is entitled to prisoner of war status. There are no prisoners of war in NIAC, apart from the situation where the belligerent parties conclude special agreements or decide unilaterally to grant a treatment not less favourable than that of prisoner of war to their captives.

2. Secondly, the separation will continue to prevail for *belligerent occupation*. Such occupation supposes international warfare, in other words, the involvement of foreign territory. Governmental forces re-conquering national territory against the rebels will not consider themselves as occupiers, nor will rebels controlling a part of the national territory.

3. Thirdly, there are certain specific areas in the law of IAC which actual practice has not yet extended significantly to NIAC. This is the case for a series of institutions of the *law of maritime warfare*. The rules on contraband and on prizes of ships have remained conditioned on the exercise of belligerent powers by a State. Some basic rules of maritime warfare were considered in the Sri Lankan civil war, where rebels were involved in maritime operations. But the law of maritime warfare in NIAC is still in its infancy. The situation today is thus the reverse of the one in the nineteenth century, when the institution of recognition of belligerency for rebels was essentially based on the interests of third States applying the rules of neutrality for the benefit of their neutral shipping. NIAC was thus at that time essentially

internationalized as a consequence of maritime warfare rules. A change could, however, occur in international practice, and could more easily so than in the two previously mentioned areas of law, where strong systematic and ideological arguments militate against any analogy between IAC and NIAC.

4.   Finally, there is no *neutrality* law applicable in NIAC. Neutrality supposes an IAC.

2.5.4   Written law

Fourth, what is the stock of written IHL in NIAC rules today? We have already seen that CIL has considerably developed the applicable law of NIAC. But there remains to take a quick stock of applicable written rules. These rules can be found in common article 3 of the Geneva Conventions, in AP II and in a series of other and applicable conventions.

1.   *Common article 3* is based on three normative layers, all relating to the protection of persons. There is thus only "Geneva Law" (protected persons) and no "Hague Law" (conduct of hostilities, means and methods of warfare) in common article 3. The first layer relates to the principle of "humane treatment" without adverse distinction (discrimination). It will be noted that among the criteria of prohibited discrimination the one of "nationality" is not listed. The reason is manifestly that the drafters took as granted that in a civil war the persons fighting each other normally have the same nationality. To the extent, however, that persons of foreign nationality participate in such conflicts, the rule on non-adverse distinction (as in the vocabulary of 1949) has to be applied to them, under the cover of the words "any other similar criteria" contained in article 3. The second layer contains specific prohibitions, listed in letters a to d. These prohibitions reflect the experiences of the Spanish Civil War and of World War II. The prohibitions are against attacks on life and limb, degrading treatment, the taking of hostages and unfair trial. The third layer concerns the care for the wounded and sick. The content of Geneva Convention I is here miniaturized in one single sentence. The fourth layer is concerned with the faculty of an impartial humanitarian body, such as the ICRC, to offer its services, for example, by proposing humanitarian assistance. The two last sentences of the article deal with special problems, not directly linked with the protection of persons. Overall, it can be said that common article 3 is a sort of convention in miniature, a spelling

out of the Martens Clause, covering the most egregious ugliness of armed conflict – and not more.

2.   *AP II*. AP II develops common article 3 and extends it in various directions. There are three normative layers in AP II. The first expands on the principle of humane treatment. It adds to the four types of prohibited acts under common article 3 a series of further acts such as prohibition of collective punishment, refusal of quarter, acts of terrorism, enforced prostitution and rape, slavery, pillage, and even any threat to commit such prohibited acts (article 4, § 2). It further contains detailed rules for detained persons (article 5) and for fair trial (article 6). The second layer expands on the care due to the injured and sick (articles 7–12). This is a notable expansion on the situation prevailing in 1949 under common article 3. We will notice in particular the duty to search for the injured and sick according to the conditions contained in article 8. The third and last substantive layer relates to the protection of the civilian population in the context of hostilities. This is the layer of "Hague Law". It echoes the provisions in articles 48ff of AP I. Thus the principle of distinction (article 13), the protection of objects indispensable for the survival of the civilian population (article 14), the protection of works and installations containing dangerous forces (article 15), the protection of cultural objects (article 16), the prohibition of forced displacements (article 17) and the right of relief societies to offer their services (article 18), are codified. The prohibition of refusal of quarter should be added, albeit it is mentioned in article 4, § 1 (perhaps not entirely satisfactorily from the systematic point of view). It has already been said that the provisions contained in AP II are much skinnier that the related ones for IAC in AP I.

3.   *Other Conventions*. There are finally a series of other conventions which apply either to any type of armed conflict (according to their wording "in any circumstances"), or provide expressly as an extension of their content to NIAC. Examples of the first category can be found in the context of weapons law. Thus, for example, the Convention on the Prohibition of Development, Production and Stockpiling of Bacteriological (Biological) and Toxin Weapons and on Their Destruction (1972), article 1. A similar formula is used in article 1, § 1, of the Convention on the Prohibition of the Development, Production, Stockpiling and Use of Chemical Weapons and on their Destruction (1993): "never under any circumstances". Such formulae cover both peacetime and times of armed conflict, and both IAC and NIAC. Examples

of the second category can be found in different areas of IHL (for example, in the context of cultural objects and their protection,[47] or the protective emblems (as AP III of 2005 to the Geneva Conventions shows, in its article 1), and again in the context of weapons law). Thus, the amended Protocol II on Mines, Booby-Traps and other Devices (1996) to the Conventional Weapons Convention of 1980, states that its content shall also apply to NIAC's covered by common article 3 of the Geneva Conventions (article 1, §§ 2 and 3).[48] There is thus a growing conventional body of IHL in NIAC, which must, however, be painstakingly searched for in the different conventions and protocols of IHL.

2.5.5 Limits of reasoning by analogy

Fifth, there remain doubts as to the extent to which reasoning by analogy can be heeded in order to fill gaps in IHL in NIAC by recourse to other bodies of international law, mainly IHL in IAC, but also HRL, or regulations of the law of peace (for example, on humanitarian assistance). Two examples may show the problem in operation. The first example relates to a situation in which the reasoning by analogy does not seem to pose any difficulty; the practice of States does not oppose any obstacles to its reign. This is the case of perfidy. The second example puts into spotlight a situation in which analogous reasoning remains shrouded in doubt, at least when applied to objects rather than to protected persons. This is the case with armed reprisals, also called belligerent reprisals.

1. *Perfidy.* Perfidy is defined in article 37 of AP I for the purposes of modern IHL as killing, injuring or capturing an adversary by resort to acts inviting the confidence of an adversary to lead him to believe that he is entitled to, or obliged to accord, protection under the rules of international law applicable in armed conflict, with intent to betray that confidence (the definition of treacherous acts was wider in the past). Thus, perfidy is characterized by an action contrary to good faith, the gist of which consists of using the rights and obligations under IHL for hostile purposes

---

47 See article 22 of the Second Protocol on Cultural Property to the 1954 Hague Convention (1999) and V. Mainetti, "De nouvelles perspectives pour la protection des biens culturels en cas de conflit armé: l'entrée en vigueur du Deuxième Protocole relatif à la Convention de la Haye de 1954", *RICR*, vol. 86, 2004, pp. 337ff.

48 For an analysis, see W. H. Boothby, *Weapons and the Law of Armed Conflict*, Oxford, 2009, pp. 165ff.

against life, limb or freedom of the members of the adverse party. It is prohibited for the obvious reason that otherwise no belligerent would be imprudent enough to implement IHL obligations, if there must be a constant and well-founded fear that these obligations are used for hostile purposes. An example of perfidy would be to feign surrender in order to be able to open fire under more favourable conditions. Conversely, it is not perfidious to feign incapacitation or injury for other than hostile purposes, for example, for being captured by the other party in order to desert or in order to escape fighting because of cowardliness. There is no perfidy even when an injury is feigned in order to be transported to the lines of the adverse party in the hope of spying. The feigning here is not placed in sufficiently direct connection to an attack on life, limb or freedom of members of the adverse party. However, under articles 38 and 39 of AP I, certain action is prohibited as such, independent of the aim for which it is used, and also unconnected to the attack on life, limb or freedom. This is, for example, the case of abuses of protective emblems. The general confidence in the proper use of such emblems is here protected. The aim pursued is to secure their constant functionality. Thus, transporting weapons in a vehicle under the cover of the protective emblem is a "perfidy" under the definition of article 38, even if there is no direct link to an attack on life, limb or freedom. All these regulations relating to perfidy and quasi-perfidy are contained in the rules of IHL in IAC. To be sure, a prohibition of perfidy was included in the Conference Draft AP II, but it was finally deleted. However, it is not disputed that a series of military manuals and national legislation prohibit perfidy in any type of armed conflict. No State has claimed that perfidy is allowed under the law of NIAC. This picture provided the decisive argument for the ICRC Study on Customary Humanitarian Law to state that the prohibition of perfidy also extends to the law of NIAC.[49] The basis for this induction in State practice may not be of a considerable strength and breadth, but in view of the absence of divergent practice, the conclusion drawn by the ICRC Study can stand. Obviously, there remains a point of imbalance in the determination of the law of IHL in NIAC, as in the law of IHL in IAC, since it is generally held that only State practice is decisive. While this stance is understandable in the situation of IAC, where

---

49 J. M. Henckaerts and L. Doswald-Beck, *Customary International Humanitarian Law*, vol. I, Cambridge, 2005, pp. 222–3.

States confront each other, it could be considered that the practice of the armed groups should be given more weight in the case of NIAC, where these groups are parties to the conflict. But the present writer has no knowledge of claims by such groups that perfidy is an acceptable method of warfare in NIAC.

2.   *Armed Reprisals.* Under certain restrictive conditions,[50] a party to the conflict may respond to the previous violation of rules of IHL by the other party with a violation of such rules. The rules on belligerent reprisals have developed under IHL for IAC. The effort there is to square two countervailing interests: on the one hand to keep alive the faculty to take reprisals as a means of last resort to sanction violations of IHL by the other party; and, on the other hand, to avoid an escalation and abuse of such reprisals, which would quickly lead to a complete breakdown of the law of armed conflicts (World War I illustrated this with regard to maritime warfare law[51]). Thus, reprisals against civilian, protected persons and objects are prohibited in any case. Where reprisals are allowed (for example, in the law on weapons), their purpose must be exclusively to induce the other party to comply with the law and not to punish; they must be a measure of last resort; they must be a proportionate reaction; the decision must be taken at the highest level of government or of the army; and reprisal action must terminate as soon as the adversary resumes compliance with the law. Conversely, the position is far from clear in the context of NIAC. In this case, the recourse of an analogy with IAC is difficult, since the underlying practice and legal opinion is uncertain. Many States traditionally voted against any regulations on reprisals in NIAC because they felt that that very concept had no place in internal conflicts. These conflicts are not based on a strict equality of belligerents; they are covered by the sovereignty of the State over its territory. Thus, for a significant number of States, there should remain a freedom of fact to take such action as deemed necessary, in the shadow of the voluntary absence of international regulation. Consequently, the ICRC Customary Law Study comes to the conclusion that "[t]here is insufficient evidence that the very concept of lawful reprisal in non-international armed conflict has ever materialized in international law";[52] the idea of enforcing

---

50 See *ibid.*, pp. 513ff.

51 W. E. Hall, *Law of Naval Warfare*, London, 1921.

52 J. M. Henckaerts and L. Doswald-Beck, *Customary International Humanitarian Law*, vol. I, Cambridge, 2005, p. 527.

the law through reprisals has in this view remained largely alien to that branch of IHL.[53] On the other hand, it is now accepted that reprisals against protected persons are implicitly prohibited under IHL in NIAC, because of common article 3 of the Geneva Conventions and article 4, § 2, of AP II: the words "prohibited at any time and in any place" contained in these provisions (common article 3, § 2, Geneva Conventions, chapeau, and article 4, § 2, AP II, chapeau) are interpreted to exclude reprisals against protected persons, in other words, persons *hors de combat*. This was also why the ICTY could come to the conclusion that reprisals against protected persons were condemned both in IAC and in NIAC.[54] The prohibitive result is here reached by interpretation of rules whose purpose is not to regulate reprisals, but which may be taken to implicitly exclude them. However, this does suppose that the concept of armed reprisals exists in NIAC; and that point is not altogether completely clear. Attacks on protected persons, whatever the cause (and whether or not called reprisals) are, however, rightly considered to be unlawful. Further, NIAC rules analogous to the ones for IAC also prohibiting reprisals against objects cannot be found. At this point, the analogy, if at all possible, seems to break down.[55] Thus, summing up, the uncertainty as to the existence of a legal category of reprisals in NIAC, a certain will to maintain a freedom of fact, and the greater uncertainty as to the entities protected against reprisals, make the operation of the analogy from IAC to NIAC quite delicate. At best, the analogy may hold well for protected persons; but it is not solid for action against persons not *hors de combat*, or against objects.

The two foregoing examples were meant to show that analogies from IHL in IAC to IHL in NIAC are not always obvious and that they depend heavily on the legal environment into which they are cast. Sometimes they are supported by practice, sometimes they are not. No automatic conclusions are warranted. Some careful analysis must always take place. Absent State practice, the analogy from IAC to NIAC is largely an act of legislation in place of the formal legislator.

---

53 *Ibid.*, p. 528.
54 *Martic* case (Review of the Indictment, 8 March 1996), §§ 9–12, 15–16, notably 16. See also the *Kupreskic* case (Trial Chamber, 2000), §§ 515ff. Sometimes the point is made under the guise of the unavailability of the *tu quoque* argument, in other words, the fact that the other party violated the provisions on the protection of civilians is not a justification for atrocities by the aggrieved party: see *Kunarac* case (Appeals Chamber, 2002), § 87.
55 See J. Hebenstreit, *Repressalien im humanitären Völkerrecht*, Baden-Baden, 2004, pp. 169ff, 173.

Any argument in this sense should thus be buttressed by good and solid reasons of legal policy, and by some urgency of action. A cogent humanitarian concern, which may be quite largely shared, is certainly a point to be taken into account in this context. That is the most that can be made of the famous § 119 of the *Tadic* judgment of 1995, mentioned above.

2.5.6   Two general principles

Sixth, in cases of gaps (and freedoms of fact) within the body of NIAC, two legally applicable general principles should always be taken into account. First, with regard to protected persons (*hors de combat*), there is the principle of "humane treatment" enshrined in common article 3 of the Geneva Conventions ("shall in all circumstances be treated humanely"). Second, and pulling in the same direction, is the Martens Clause, which today undoubtedly applies to NIAC, as can be seen by its insertion in the Preamble of AP II. The reach of the two principles is largely the same, but not identical. Common article 3 is limited to persons *hors de combat*, who find themselves in the control of the adverse party. The Preamble of AP II and CIL benefit "the human person" in general. This includes combatants during the phase of hostilities. Certainly, the parties to NIACs do not do enough to implement the dictates contained in these two provisions. Situations such as those in Syria (2012 to present) are hardly suitable to modify this pessimistic conclusion. But according to the situation, much can be obtained through patient and not heavily publicized action on the spot, such as the actions the ICRC routinely performs.

2.5.7   The interplay of international humanitarian law and human rights law

Seventh, situations of NIAC evidence a close interplay, interrelationship and cooperation of IHL and HRL, in particular between what is called "conduct of hostilities" (IHL) and "maintenance of order" or "law enforcement" (HRL).[56] The distinction is not exclusive to NIAC. It also applies in the context of IAC, but it is certainly of particular

---

56 On this question, see for example, N. Melzer, "Conceptual Distinction and Overlaps between Law Enforcement and the Conduct of Hostilities", in T. Gill and D. Fleck (eds), *The Handbook of the International Law of Military Operations*, Oxford, 2010, pp. 33ff; D. Fleck, "Law Enforcement and the Conduct of Hostilities: Two Supplementing or Mutually Exclusive Legal Paradigms?", in *Essays in Honour of M. Bothe*, Baden-Baden, 2008, pp. 391ff.

relevance in NIAC. The problem is inherent in the tasks of an army. However, it has been sharpened recently by the considerable broadening of the functions to be performed by modern armed forces, vested with multi-functional mandates, often in close cooperation with civilian actors. Such functions include, but are not limited to, conducting hostilities, maintaining order (as would do the police), the transport of humanitarian aid, clearing mines and other war remnants, fighting crime and helping in the reconstruction of State structures, and so on.[57] During the "hot phase" of the conflict, the conduct of hostilities under IHL will prevail, without, however, being exclusive; during the "soft phase" of the conflict, especially in the *post bellum* phase, the law enforcement paradigm will tend to prevail, albeit again without exclusivity.[58] The rules applicable to both types of activities are not identical: IHL dominates the first, HRL the second. There thus arise complex problems of interplay between both bodies of law, which are not yet fully elucidated and continue to shift as practice evolves. The relationship has been to some extent clarified in the context of the taking of life, in other words, in the trade-off between the relative right to kill during warfare and the somewhat stronger protection of the right to life under HRL.[59] The divide between the two mentioned bodies of law will here be applicable as a function of the different situations in which the taking of life will occur, for example during open combat or in a counter-insurgency operation attempting to arrest a fighter.[60] The relationship of IHL to HRL is open to more doubt in other areas, which, however, are not of particular interest with regard to our problem relating to the conduct of hostilities and the law enforcement paradigms.

In IAC, the question of the relation between the two bodies of the law and the two paradigms arises in different complexions, for example in

---

57 On the many functions of modern peacekeeping operations, see P. Dailler, "Les opérations multi-nationales consécutives à des conflits armés en vue du rétablissement de la paix", *RCADI*, vol. 314, 2005, pp. 233ff.

58 On this *jus post bellum*, see for example, C. Stahn and J. Kleffner (eds), *Jus post bellum: Towards a Law of Transition From Conflict to Peace*, The Hague, 2008. See also N. D. White and C. Henderson (eds), *Research Handbook on International Conflict and Security Law, Jus ad bellum, Jus in bello and Jus post bellum*, Cheltenham, 2013.

59 See G. Gaggioli, *L'influence mutuelle entre les droits de l'homme et le droit international humani-taire à la lumière du droit à la vie*, Paris, 2013.

60 The *lex specialis* approach of the ICJ makes sense only if taken within this activities-related or functional view. See the *Nuclear Weapons* advisory opinion, ICJ, *Reports*, 1996-I, p. 240, § 25; and the *Wall* opinion, ICJ, *Reports*, 2004-I, p. 178, § 106.

the context of occupied territories, where in almost all cases,[61] after the phase of combat, comes the phase of occupation and the duty to maintain public order (article 43 of the Hague Regulations of 1907).[62] The question also arises in other contexts: for example, the establishment of a military checkpoint, where law enforcement rules will apply, rather than conduct of hostility rules. The question arises again in the context of prisoner of war camps. There are no hostilities here. If a prisoner of war attempts an escape, law enforcement logic will apply. The use of force against the fugitive will have to be progressively escalated in order to remain compatible with the polar stars of the law enforcement paradigm, namely necessity and proportionality. Thus, article 42 of Geneva Convention III reads: "The use of weapons against prisoners of war, especially against those who are escaping or attempting to escape, shall constitute an extreme measure, which shall always be preceded by warnings appropriate to the circumstances". This provision is manifestly inspired by a HRL paradigm *avant la lettre*. We may therefore note that the two paradigms are not necessarily successive in time: first, a phase of conduct of hostilities; later, a phase of maintenance of order. If it is true that there will sometimes be a shift in emphasis according to such different phases, the two paradigms are intertwined in the sense that they often apply at the same time, in the same phase, but to different activities and situations.

In NIAC, the relationship between the two paradigms is particularly close. Especially in the low-threshold NIACs, to which common article 3 of the Geneva Conventions applies, there will be few open military confrontations and a lot of law enforcement measures. This is the case, for example, when there is an attempt to arrest a fighter or a civilian directly participating in hostilities, when this happens outside the context of actual fighting (and albeit such arrest operations may easily lead to small armed clashes). Such counter-insurgency operations are particularly frequent in NIAC. Moreover, the greatest number of NIAC take place within the territory of a State, in other words, in the sphere of jurisdiction in which HRL most normally applies and continues to apply in times of NIAC. The parallel application of HRL and IHL is here particularly important since, as we have seen, IHL in NIAC is replete with uncertainties and gaps. HRL is therefore providing a

---

61 Apart from the one envisaged in article 2, § 2, of the Geneva Conventions I–IV, a territory occupied without armed resistance and thus without hostilities.

62 See M. Sassòli, "Legislation and Maintenance of Public Order and Civil Life by Occupying Powers", *EJIL*, vol. 16, 2005, pp. 661ff.

safety net to the benefit of civilians. It often goes beyond the protections offered by IHL in NIAC, especially when a State has not ratified AP II with its HRL-related provisions (articles 4–6) and there is some quibbling about the customary status of those rights. Thus, in many NIAC, HRL was applied in a law enforcement context, for example, in the Turkish-Kurdish NIAC in the 1990s. A single example may suffice. The *Ergi v. Turkey* (1998) case[63] concerned a situation where the State armed forces had not taken all the necessary precautions in order to minimize civilian losses while attempting an arrest. Not having the jurisdiction to apply the relevant IHL rules directly, the ECtHR reverted to the HRL enforcement paradigm under article 2 of the ECHR, in other words, the right to life. This implies a strict control of the use of "minimum of force necessary". Force can be used only as a means of last resort; the least violent means must be selected; the use of force must appear unavoidable; it must be strictly proportionate to the threat posed and to the aim pursued, and so on.[64] In this way, even during NIAC, law enforcement lurks behind the scenes and frequently comes forward. It cannot be said, however, that all the problems have been solved with regard to its application. Especially in more intense NIAC, there remains the question to what extent the conduct of hostilities model should prevail as a *lex specialis*. But there is here also a problem of jurisdiction of the human rights bodies, which are not entitled to apply IHL as such. A too bold application of HRL may lead to a certain disaffection of the military forces against a law considered to be badly tailored to the situations and needs on the spot. This would weaken respect for the law and also reduce commitment and engagement, two key words in the context of IHL.

Different criteria can be devised in the choice of the correct body of law, but there remains a grey area. The relevant criteria include the following. The conduct of hostilities model should prevail when there is an armed conflict and the action takes place in the context of fighting enemy forces (causal and functional nexus); there is a use of force against combatants, fighters, military objectives or civilians participating directly in hostilities; there is no control over the persons against whom violence is used; and in general when there is a high-level exchange of violence of a belligerent type. The law enforcement model should prevail in the following contexts: partially and in conjunction

---

63 See http://hudoc.echr.coe.int/sites/eng/pages/search.aspx?i=001–58200.

64 See G. Gaggioli, *L'influence mutuelle entre les droits de l'homme et le droit international humanitaire à la lumière du droit à la vie*, Paris, 2013, pp. 341ff.

with applicable rules of IHL when there is control and exercise of authority over persons (for example, detained persons); in situations of public disorder or unrest, characterized by non-organized violence; in case of attacks by persons whose status is not determined, in particular in the context of rioting or criminality. The interplay of the two paradigms and the two branches of the law has led to a palpable increase of complexity in the pertinent legal analysis.

3   The sources of international humanitarian law and their subject matter specificity

3.1 Definition of the term "sources"

In legal science the term "sources" is used to designate the law-creating agencies, in other words, the facts of legal production. There are certain facts or procedures by which the law is created; and there are also places where the law can be found. These facts, procedures and places whereby law is made and where law can be found are the sources of the law. They contain the legal norms applicable in the particular situations. Thus, a treaty (and the treaty-making process) is a way of producing norms of international law; it is thus a source of international law. In contrast, general principles of law are not created by the legislator, but found through an exegetic perusal of the body of legal rules, either on the plane of international law (general principles of international law) or on the plane of comparative municipal law (general principles of municipal law to be transferred analogously into the body of international law); it is also a source of international law, in other words, a place where legal rules can be found. The main sources of international law are agreements (called treaties when written), CIL and general principles of law. All three sources have a distinctive role in IHL. The purpose of this chapter is not to discuss the sources of international law from a general standpoint. It is rather to show with what particularities and idiosyncrasies these sources are applied in the context of IHL. The principles of IHL will be discussed in Chapter 4.

3.2 The significance of treaties in international humanitarian law

Treaty law (in other words, written agreements between States) remains a particularly significant source of IHL. Indeed, IHL is one of the branches where the codification of the law has been pushed furthest. In addition to the general factors which account for the importance of treaty law within the body of international law, there are specific reasons why this is so in the specific realm of IHL.

3.2.1   The importance of treaty law in general

Among the reasons accounting for the importance of treaty law in general, three aspects may be briefly mentioned. First, treaty law reflects the typical-law making mechanism in a decentralized society characterized by the absence of a common superior power. If some law is to be made between equals, such as sovereign States, where no one holds power or sway over the other, there remains only some form of consent or agreement to fix common rules of behaviour. Second, treaty law allows the parties to obtain, with regard to certain matters, for a certain time-span (or also in the long run), an appreciable degree of legal certainty. On the one hand, there are subject matters where States want to keep a high degree of freedom of action for their foreign policy and which they do not subject to a legal regime of any tightness. In such a situation, an agreement is normally not concluded. On the other hand, there are matters where there is a reciprocal interest in some degree of stabilization. The treaty is the best vehicle for achieving this aim. Its written rules normally provide a greater degree of stability than the mobile rules of CIL. True, a text can be bent to subjective interpretations and contortions, but such an exercise is generally more arduous in the face of written provisions rather than unwritten ones. To make a written provision say the opposite of what its text conveys is not an obvious exercise. Third, the treaty allows for the regulation of technical matters of detail which are not suitable for unwritten norms. Thus, it is unthinkable to create an international organization, with its institutions, procedures, financing, and so on, on the sole basis of customary rules; nor is it feasible to set up detailed regimes for environmental protection, like those of Kyoto (1997), solely on the basis of customary rules. In IHL it would not be possible to set up a fact-finding commission like the one provided for in article 90 of AP I by unwritten rules.

3.2.2   The importance of treaty law to international humanitarian law

To the above general reasons, others, relating to IHL in particular, may be added. Also, some of the general reasons hold in the context of IHL, but require some specification.

First, questions of warfare are relatively detailed and technical matters. Thus, apart from a body of broad customary principles and flexible general rules, adaptable to the ever-changing circumstances of war, there must also be a set of detailed rules. IHL is an area of international law most intimately characterized by the complex interplay of some general principles (necessity, proportionality, prohibition of unnecessary suffering, distinction, humanity, and so on) with a dust of detailed rules containing specific prescriptions, procedural and substantive. Such specific rules can be set out reasonably only in a written form. For example, a regulation of rights and duties in the complex web of a prisoner of war camp, with rules on prisoner hygiene, labour, personal belongings, representatives, visits by the ICRC, and correspondence with families, and so on, cannot reasonably be left to the simple progressive growth of customary law. On the contrary, customary rules must here be rooted in some written legal regime on which they can take a firm hold.

Second, one has to bear in mind that IHL addresses itself to non-lawyers. IHL has to be applied mainly by soldiers and higher military officials, sometimes also by private individuals in IACs[1] or in NIACs. These persons are most often not lawyers. They cannot be asked to undertake complex and subtle tasks of determining the existence of customary rules and of interpretation. The law must tell them clearly and in some detail what conduct is expected from them in a large set of particular situations. Only treaty law allows for such detailed legal regulation. Alberico Gentili, one of the founding fathers of classical international law, wrote with some sense of derision: "In fact, a soldier ought to know arms and not the law, and it is proper that military men should be ignorant of the law. It is military custom to regard as ridiculous and silly the subtleties of the courts".[2] The written form of the rules is all the more precious in this regard. Moreover, since the creation of the Geneva Committee after the battle of Solferino (1859) IHL has been based on the idea of dissemination of its rules and education of its prescriptions to the largest possible number of persons. This imperatively requires a set of precise and written norms.

Third, IHL is mainly bound to apply in situations of great social and psychological stress, namely during warfare. In such situations, there

---

1 For example, industrialists in whose factories prisoners of war may work: see for instance the *I.G. Farben* or *Krupp* cases, in United Nations War Crimes Commission, *Law Reports of Trials of War Criminals,* vol. X, London, 1949, pp. 1ff, 69ff.
2 A. Gentili, *De iure belli, libri tres* (1598), Oxford Carnegie Classics, 1933, p. 204.

is ordinarily no time and no possibility to consult legal writings, which are most often unavailable on the battlefield, or to have complex discussions, balancing general principles, in order to shape a contextual rule. To be sure, such a process of balancing is also sometimes required. For instance, higher officials will perform it in the targeting phase, when weighing up one course of action against another in terms of the expected concrete military advantages and the expected collateral civilian damage. But for most military and administrative operations of warfare, there must be some ready-made and concrete rules at hand. These can be provided for only in the form of a written treaty.

Fourth, IHL regulates situations of hostility during combat and after combat, when enemies or other adverse persons are held in custody or under control. In such situations of clashes of interests interacting in an overall context of heightened nervous tension, the danger of harsh, abusive or self-serving action is particularly pronounced. It is generally true that each of us will try to impose interpretations suiting our own interests of the moment. But the propensity of such a course is particularly pronounced in the phase of warfare. Moreover, since in international law the general rule is that each party interprets its legal commitments for itself, without the regular presence of a court of justice to settle any disputes (and with no court at all during wartime), the danger of excessively self-serving interpretation is further increased. Norms of customary nature are not usually the most qualified to forestall such excesses. They are less easily available, less precise and often more controversial; in other words, they often leave greater margins of discussion and appreciation. Here, treaty law has a fundamental role to perform: to set clear and detailed rules, such as to effectively constrain the action of the military personnel with regard to the "enemy". The function of providing legal certainty is thus particularly pronounced in the context of IHL.

Fifth, treaties are important as a device for unifying the law. National legislation and military manuals could certainly satisfy all the requirements set out above. The soldiers would possess the detailed technical rules they need for performing their duties. But the law would differ considerably from one State to the other. This fact would be highly problematic in the light of the paramount principle of reciprocity and of equality of belligerents. To a large extent, IHL can only practically function if it is premised on the equality and non-discrimination of the belligerents. No party to the conflict will bow to the application of rules to which its adversary will not show obedience or pay only lip service.

No party to the conflict will accept adverse discrimination, putting it at a comparative military disadvantage. This is particularly true in IACs, where two sovereigns endowed with belligerent powers confront each other. Treaties ratified by a large number of States of the world create such a unique legal space by making the applicable rules uniform and consequently by extending the practical scope of reciprocity and equality of the belligerents. This function could obviously also be displayed by CIL. However, its evolution would be longer, more burdensome and haphazard, and also riddled with more uncertainties. Therefore, since the customary rules could give rise to conflicting interpretations more easily, some of the desired effect of uniformity would be lost.

Sixth, treaties allow in some situations for a quicker and more rational modification of the law when some change is needed. This is frequently the case in IHL, which has to keep pace with a highly complex and evolutionary field of human experience, namely warfare. It is an old commonplace to affirm that IHL tends to become outdated by one war.[3] By crafting some protocol or modifying some rules, changes can sometimes be achieved relatively quickly through the conventional process. The same is true for minor or technical amendments, which may be felt to be urgent. Thus, it is only by a treaty that the new emblem of AP III of 2005 to the four Geneva Conventions could reasonably be adopted and translated into the law. It is, however, true that CIL, by its flexibility and its closeness to the practice of States, also has the potential of effecting rapid and sensible adaptations of the law. Thus, many gaps of IHL in NIAC were progressively filled by unwritten rules. It must, however, be stressed that a reflected and rational change in the law on technical matters can best be achieved through a process of multilateral discussion and negotiation, in other words, through the process of adoption of a treaty. Such a process will, moreover, have a decisive advantage over the customary process from the standpoint of the great majority of States. Indeed, in the process of creation of customary norms the great powers and the developed States tend to have even more preponderance than they use to have in the treaty-making process. True, in the latter the greater skill of the developed States will still ensure a greater weight to them. But at the end of the day, the "one State one vote" rule will provide the basis for a more "democratic" process of norm-making. This larger forum of adoption retroacts on the acceptability of IHL norms; these should be universally applicable.

---

3 See for example, the "Editorial" in the *International Review of the Red Cross*, vol. 84 (no. 847), 2002, p. 518.

Contrary to HRL, where the rules are split between the regional systems and the universal plane, IHL is creating norms on the universal plane. There is no regional IHL. Hence, this issue of acceptability is of great importance for IHL.

3.3 Important treaties of international humanitarian law

There are a series of important IHL conventions. The following is a short presentation of the most salient of them.

3.3.1 St. Petersburg Declaration Renouncing the Use, in Time of War, of Explosive Projectiles under 400 Grams Weight (1868)

The St. Petersburg Declaration was adopted in response to a technical development of warfare in Russia.[4] In 1863, Russian military authorities invented a bullet exploding on contact with hard substances. Its primary aim was to blow up ammunition wagons. In 1867, the projectile was modified in a way so as to explode on contact with a soft substance, such as the human body. Considered as an inhumane and unnecessary instrument of war in the latter context, the prohibition was adopted in the Declaration under consideration. This text is important today mainly for the general principles stated in the Preamble as to the legitimate war aims and the principle of limitation of means allowed in warfare. It is, moreover, the first treaty to prohibit the use of a certain type of weapon in armed conflict. As to its content, it continues to apply today, as treaty and customary rule, but has been modified by subsequent practice of States. The 400 grams weight-criterion was initially adopted because at the time of adoption of the treaty that was the current distinction between infantry and artillery bullets. It was understood that explosive ammunition could and should not be prohibited when used for artillery purposes, in other words, when it was not specifically directed against an enemy soldier. Conversely, it was considered that infantry bullets, used in man-to-man fighting, should not be explosive. Such explosive ammunition wreaks horrendous and

---

4 D. Schindler and J. Toman, *The Laws of Armed Conflicts*, Leiden/Boston, 2004, p. 91. See also H. Meyrowitz, "Reflections on the Centenary of the Declaration of St. Petersburg", *International Review of the Red Cross*, vol. 8, 1968, pp. 611ff; H. P. Gasser, "A Look at the Declaration of St. Petersburg of 1868", *International Review of the Red Cross*, vol. 33, 1993, pp. 511ff.

extremely painful wounds, producing a great amount of "unnecessary suffering". The suffering is unnecessary in the sense that there is no corresponding military advantage for the use of such bullets. Other classical bullets would produce a similarly useful military result, but would not cause the same amount of suffering. Thus, such ammunition could (militarily) and should (morally and legally) be prohibited. However, soon after the adoption of the Declaration, technological progress erased the 400 grams limit. Explosive man-to-man bullets could be of lesser or of greater weight. Thus, State practice modified the rule contained in the Declaration, which today is limited to stating that explosive bullets are prohibited in infantry use.[5] This historical event provides an interesting example of the modification of a treaty provision by subsequent (customary) practice of the treaty parties.

3.3.2   The Hague Conventions I–XIV of 1907

The Hague Conventions of 1907 include in particular Convention IV, respecting the Laws and Customs of War on Land, with its annexed Regulations on Land Warfare, and Convention V respecting the Rights and Duties of Neutral Powers and Persons in Case of War on Land. Conventions VI–XIII concerned issues of warfare at sea. These latter conventions are today largely, but not on all points, outdated. The Hague Convention IV with its Regulations is still applicable to a wide array of situations. It remains relevant namely for the prohibited means and methods of warfare (see especially articles 22 and 23 of the Regulations) and for occupied territories (see articles 42ff of the Regulations). The Hague Convention V contains relevant rules on the law of neutrality in land warfare. Regulation IV of 1907 is rooted in the conceptions of the nineteenth century. This bent is reflected in many of its salient features. First, the civilian is largely absent. He surfaces only in some protective provisions for occupied territories, in other words, articles 44–7. Second, the provisions are mainly of a military and administrative character. Their points of vantage are the powers of the army, the means and methods of warfare, the treatment of adverse military personnel and the administration of occupied territories. Thus, the section on occupied territories is not centred on the protection of the local population (as in Geneva Convention IV, articles 47ff). It is rather concentrated on how the adverse forces have to administer occupied territory: keeping the public order (article 43),

---

5 J. M. Henckaerts and L. Doswald-Beck, *Customary International Humanitarian Law*, vol. I, Cambridge, 2005, pp. 273ff.

imposing taxes, dues and tolls (article 48), requisitions (article 52), seizure of war booty (article 53), usufructuary administration of the public property (article 55) and the treatment of certain municipal or charitable goods as private property (article 56). Third, the provisions of the Regulations are generally very short, in other words, skinny and replete of gaps. The old idea according to which there is no point in drafting detailed rules of IHL, still reigns for the reason that belligerents will spontaneously respect the rules they accepted as treaty commitments and as necessities of civilization.

The Hague Regulations originated in the Hague Peace Conference of 1899 (revision Conference in 1907), where for the first time States pursued the aim of agreeing on some instruments susceptible to maintain international peace.[6] To achieve that aim, two main issues were pursued: first, mandatory arbitration to secure peaceful settlement of the disputes among States; and, second, disarmament. It quickly became apparent that no decisive progress could be made on the first issue: no more than optional arbitration was acceptable to some States. It also became apparent that no progress at all could be made on the second issue. Some States were rapidly arming, while others did not have the necessary resources to keep pace. In such a setting, it is impossible to reach disarmament, since the arming States will not renounce their strategic advantage. In order to save the Conference from an almost complete failure, the issue of the laws of war was taken up. Much preparatory work had been done at the Brussels Conference of 1874.[7] The matter was thus ready for immediate consideration. Thus, in 1899 and 1907, conventions on the laws of war were finally adopted in place of conventions on disarmament.

3.3.3   The Geneva Conventions I–IV of 1949[8]

There are four Geneva Conventions: Convention I for the Amelioration of the Condition of the Wounded and Sick in Armed Forces in the Field; Convention II for the Amelioration of the Condition of the Wounded, Sick and Shipwrecked Members of Armed Forces at Sea; Convention III relative to the Treatment of Prisoners of War; and

6 See D. Schindler and J. Toman, *The Laws of Armed Conflicts*, Leiden/Boston, 2004, p. 41.

7 On this Conference, see the short overview in D. Schindler and J. Toman, *The Laws of Armed Conflicts*, Leiden/Boston, 2004, p. 21.

8 On these new Conventions, see J. A. C. Gutteridge, "The Geneva Conventions of 1949", *BYIL*, vol. 26, 1949, pp. 294ff; F. Bugnion, "Les Conventions de Genève du 12 août 1949", *RSDIE*, vol. 9, 1999, pp. 371ff.

Convention IV relative to the Protection of Civilian Persons in Time of War. These are currently the major IHL conventions in force. The Geneva Conventions of 1949 are universal in reach, having been ratified by almost all existing States. The Geneva Conventions reflect in three respects a tangible ideological shift with respect to the Hague Law of 1907. First, the Hague Law is essentially based on a military and administrative approach to warfare. Primarily, it contains rules for the military branch, spelling out their rights during warfare and their powers in certain situations, such as occupied territories. The Geneva Law for its part is based on the protection of individuals, namely the actual or potential victims of war or persons in need of protection when *hors de combat*. A military approach has given place to a humanitarian one. Second, the Hague Law is formulated in a series of short provisions containing general rules, with an important number of gaps or uncertainties lurking behind the surface. In 1899 and 1907, the participating States were not ready to limit their sovereignty significantly during wartime. After the appalling experiences of World War II, the Geneva Conventions mark a shift towards a much more detailed and complete codification of the rules applicable. The norms of Geneva are much more numerous, much more detailed and much more comprehensive. Third, the Hague Law does not make clear to what extent it can be derogated from by way of special agreements. The Geneva Law, on the contrary, contains specific rules ensuring that the provisions it contains will not be displaced by all sorts of ingenious devices invented by the States parties: see articles 6/6/6/7 and 7/7/7/8 of Geneva Conventions I–IV, and article 47 of Geneva Convention IV. Thus, the Geneva Law considers itself as a public order or public policy law, not to be derogated from in any circumstance.[9]

It is most important to stress that the Geneva Conventions concern only the protection of persons *hors de combat* in their relations with the adverse belligerent. The relevant scene is set outside the context of actual hostilities. Thus, the Geneva Conventions do not revise the "conduct of hostilities" limb of the Hague Conventions. The civilians protected by Geneva Convention IV are only those who find themselves "in the hands of the enemy",[10] either because they are on the territory of the adverse belligerent or because the belligerent occupies their

---

9 See also common article 1 of the Geneva Conventions, where the States pledge themselves to ensure respect of the Convention "in all circumstances".

10 Article 4, § 1, Geneva Convention IV.

territory. The protection of civilians against the effects of hostilities was codified only in AP I and AP II, notably, for IAC, in AP I, articles 48ff.

The origins of the Geneva Conventions of 1949 lie in the feeling that the old "laws of war" had not given the results hoped for[11] and that, therefore, a fresh start was necessary. The old military law conception gave way to a new protected persons conception, due to the horrendous experiences of World War II, with is deportations, killings and cruelties. The ICRC prepared drafts revising the two Geneva Conventions of 1929 (injured and sick; prisoners of war), the Hague Convention X of 1907 for the Adaptation to Maritime Warfare of the Principles of the Geneva Convention, and an entirely new draft on the protection of civilians. These drafts eventually ushered in the adoption of the four Geneva Conventions of 1949.

3.3.4 The Convention for the Protection of Cultural Property in the Event of Armed Conflict (Hague Convention of 1954), with its Two Additional Protocols of 1954 and of 1999[12]

This Convention deals with the protection of monuments and works of art, in other words, buildings, libraries as well as other objects of cultural interest, or deposits of protected objects. A definition of protected cultural property can be found in article 1. The States parties draw up lists of these objects and communicate them to the other parties. The lists of world cultural heritage of the UNESCO contribute to the determination of such sites and objects. There is a distinctive emblem by which the protected objects are marked in case of armed conflict. The protection of these objects is not absolute. If they are used militarily, they may become a military objective. However, the degree of protection has been increased for certain objects by the Protocol of 1999 through an "enhanced protection" (article 10ff) and the tight definition of military necessity in article 6, as well as the precautions during attack in article 7.

---

11 Even the delegates of the ICRC, who could hardly be described as hostile to IHL, were full of discouragement. See for example, M. Junod, *Le troisième combattant*, Lausanne, 1947, p. 119.

12 On the protection of cultural property during armed conflict, see J. Toman, *The Protection of Cultural Property in the Event of Armed Conflict*, Aldershot/Paris, 1996; R. O'Keefe, *The Protection of Cultural Property in Armed Conflict*, Cambridge, 2006.

3.3.5   Additional Protocols I and II to the Geneva Conventions of 1949 (1977)

Two Protocols were adopted in 1977:[13] Protocol Additional to the Geneva Conventions of 12 August 1949 relating to the Protection of Victims of International Armed Conflicts (AP I) and Protocol Additional to the Geneva Conventions of 12 August 1949 relating to the Protection of Victims of Non-International Armed Conflicts (AP II). The reasons that led to the adoption of the Additional Protocols are discussed in Chapter 1. AP I is an important update to the Geneva Conventions, developing the rules as to the protection of persons and inserting rules on means and methods of warfare, such as attacks against military objectives and the correlative immunity of civilian objects and persons (articles 48ff of AP I). AP II is the first IHL treaty dedicated exclusively to NIACs (in other words, "civil wars"). In 2005, a third Additional Protocol was adopted, adding a further protective emblem to the first two.[14] It should be stressed that the two Protocols of 1977 largely merge so-called "Geneva Law" and "Hague Law". In other words, in both Protocols there are rules on the protection of persons outside the context of hostilities (Geneva Law) and rules on the conduct of hostilities (Hague Law). For example, in AP II, the Geneva Rules can be found in articles 4–12, while the Hague Rules feature in articles 13–17. In AP I, articles 48ff (protection of civilians during hostilities) belong to the Hague Law, whereas articles 8ff (on the wounded, sick and shipwrecked) are typically Geneva Law. AP I has been applicable in many IACs, for example, in the Kosovo War of 1999 between the Federal Republic of Yugoslavia and those NATO States that had become a party to that Protocol. The greatest achievement of the two Protocols of 1977 is that they have brought IHL up to the needs of modern warfare. Neither the Hague Regulations, nor the Geneva Conventions, would have sufficed to fully maintain the relevance of IHL in the context of the armed conflicts of the last 40 years.

---

13 On these Protocols, as well as the two Commentaries mentioned in the Select bibliography, see: R. Kosirnik, "The 1977 Protocols: A Landmark in the Development of International Humanitarian Law", *International Review of the Red Cross*, vol. 79, 1997, pp. 483ff.
14 See J. F. Quéguiner, "Commentary on the Protocol Additional to the Geneva Conventions of 12 August 1949, and Relating to the Adoption of an Additional Distinctive Emblem (Protocol III)", *International Review of the Red Cross*, vol. 89, 2007, pp. 175ff.

3.3.6   Rome Statute on the International Criminal Court

The Rome Statue of the International Criminal Court (ICC) was adopted at Rome in 1998.[15] This treaty does not deal directly with IHL; rather, it deals with criminal international law. However, the violation of IHL rules sometimes constitutes a war crime. This is the case when such violations are serious enough and when they give rise, under customary or conventional international law, to individual criminal responsibility. Thus, killing prisoners of war will constitute an ordinary war crime under CIL and even a "grave breach" under the Geneva Conventions conventional regime.[16] Conversely, the fact of not filling in and filing in due time the capture cards provided for in article 70 of Geneva Convention III will not be a war crime. The ICC Statute contains a long provision (article 8) dealing with the substance of war crimes. Therein it also defines the conditions of applicability of war crimes and indirectly touches upon and hence develops IHL. Thus, for example, it declares certain conducts prohibited by AP II to be war crimes, without, however, requiring the "territorial control" by rebels that is a condition for the treaty law applicability of AP II.[17] Consequently, the conduct is criminalized even when it takes place in a common article 3 NIAC, which does not presuppose any territorial control by rebels. This state of affairs may have its effects on the development of customary IHL and re-evaluate the conditions of applicability of certain rules relating to NIAC. However, it also induces a certain degree of legal uncertainty, since CIL and conventional international law may then differ in their conditions of applicability. The conventional law may then have precedence for the parties to a convention in their dealings *inter se*, under the rule of *lex specialis*, and the customary international rule will prevail as among non-parties or between parties and non-parties.

In addition to the above, there are a number of treaties limiting the production or use of particular weapons. Some prominent examples include the following.

---

15 On the Statute, see the two English Commentaries: A. Cassese, P. Gaeta and J. Jones (eds), *The Rome Statute of the International Criminal Court: A Commentary*, Oxford, 2002; O. Triffterer (ed.), *Commentary on the Rome Statute of the International Criminal Court*, 2nd edn, Munich, 2008.

16 For the grave breaches regime, see articles 50/51/130/147 of the Geneva Conventions I–IV, and article 85, AP I.

17 See article 8, § 1, letter e, of the ICC Statute.

3.3.7 Protocol for the Prohibition of the Use in War of Asphyxiating, Poisonous or Other Gases, and of Bacteriological Methods of Warfare (Geneva, 1925)

The 1925 Gas Protocol is still in force. The Protocol puts a ban only on the use of such arms, not on their production or possession. This was due to the fact that many States in 1925 insisted – through apposite reservations – that they remained free to use prohibited gases to the extent that such weapons were first used against them or their allies (armed reprisals). Thus, it remained necessary to adopt further later instruments limiting the production and possession of biological and chemical weapons (see below). The Protocol of 1925 covers both chemical weapons and biological (bacteriological) ones, in other words, weapons based on non-organic poisonous substances or on organic (living) poisonous substances.[18] During the Ethiopian War of 1935 Italy did not respect this prohibition,[19] but World War II remained largely free of chemical warfare, due to fear of armed reprisals.

3.3.8 Convention on the Prohibition of Development, Production and Stockpiling of Bacteriological (Biological) and Toxin Weapons and on Their Destruction (London, Moscow, Washington, 1972)

The 1972 Convention was drafted by the UN Committee on Disarmament and recommended for accession by Resolution 2826 of the United Nations General Assembly (UNGA) in 1971. This agreement was limited to biological weapons, as no agreement on the international supervision of a prohibition on chemical weapons could be agreed upon (the Vietnam War was still in all minds). With regard to biological weapons, the problem of supervision was thought to be dispensable, since by that time such weapons did not present any direct military usefulness or advantage anymore. Chemical weapons were considered sufficient as a "weapon of mass destruction of the poor(er)". Moreover, chemical weapons were of much easier handling than biological weapons. Article 1 of the Convention defines the types of substances covered by the treaty. The ban on those weapons has up to this date been most successful. This is not likely to change in the foreseeable future.

---

18 See § 1 of the Preamble and § 1 of the text. The latter reads: "[The High Contracting Parties accept such prohibition, in other words, that on chemical weapons and] agree to extend this prohibition to the use of bacteriological methods of warfare. . .".

19 See M. Junod, *Le troisième combattant*, Lausanne, 1947, pp. 48ff.

3.3.9 Convention on the Prohibition of Military or Other Hostile Use of Environmental Modification Techniques (New York, 1976)

The 1976 Convention was drafted by the UN bodies. It originated because of concerns about environmental protection raised by the US military campaign during the Vietnam War at the end of the 1960s and beginning of the 1970s. It does not protect the environment in general terms, but only seeks to prohibit the deliberate and large-scale manipulation of the environment for military purposes, such as, for example, climate change for hostile purposes. Article I of the Convention sets out clearly that only "widespread, longlasting or severe effects" on the environment are covered; and article II adds that the point is only to prohibit certain hostile "environmental modification techniques", changing the dynamics, composition or structure of the Earth. The term "widespread" was taken to mean several hundreds of square kilometres; "longlasting" meant for at least a season; "severe" meant involving serious or significant disruption or harm to human life and natural resources. These terms are alternatives (unlike article 55 of AP I). This means that environmental damage is prohibited if it is either widespread *or* longlasting *or* severe. In AP I, the three mentioned conditions are cumulative. To qualify, a damage must be widespread *and* longlasting *and* severe. The idea was to prohibit weather manipulation for flooding adverse lands, the provocation of earthquakes or tsunamis, or the like. As can be observed, only extremely high-level damage is covered.[20] Overall, the environment is not protected because of its own value; it is mainly protected as the medium necessary for the survival of human beings. This shows again the completely anthropocentric outlook of the human race, which considers itself the crown jewel of all creation.

3.3.10 Convention on Prohibitions or Restrictions on the Use of Certain Conventional Weapons Which May Be Deemed to Be Excessively Injurious or to Have Indiscriminate Effects (Geneva, 1980)

The 1980 Convention is accompanied by a number of Protocols: Protocols I on non-detectable fragments; Protocol II on Mines, Booby-traps and Other Devices; Protocol III on Incendiary Weapons;

---

20 See W. H. Boothby, *Weapons and the Law of Armed Conflict*, Oxford, 2009, pp. 86ff, 92–4. On environmental protection in times of armed conflict, see also K. Mollard Bannelier, *La protection de l'environnement en temps de conflit armé*, Paris, 2001.

Protocol IV on Blinding Laser Weapons; Protocol V on Explosive War Remnants.[21] The 1980 Convention is the most important modern treaty for restriction on use of conventional weapons. It is an umbrella treaty, which is concretized through successive protocols on the prohibition of specific weapons. It thus sets in motion a living process, with its periodic review conferences (article 8). Each State party is required to accept at least two Protocols (article 4, § 3). The Convention was drafted as a by-product of the negotiation process of AP I and AP II. At that time, the glaring opposition over weapons of mass destruction had overshadowed the whole quest for the prohibition of weapons. Since the nuclear powers refused to discuss restrictions on the use of nuclear weapons from the point of view of IHL, as a retaliation the Third World States refused to discuss the issues posed by chemical or other weapons. The ICRC could finally make some progress after the Conference of 1977, once the controversial problem of weapons of mass destruction had been eliminated from the process. The focus was now put on conventional weapons and the result was the 1980 Convention. By an amendment of 2001, the scope of the Convention was extended to common article 3, NIAC (article 1, § 2); however, this does not mean that each Protocol to this Convention will necessarily extend to such NIAC. According to article 1, § 7, future Protocols may determine their material scope of application in an autonomous way.

3.3.11   Convention on the Prohibition of the Development, Production, Stockpiling and Use of Chemical Weapons and on Their Destruction (Paris, 1993)

The 1972 Convention on biological weapons left open the prohibition of chemical weapons. The question came to the fore during the Iraq–Iran War in the 1980s. There was now readiness, at the end of the Cold War, to completely eliminate chemical weapons. The Convention was finally adopted through the channelling efforts of UNGA.[22] Article 2 of the Convention contains a definition of the prohibited substances and devices. It stipulates for a comprehensive ban of such weapons, extending to possession and use, and providing for destruction of existing stocks. Chemicals may be used in the law of peace, for medical purposes, or even in the context of riot control. Conversely, even non-lethal chemical substances are completely banned in times of armed conflict in the conduct of hostilities,

---

21 W. H. Boothby, *Weapons and the Law of Armed Conflict*, Oxford, 2009, pp. 106ff.
22 *Ibid.*, pp. 129ff.

although they are not banned, even in times of armed conflict, for law enforcement purposes, for example, in occupied territories. A detailed mechanism of control was agreed upon. It includes in site verification. The mechanism has recently featured quite prominently during the Syrian civil war (2013).

3.3.12   Convention on the Prohibition of the Use, Stockpiling, Production and Transfer of Anti-Personal Mines and on Their Destruction (Oslo, 1997)[23]

A landmine is a device designed to explode by the proximity of a person or vehicle. Weapons having only accidentally the effect of so detonating are not mines and do not share the legal regime of mines. Anti-personnel mines are those designed to explode by the proximity of a person. Thus, cluster ammunition is not a mine, since it is designed to detonate on impact and not on the passage of a person. The amended Protocol II on Prohibitions and Restrictions on the Use of Mines, Booby-Traps and Other Devices (1996) annexed to the 1980 Weapons Convention did not satisfy all those circles, namely within non-governmental organizations (NGOs), that wanted to place a general ban on anti-personnel mines. Indeed, the mentioned Protocol II did restrict the use of anti-personnel mines, but did not contain a general prohibition. It was estimated that more than 100 million such mines were scattered throughout the world. Such mines were killing and injuring thousands of persons every month. The 1997 Convention seeks to fill the gap left by the previous conventions by providing for a total ban. Its humanitarian purpose is neatly set out in its Preamble, where the protection of civilians from the perverse effects of anti-personnel mines is mentioned. However, the 1997 Convention has not been ratified by some important mine-producing States. It is mainly the fruit of intense lobbying by civil society and NGOs. In 2006, a non-binding Declaration on "Mines other than Anti-Personnel Mines" was added to the 1980 Conventional Weapons Convention, covering some anti-vehicle mines. Its main content is to recommend not using such mines outside a marked area, if that mine is not detectable or if that mine is not equipped with a self-neutralization device.

---

23 *Ibid.*, pp. 181ff.

3.4   The importance of customary international law

If IHL is essentially governed by treaties, what are the roles CIL can perform, or does perform, in that area of the law? What are the advantages of CIL when compared to treaty law? Are there certain needs that only CIL can satisfy?

First, CIL provides for a minimum standard of universally applicable IHL rules independent of the particular state of ratification or accession to a treaty. CIL is therefore the "common law" within the realm of international law. Treaty law, conversely, is relative or particular law: it applies only to States (or other actors) having assumed the treaty obligations by a formal act of subjection (ratification or accession). The rule here is: *pacta tertiis nec nocent nec prosunt*. An agreement not ratified or acceded to remains *res inter alios acta*. Its rights and obligations do not benefit or bind third entities.[24] Some IHL conventions of major significance have far from universal ratification or accession. The most famous examples are AP I and AP II. These Protocols contain some rules of paramount importance, such as the rules on the protection of civilian populations from attack.[25] To the extent the rules of such multilaterally – but not universally – ratified conventions can be labelled as customary law, in other words, when supported by general state practice and *opinio juris*, they will be applicable to all the States of the world. The rules of the treaties can thus be transformed into general or universal international law by CIL. This is an important function in a world divided into increasing numbers of States; in a world where new States regularly emerge, that for a transient time will not be bound by the conventions; and in a world where armed conflicts are endemic. In other words, customary law insures a common standard of rules applicable in all situations of armed conflict everywhere in the world, independent of the particular state of acceptance of treaties by the States concerned. Moreover, the non-ratification of a treaty by one party to the conflict does not simply entail the non-application of that treaty only to its own action, but rather to all the relationships of that State with all the other belligerent parties (in other words, also to the action of all other belligerent parties). Thus, since the Korean War of 1950,[26]

---

24 Rights and obligations flowing from a treaty can, however, be accepted by a third State under the conditions set out in articles 35 and 36 of the Vienna Convention on the Law of Treaties (1969).
25 Articles 48ff, AP I, and the weaker rules of articles 13ff, AP II.
26 D. W. Bowett, *United Nations Forces, A Legal Study of United Nations Practice*, London, 1964, pp. 53ff.

where the Geneva Conventions were still widely non-ratified, through the Eritrea/Ethiopia War of 1998–2000, where Eritrea did not accede to the Geneva Conventions until August 2000, there has been experience with falling back on CIL because of formally inapplicable treaty norms.

The example relating to the Eritrea/Ethiopia War shows a point of significance: even when a set of conventions is said to be universally or quasi-universally ratified, the conventional norms remain norms of particular law. Especially in the context of the Geneva Conventions, this is highly relevant. It is often new States that are entangled in armed conflicts. They are prone to instability during a first phase of their life, especially in Africa. During that phase of infancy, such States have not always yet acceded to the Geneva Conventions. The result will be that the Geneva Conventions are frequently not applicable as conventional rules. The fall-back on CIL is here of paramount importance for keeping a certain minimum standard of IHL applicable throughout the world and throughout the different situations that may arise. In the case mentioned above, Eritrea, as a new State, had not acceded to the Geneva Conventions prior to the 14 August 2000. However, the war with Ethiopia had started in 1998. In the intermediary phase between 1998 and August 2000, the Geneva Conventions were not applicable to this armed conflict. Thus, the Permanent Court of Arbitration (PCA) fell back on CIL, which it applied to the belligerent relations of the two States between 1998 and 2000.[27] It may be added that even for States that have ratified or acceded to a specific convention, CIL remains relevant under the aspect discussed here. Indeed, such a State may ratify or accede to the convention, and enter one or more than one reservation to its provisions. To the extent these provisions reflect CIL, the effect of the reservation will be next to naught. The State may have validly reserved to the treaty provision (if that is not prohibited by the treaty or contrary to its object and purpose), but the reservation does not extend to CIL. There are no reservations against CIL norms. It is obvious that the entry of a reservation to a treaty provision most often expresses the claim of the reserving State that the content of this provision does not reflect CIL, or at least does not reflect CIL in all its points. Otherwise the reservation would make little sense. But a single State does not determine international law. The majority of States, on whose practice and opinion the CIL rule will rest, may reject its claim. Conversely, if there are many States entering a certain type of

---

27 See for example, the *Central Front* case, Ethiopia's Claim 2 (judgment of 28 April 2004), §§ 13ff.

reservation, this may be an argument for considering that the content of the reserved provision is not, or not in all aspects, part of CIL. That arguments linking reservations to the state of CIL may have a certain weight is shown by the International Court of Justice (ICJ) judgment on the *North Sea Continental Shelf* cases of 1969.[28]

Second, CIL remains the paramount vehicle for binding different non-State subjects and entities to IHL. The conventions are open to accession only by States[29] or "Powers",[30] this last term being customarily interpreted as meaning States. Thus, if armed forces under the command of an international organization participate to hostilities – as happened to UN blue helmets, dragged into an armed conflict in the Congo in 1960–1963[31] – CIL humanitarian law will apply to them. The organization is not a party, and under the current interpretation could not become a party, to the relevant conventions.[32] Thus, CIL can provide a minimum common yardstick with respect to international peace operations of the UN. There, independent of particularly framed military Rules of Engagement (ROE), the conventional law applicable to the different national contingents may greatly differ, because of unequal ratification/accession to treaties by their respective home States. In Somalia, during the phase of ONUSOM II in 1992, there were 23 national contingents participating in the operation, with a potential split of the applicable law with regard to each contingent.[33] The ROE and CIL here provided a powerful bracket of common law. The same common normative yardstick through CIL may be provided for insurgents or other similar entities in a NIAC. In this latter case, conventional law is ordinarily held to be applicable by the device of a direct reach of the treaty to individuals on the territory of the State having ratified the treaty or acceded to it. The conception is that the ratification or accession to a treaty and its incorporation into the municipal law of a State has as a corollary effect that all individuals on the territory will be bound by those rules, especially in the case they take up

---

28 ICJ, *Reports*, 1969, p. 39, § 64.

29 See for example, article 4 of the Convention on Certain Conventional Weapons of 1980.

30 See for example, article 6 of the Hague Convention IV of 1907; articles 60/59/139/155 of the Geneva Conventions I–IV.

31 F. Seyersted, *United Nations Forces, in the Law and Practice of War*, Leiden, 1966, pp. 192ff. It must be noted that these troops were also under the tactical command of their home State.

32 On the whole question, see R. Kolb, *Droit humanitaire et opérations de paix internationales*, 2nd edn, Geneva/Basel/Munich/Brussels, 2006, especially pp. 21ff.

33 UN (Blue Book Series), *The United Nations and Somalia, 1992–1996*, New York, 1996.

arms for an insurrection.[34] However, apart from that reach of conventional law, CIL also applies to such actors (albeit only that branch of customary IHL applicable in NIACs). This general reach of CIL *ratione personarum* was stressed by the *Institut de droit international* in its Resolution on "The Application of International Humanitarian Law and Fundamental Human Rights in Armed Conflicts in Which Non-State Entities are Parties" (1999), in articles II and IV.[35] Consequently, CIL here again plays a unifying function. It is a common law not only with regard to States, but also with regard to other belligerent subjects of international law.

Third, CIL is a subsidiary source of IHL. It may in appropriate circumstances fill gaps and/or remove uncertainties lurking behind the interstices of conventional law. Such gaps are particularly numerous in underdeveloped areas of IHL and in areas subjected to rapid evolution. The best example is the branch of NIACs. To a tiny set of conventional rules, mainly in common article 3 of the Geneva Conventions and AP II, there is today the complement of a great series of rules having progressively emerged through international jurisprudence as well as through institutional and State practice.[36] In the same vein, specific norms may benefit from some complement flowing from unwritten practice. CIL can thus also develop conventional rules by adding some precision to them. In that process, customary practice can derogate from some written norm, as it can also just complement or develop it.

An example of the first situation is the application of article 118, § 1, of Geneva Convention III requiring that prisoners of war *shall be* released and *repatriated* without delay after the cessation of active hostilities. This article has today to be interpreted in the light of the derogatory customary practice according to which repatriation to the country of origin of the prisoner shall not be effected against the express wish of the prisoner. The concern of the mandatory rule in Geneva Convention III was to impede any delay and excuses for the non-repatriation of prisoners, as had been notably witnessed after World War I, and also,

---

34 On this construction, see Y. Sandoz, C. Swinarski and B. Zimmermann (eds), *Commentary on the Additional Protocols of 8th June 1977 to the Geneva Conventions of 12 August 1949*, Commentary, Geneva, 1987, p. 1345.

35 See D. Schindler and J. Toman, *The Laws of Armed Conflicts*, Leiden/Boston, 2004, pp. 1206–7.

36 See T. Meron, "International Law in the Age of Human Rights", *RCADI*, vol. 301, 2003, pp. 24ff. See also the ICRC study on CIL, J. M. Henckaerts and L. Doswald-Beck, *Customary International Humanitarian Law*, vols I–III, Cambridge, 2005.

specifically, to impede manipulated demands to be sent to a place other than the home State. It thus provided for mandatory return to the country of origin of the prisoner. However, since the Korean War of 1950, the concern has shifted to the case of prisoners who do not wish to be sent back by force to their country of origin, because of well-founded fears of persecution.[37] The relevant State practice – not reflected in the text of the Geneva Conventions – eventually changed under the conjunct pressure of refugee and HRL. In order to avoid unwelcome pressures by the detaining power, the ICRC attempts to find out the true will of the prisoner during individual interviews. Once his or her will not to return to his or her country of origin had been ascertained, any destination of release corresponding to the free will of the prisoner would be accepted. The PCA in 2003 ruled that this practice amounted to a customary rule.[38] Thus, CIL modified a treaty rule of Geneva Convention III or filled a "justice gap" (*rechtspolitische Lücke*) within that rule. This is also an example of the influence of HRL on IHL.

The following example shows how CIL can complement a treaty norm by lending more precision to it. Article 30 of Geneva Convention I stipulates that medical and religious personnel whose retention is not indispensable for the care of prisoners of war of their country shall be returned to the party to the conflict to whom they belong, as soon as the road is open and military requirements permit. In the practice of States, initiated by requests of the ICRC, these release operations are usually linked with the repatriation of seriously wounded and sick prisoners of war. These latter prisoners must be sent back to their State of origin as quickly as circumstances allow, according to article 109 of Geneva Convention III. This consolidated solution linking the two sets of repatriation avoids multiple flights or convoys. It also insures the care of the seriously injured prisoners during transit. The link of both provisions can only be understood in the light of customary practice or usage.[39]

Finally, CIL shaped by military practice can sometimes also be used to interpret conventional rules or general principles, which need to be

---

37 C. Shields Delessert, *Release and Repatriation of Prisoners of War at the End of Active Hostilities*, Zurich, 1977, pp. 157ff.

38 Arbitral Award of 1 July 2003, *Prisoners of War*, Eritrea's Claim 17, § 147: "[T]here must be adequate procedures to ensure that individuals are not repatriated against their will".

39 F. Bugnion, *Le Comité international de la Croix-Rouge et la protection des victimes de la guerre*, Geneva, 1994, p. 790.

concretized. Thus, for example, in the context of "military necessity", it is indispensable for the lawyer to have some intimate knowledge of field practice in order, for example, to assess when the destruction of enemy property is normally considered to be "imperatively demanded" (article 23, letter d, of the Hague Regulations 1907).

Summing up, CIL presents the advantage of offering a minimum standard of rules applicable in all circumstances of armed conflicts and for all actors effectively participating in it. CIL is not affected by the loopholes and inequalities flowing from differing ratification or accession, from participation in the armed conflict of non-State entities not bound by treaty rules or from other limitations (denunciation, reservations, and so on) which may flow from treaty engagements. Moreover, CIL may fill gaps in, or guide interpretation of, conventional rules. CIL is thus the "common IHL" on which it is always possible to fall back if more special conventional sources (*lex specialis*) do not apply in a particular case.

3.5 The content of customary international law with regard to international humanitarian law

Which rules of conventional IHL reflect existing CIL? Which rules of conventional IHL shaped new CIL? The two questions relate to codification of pre-existing CIL and to progressive development of CIL through conventional impulses. A great many rules in IHL conventions codify pre-existing CIL. After all, conventional IHL seeks to reflect effective military and humanitarian practice. Thus, the provisions on the right of humanitarian initiative by the ICRC (articles 9/9/9/10 and common article 3 of Geneva Conventions I–IV) codify an old practice going back to the formative stage of the 1860s. Conversely, article 54 of AP I on the protection of objects indispensable to the survival of the civilian population during the hostilities phase was hardly expressive of CIL in 1977. However, the PCA in the Eritrea/Ethiopia *Western Front, Aerial Bombardment and Related Claims* case (Eritrea's Claims 1, 3, 5, 9–13, 14, 21, 25 and 26, judgment of 19 December 2005), found that the provision had become customary in the meantime, even without any compelling State practice to that effect.[40] There is thus a double movement here: CIL that inspires conventional rules (codification of IHL); and conventional rules that crystallize or constitute new CIL rules.

---

40 At §§ 96ff.

Overall, what rules of conventional IHL are to be considered CIL? The rule of thumb today is that the substantive rules (as opposed to procedural provisions) contained in the great multilateral conventions on IHL represent CIL. This tendency to harmonize and to equalize the two sources stems from the fact that military and State practice can be only one and the same. This action cannot split according to the sources. If the conventions are expressive of, and seek to influence, the actual practice of warfare, they must perforce reflect what the States and other actors use (or consider they should use) in armed conflicts. If the two sources contained significant differences, a legal schizophrenia would ensue: the actors would be bound by CIL reflecting their practice and *opinio juris*, whereas the conventional law would largely be irrelevant or modified by subsequent practice.[41] Thus, as manifested in the *Nicaragua* (1986) case,[42] we are confronted with two sets of largely (albeit not completely) identical rules of behaviour in conventional international law and CIL.

However, a precise proof of actual military practice is exceedingly difficult to obtain, especially if it is based not only on the dealings of some selected States, but on a universal approach confronting the practice of all the States of the world. Thus, there is a significant temptation to find a proper expression of *opinio juris* (which in turn is supposed to underlie the true practice) in the conventional norms. This "presumption" approach, rooted in the particular relevance of treaty law, has a long standing. The International Military Tribunal (IMT) of Nuremberg stated that the Hague Regulations of 1907 (Convention IV) were in all their parts expressive of CIL.[43] The ICJ affirmed more generally that the great majority of substantive rules of conventional IHL reflect CIL. In the *Legality of the Threat or Use of Nuclear Weapons* opinion (1996), it expressed itself:

> The extensive codification of humanitarian law and the extent of the accession to the resultant treaties, as well as the fact that the denunciation clauses that existed in the codification instruments have never been used, have provided the international community with a corpus of treaty rules the great

---

41 If the conventional law was held to prevail by virtue of the *lex specialis* rule, there would be an enormous number of violations of the law, which is an impractical solution.

42 In this case, the rules at stake were those on the use of force under the Charter and under CIL (*jus ad bellum*): ICJ, *Reports*, 1986, pp. 92ff.

43 *Nuremberg Judgment of the IMT*, 1947, in *AJIL*, vol. 41, 1947, pp. 248–9. For the customary nature of article 42 of the Regulations, see also the *Armed Activities* case (*DRC v. Uganda*), ICJ, *Reports*, 2005, p. 229, § 172.

majority of which had already become customary and which reflected the most universally recognized humanitarian principles. These rules indicate the normal conduct and behaviour expected of States.[44]

The ICTY in the *Tadic* case (1995)[45] affirmed that many rules contained in AP II concerning NIACs are reflective of CIL. More recently, in the same vein, the PCA in its Eritrea/Ethiopia cases affirmed in a more balanced way that the great majority (but not all) of the substantive rules contained in the four Geneva Conventions and AP I represented CIL.[46] The Geneva Conventions were, however, considered by this PCA to reflect CIL throughout their substantive IHL provisions. As for AP I, the PCA emphasized that most of its provisions are CIL, but not all of them, some consisting rather in progressive development of the law. However, according to the PCA, the provisions concerning the conduct of hostilities and correlative protection of the civilian population (articles 48ff) today represent CIL without any exceptions (and this albeit some States have formulated reservations to some aspects of these provisions). Moving to Protocol II on Mines, Booby-traps and Other Devices under the Conventional Arms Treaty of 1980, the PCA held that its conclusion was too recent,[47] and State practice still too uncertain, to affirm the customary nature of its provisions. However, the Court added that some of these provisions represent accepted general principles of IHL as thus reflecting CIL; for example, the provisions on registration of mines and the localities where they are placed; and the prohibition of their indiscriminate use. Finally, the PCA sets up a presumption whereby the substantive provisions of conventional IHL in the codification treaties reflect CIL. There is thus a shift in the burden of proof: the party that contests that customary status has the onus to prove its allegation.

In sum, according to recent case-law, there is a considerable tendency to merge conventional IHL and customary IHL. The equation seems roughly to be: written IHL ≈ customary IHL. The same result was reached by the ICRC Study on the subject matter.[48] This view, based on a large degree of harmonization of the conventional and custom-

---

44 ICJ, *Reports*, 1996-I, p. 258, § 82.

45 At § 117. The judgment is published in *ILM*, vol. 35, 1996, pp. 32ff.

46 See *Central Front*, Ethiopia's Claim 2, 28 April 2004, §§ 13ff and many other awards. See www.pca-cpa.org or *RIAA*, vol. 26.

47 This Protocol was adopted in 1980, with amendments in 1996.

48 Cf. J. M. Henckaerts and L. Doswald-Beck, *Customary International Humanitarian Law*, vols I–III, Cambridge, 2005.

ary sources, is today challenged only by States not having ratified or acceded to some important treaties, as is the case of the US, Israel or India, which are not parties to AP I. These States thereby seek to retain the advantage of not being compelled by some rules of this or other instruments, and do not want to be bound by the backdoor of CIL.

Conversely, in some areas of IHL, there is still no codification of the relevant rules. CIL then reigns largely alone. To the extent efforts of codification are undertaken, CIL will guide the work of the drafters of the relevant texts. This is the case, for example, in the context of aerial warfare, especially in the relations air–air.[49] An effort of "codification" has taken place in this area by the drafting of a "Third Draft Manual on Air and Missile Warfare" for the use of professional armies.[50] The same is true for cyber warfare.[51] In such subject matters, there is a rather particular relationship between CIL and conventional law: the first makes an original contribution to the second; and the second grows in the shadow of the first.

There is a last question which deserves a quick treatment. Some authors claim that IHL–CIL has certain specificity with respect to general CIL. As with CIL in the context of HRL, so also in the realm of IHL the relationship and weight accorded to the two main factors of CIL would be tilted slightly in favour of *opinio juris* and against actual State practice.[52] Said differently, the tendency would be to take the States by what they say rather than too strictly by what they do. This tendency to accord a greater weight to policy statements embodying *opinio juris*, as they are made during conferences, in UNGA, in military manuals, and so on, has its roots in HRL. The problem lies in the fact that in HRL matters there is often a great discrepancy between what States say and what they actually do. Lofty and generous statements contrast with appalling and worrisome practices. Thus, the prohibition of torture is maintained in high esteem in various statements, yet torture is a quite regular occurrence in more than 120 States of the world. There may

---

49 On air warfare, see the orientation in M. Sassoli, A. Bouvier and A. Quintin, *How Does Law Protect in War?*, vol. I, 3rd edn, Geneva, 2011, pp. 313ff. The relations air–land are covered by such treaties as AP I.

50 *Manual on International Law Applicable to Air and Missile Warfare* (Harvard), New York, 2011.

51 See M. Schmitt (ed.), *Tallinn Manual on the International Law Applicable to Cyber Warfare*, Cambridge, 2013.

52 See for example, C. Tomuschat, "International Law: Ensuring the Survival of Mankind on the Eve of a New Century", *RCADI*, vol. 281, 1999, p. 334.

thus be doubts on actual practice; but there are no doubts on legal opinion. Therefore, in such areas of rules of civilization, as is the case in HRL and IHL, the argument is to analyse with particular attention the opinion and not to give undue weight to diverging practices, when these are not accompanied by a claim to be legally entitled to depart from the rule.

It is not altogether clear if it is really necessary to alter the relationship between the two elements of CIL, since their relationship is flexible and already context-related on the general plane. But it may be accepted that legal opinion plays a particularly significant role in areas such as HRL and IHL. If a particularly crucial distinction can be made between practices disavowing a legal rule they pretend to change (violations accompanied by legal opinion for the change of the rule) and practices bound to remain simple violations of IHL, which may be discarded at the normative level (violations not accompanied by such an opinion for legal change), in this context, it may be recalled what the ICJ emphasized in the *Nicaragua* case of 1986:

> In order to deduce the existence of customary rules, the Court deems it sufficient that the conduct of States should, in general, be consistent with such rules, and that instances of State conduct inconsistent with a given rule should generally have been treated as breaches of that rule, not as indications of the recognition of a new rule. If a State acts in a way prima facie incompatible with a recognized rule, but defends its conduct by appealing to exceptions or justifications contained within the rule itself, then whether or not the State's conduct is in fact justifiable on that basis, the significance of that attitude is to confirm rather than to weaken the rule.[53]

This passage shows that the notion of "State practice" must always be qualified and differentiated with regard to subjective factors attached to it, in order to give it a correct interpretation and standing.

---

53 ICJ, *Reports*, 1986, p. 98, § 186.

4 The main principles of international humanitarian law

4.1 The role of general principles in international law

General principles of law (GPL) operate as guiding legal ideas, founding and directing the operation of a series of more particular legal rules, which appear linked to the principle or may even be considered a concretization of it. By illuminating the whole legal system with a set of generally applicable guiding legal concepts, GPL stress the centripetal or unifying forces within a legal order and throughout legal phenomena.

The generality of the principles puts them beyond the peculiarities of operation of simple rules. On the one hand, their legal content is not as narrow or defined in as precise ways as it is in rules. But at the same time, it is not as broad as in general political concepts of a given moment. Therefore, the principles can play a middle role between the *lex lata* and the *lex ferenda*, being wholly neither the one nor the other. They have the temperate degree of abstraction and concreteness to be able to be dynamic and yet filled with some specific legal meaning at the same time. Principles live on that polarity: (1) generality and flexibility on the one hand, and thus the capacity for serving in a dynamic interpretation and in substantive development of the law, especially since the class of cases they can cover is not closed; (2) anchoring in the realm of legal phenomena, on the other hand, with a definable core-meaning and a reviewable system of extensions, which gives to the principles a genetic code able to grant that minimum of certainty without which the law is opened up to the arbitrary.

Thus, for example, the rules as to reparation for damages were, in international law as in the other systems, based on case-law, developed out of a set of general principles, mainly the ideas of *neminem laedere*, equivalence (reciprocity), proportionality, *nemo ex propria turpitudine commodum capere potest*, equity and retribution. Or, as a further example, the law of armed conflicts emerged out of a re-elaboration of the principles of military necessity, of mercy and compassion (no excessive suffering, no useless destruction, duty of humane treatment) and of proportionality. All the law of armed conflicts is but a sort of *mise en équilibre* of these three legal ideas. The principle of good faith, to give a third example, has coagulated within its borders the following legal ideas: (1) the protection of legitimate expectations (for example, through doctrines such as qualified acquiescence, *qui tacet consentire videtur...*; of estoppel; of responsibility for expectations deliberately created); (2) the protection of inter-personal or social finalities attached to legal institutions, through the doctrines of prohibition of abuse of rights or *détournement de pouvoir*; (3) finally, some standard of moral correctness and reciprocity, by way of doctrines such as "none shall take profit of his own wrong". These facets of the principle were attached to it by way of prolonged jurisprudence. The same could be said of the principle of proportionality. Several legal ideas coagulated in this principle during the nineteenth and twentieth centuries. First, there was the idea that a measure taken should be able to fulfil the aim searched for; if it does not have that ability at all, it will be disproportionate. Second, the idea that among the several means able to further the aim searched for, the least onerous one should be selected (idea of "necessity"). Third, the idea that there must be some degree of equivalence in gravity between a measure taken and the fact or act giving rise to it. These aspects were slowly worked out in practice. GPL, therefore, help to fill gaps, contribute to a functional completeness of the legal system, help to understand its nodal or gravitational points and oil the wheels of the system. This is an invaluable function.

4.2 The role of general principles of law in international humanitarian law

It may be questionable to what extent GPL should have a distinctive role to play within the realm of IHL. At first sight, it may seem reasonable to expect a robust role of GPL in areas of international law characterized by poor normativity, in other words, by a significant number of gaps and generally by a conspicuous absence of legal rules. The principles then fill the gaps and give a minimum orientation to the legal operator. This has been the role equity has played for many years in the context of maritime delimitation, where, after the rejection of the equidistance criterion as a rule of CIL, there were hardly any specific rules to apply in order to effectuate the requested delimitation of maritime areas. Conversely, in IHL, where there is a profusion of detailed legal rules, so important for directing concrete military action, there would seem to remain less room for principles. But this first impression does not hold true. There are at least three reasons for that.

First, the whole body of IHL is the result of a careful and constant balancing of two great principles, namely military necessity and humanitarian need.[1] There can be no effective IHL outside the tension of these principles. A purely military law of war tends to atrophy, since the military personnel are traditionally conservative and over-emphasize their freedom of action. A too boldly humanitarian IHL tends to become ineffective, since it is not valued by the military personnel, considering it unrealistic and not properly designed for their needs.[2] The two mentioned principles do not disappear once a rule of IHL is adopted. They continue to operate on the legislative level each time new rules are devised; and they also continue on the level of positive law, by providing important arguments for the interpretation of the rules. If that is true, the whole body of IHL is constantly permeated by considerations "of principle", weighing up humanitarian with military concerns. IHL is then driven or guided by principles.

Second, it is paradoxical only at first sight that a body of law characterized by a great number of detailed rules is in need of some compensating guiding legal ideas expressed in GPL. It is only through these principles that the main values and gravitational points of the system can be correctly assessed and applied; that the dust of legal rules takes it correct meaning and its proper sense; and that the operator is able to fully see the wood for the trees. Without GPL such as military necessity, humanity, distinction and proportionality, IHL would be largely blind and in any case less operational than it is in the light of the great principles, expressing fundamental legal tenets of that system.

Third, any branch of the law, notwithstanding the degree of detailed codification to which it may have been subjected, cannot be reduced completely to detailed legal rules. There are subject matters which remain so context-related that the law cannot express more than a

---

1 This is a trite truth, often repeated. See for example, Y. Dinstein, "Military Necessity", in R. Wolfrum (ed.), *The Max Planck Encyclopaedia of Public International Law*, vol. VII, Oxford, 2012, p. 201.

2 M. Sassoli, "The Implementation of International Humanitarian Law: Current and Inherent Changes", *Yearbook of International Humanitarian Law*, vol. 10, 2007, pp. 45–73.

general guidance on the matter, to be spelled out in more detail by a contextually appreciative legal work in the changing circumstances of different situations. In IHL, this is true, for example, in the context of targeting issues (see Chapter 8). Thus, in such areas the law must work with more GPL than in other areas. For targeting, such principles as distinction, precaution and proportionality (military advantage/ collateral civilian losses) will be essential. They will determine to what extent something is a military objective and/or to what extent that military objective can be lawfully attacked in the circumstances ruling at the time of the attack.

4.3   Examples of general principles of law in international humanitarian law

The most important GPL operating in IHL will be briefly presented.[3] We will be dwelling slightly more profoundly on one of these principles, which has not been considered as much as it deserves, since to most humanitarian lawyers it is less sympathetic than the bright principle of "humanity". This is the principle of "military necessity". The overall picture of these general principles of IHL provides the legal operator in the area with a series of gravitational points of paramount importance for understanding and correctly applying the relevant rules. The principles make explicit the legal meaning of many detailed rules and provide the operator with an understanding of the fundamental tenets of the area of law at stake. It is, therefore, of great importance to study in detail the meaning and scope of the principles if one wants to achieve an advanced understanding of IHL.

4.3.1   Principle of humanity or of humane treatment[4]

The previously quoted Martens Clause[5] is but an expression of the principle of humanity. The principle permeates the whole body of modern IHL, with the so-called "Geneva Law" (protection of persons) at is core. It extends to the so-called "Hague Law" (conduct of

---

3   On the principles of IHL, see J. Pictet, *Development and Principles of International Humanitarian Law*, Dordrecht/Geneva, 1985.

4   See *ibid.*, pp. 61ff. See also J. Corn, "Humanity, Principle of", in R. Wolfrum (ed.), *The Max Planck Encyclopaedia of Public International Law*, vol. V, Oxford, 2012, pp. 72ff.

5   See Chapter 1.

hostilities), as can be seen, for example, in the prohibition of weapons causing "unnecessary suffering". This originally moral principle, inspired by mercy, compassion and solidarity, has been inserted into the positive law of armed conflicts by express provisions of the Geneva Conventions, namely common article 3 for NIAC ("shall in all circumstances be treated humanely") and in articles 12/12/13/27 of Geneva Conventions I–IV ("shall be treated humanely"; "shall at all times be humanely treated"). Within IHL, the principle has the following distinctive functions. First, it is the inspiration of a series of more detailed rules, which are all based on it. This is especially the case for the rules contained in the Geneva Conventions, which are all mainly specifications of the principle of humanity. Thus, this principle can be taken into account when interpreting these provisions, but without forgetting the counterbalancing aspect of military necessity, in other words, of what is militarily possible and reasonable. Second, especially in the complexion of the Martens Clause, the principle runs to counter the rule according to which "all that is not prohibited is allowed". In IHL, this argument does not hold true, even if IHL is mainly prohibitive law. An action or omission, to be lawful, must first be checked against the dictates of humanity. If it is utterly inhumane, it cannot be considered lawful. The moral principle is here quite directly translated into the law – a quite unique occurrence in international law. Third, the principle has certain typical features. It requires a belligerent to "respect" persons *hors de combat* in its control. This is a negative obligation prohibiting detrimental acts, sparing persons, not threatening them, and so on. It further requires a belligerent to "protect" persons *hors de combat* under its control; this is a positive obligation requiring action in order to preserve the persons from evils and dangers. It also requires the belligerent not to adversely distinguish (discriminate) between the persons, for example, on the basis of sex, race, nationality, religion, political opinion. This is remarkable in the context of the care of the wounded and sick: priority may be given only with regard to medical urgency, not with regard to nationality; a belligerent would have to take care of enemy soldiers before his own soldiers when the medical urgency lies on the enemy. Conversely, some distinctions are not considered adverse but are accepted, such as a differential treatment of prisoners of war according to sex and rank (article 16 of Geneva Convention III), to which later practice has added the differential treatment according to age, when child soldiers were detained in camps during the Iran–Iraq war of 1981–1988. Finally, humane treatment may also be taken to mean that a human being shall never be considered by a belligerent as a simple means, but always also as an end in itself, according to the famous Kantian distinction. As can be seen, the principle of humanity has a rich array of content. It moreover supposes some form of universal human morality, which may indeed exist in this extremely concrete context of compassion. All the great religions have valued such mercy, and there is thus some concrete cultural basis throughout the world for giving meaning to the eminently practical principle at stake here.

4.3.2 Principle of limitation

The *principle of limitation* negates the admissibility of total war, where a belligerent could do everything it sees fit in order to overpower the enemy. If total war prevailed, if any means and methods were allowed, there could clearly be no IHL, since there would be no limitation in warfare. It may be recalled that IHL is mainly a body of prohibitive rules for belligerents. Their very existence and binding character is the negation of total war. Thus, article 22 of the Hague Regulations proclaims: "The right of belligerents to adopt means of injuring the enemy is not unlimited". Article 35, § 1, of AP I echoes this principle: "In any armed conflict, the right of the Parties to the conflict to choose methods and means of warfare is not unlimited". The term "any armed conflict" must be taken also to cover NIAC. The principle of limitation applies directly only to means and methods of warfare, in other words, the conduct of hostilities. But it is applicable also in the context of protected persons, where it takes the form of the principles of humanity previously discussed. The principle of limitation operated as a break on the principle of permissive military necessity. This principle clearly applies in all armed conflicts, IAC and NIAC. The existence of any IHL stands and falls with it.

4.3.3 Principle of distinction

The *principle of distinction* is the cardinal principle of the "Hague Law", in other words, the law relating to the conduct of hostilities. This principle requires that the belligerents "shall at all times distinguish between the civilian population and combatants and between civilian objects and military objectives and accordingly shall direct their operations only against military objectives" (article 48 of AP I). Military objectives are then defined in article 52, § 2, of AP I. The operations of war shall be limited to breach the resistance of the adverse party in order to overpower it. The aim of war is not to achieve the greatest destruction and death possible. Therefore, since the civilians not directly participating in hostilities are not militarily active, there would be no gain in attacking them; there is no adverse resistance to over-power here. The principle of distinction thus operates by directing all the military theatre towards "military objectives". It considerably limits the scope of action and destruction. The principle also applies in NIAC (see article 13 of AP II). It may be added that the principle is realistic, since no belligerent wants to waste time and energy attacking objects and persons whose destruction will not secure any military advance.

4.3.4 Principle of proportionality

The detail of the *principle of proportionality* will be discussed later in Chapter 8. Its main meaning in IHL is to require a certain type of balancing in any targeting operation. A military objective may in principle always be attacked. However, there are situations where the attack on the objective yields only a limited military advantage, while the expected civilian losses appear excessive when compared to that advantage. In such a case, the attack is prohibited in the circumstances, in other words, as long as the advantage and the collateral losses remain roughly the same. The equation could obviously be changed, for example, by using laser-guided precision bombs that decrease the expected number of civilian losses; or by changing the timing of the attack to a moment when there are fewer civilians in the surroundings, and so on. Thus, article 51, § 5, letter b, of AP I stipulates that: "an attack which may be expected to cause incidental loss of civilian life, injury to civilians, damage to civilian objects, or a combination thereof, which would be excessive in relation to the concrete and direct mili-tary advantage anticipated" is considered as being indiscriminate and thus prohibited. The principle of proportionality also applies in NIAC, by virtue of customary rules.

4.3.5 Principle of precaution

The *principle of precaution* means that no attack shall be launched without a careful preparation with a view to sparing civilians and civil-ian objects from the adverse effects of the attacks as much as feasible. The principle of precaution is thus directly linked to the principle of distinction, and has in relation to it a serving function. The point is to lend strength to the principle of distinction by ensuring both in the preparation phase and in the carrying out of an attack, the maximum effort will be made to live up to the expectations formulated under the cardinal tenet of distinction. This principle will be discussed in more detail in the context of targeting (Chapter 8). It is codified in article 57 of AP I. It applies also to NIAC, by virtue of CIL.

4.3.6   Military necessity

The principle of *military necessity* will be considered in greater detail.[6] The notion of military necessity has been given various definitions, and is indeed a multifaceted notion.

Some definitions of military necessity are centred on military necessity as a fact. Military necessity here becomes an action considered necessary to achieve a war aim. Other definitions are a mixture of fact and legal entitlement. Consider the words of the Manual for the naval forces of the US (1959): "The principle of military necessity permits a belligerent to apply only that degree and kind of regulated force, not otherwise prohibited by the laws of war, required for the partial or complete submission of the enemy with the least possible expenditure of time, life, and physical resources".[7] Still other definitions of military necessity focus on its normative side, in other words, consider it as a legal principle. To the necessity as an action of fact, is here added the necessity as a legal circumstance excluding wrongfulness and as a principle requiring a careful balancing of any lawful exemption from the law of armed conflicts with regard to its necessity in regard to the war aim to be achieved.[8] The various writings and conventions do not always use the term in an equivalent meaning. Apart from military necessity, one may find "military needs", "imperative military necessities", "imperative military reasons", "urgent necessity", "absolutely necessary by military operations", "necessities of war", and so on. The legal meaning of all these expressions is essentially the same. However, the meaning can vary through qualification by various adverbs, such as "absolutely" or "imperatively". Indeed, sometimes an action which is in principle contrary to the law of armed conflicts is allowed in case of military necessity, and sometimes it is allowed only in case of absolute military necessity. The adverb is here to be interpreted as requiring a restrictive, or most restrictive, interpretation of the allowance.

The principle of military necessity operates on different levels of IHL.

---

6 On this principle, see Y. Dinstein, "Military Necessity", in R. Wolfrum (ed.), *The Max Planck Encyclopaedia of Public International Law*, vol. VII, Oxford, 2012, pp. 201ff.

7 M. Whiteman, *Digest of International Law*, vol. 10, Washington, 1968, p. 300.

8 P. Verri, *Dictionnaire du droit international des conflits armés*, Geneva, 1988, pp. 81–2.

4.3.6.1   A constitutional principle

First, it is a constitutional principle in the sense that it operates in the phase of adoption of new rules of that body of law (legislative principle). As we have already seen, it here requires a balancing between humanitarian aims to be pursued though a legal rule, and the military needs manifested in the subject matter. As has already been explained, IHL can properly perform its function only if and when the rule adopted expresses a workable and careful equilibrium between these two notions. Too much militarism makes the rule useless, since it does not constrain military action in any significant way; too much humanitarianism discredits the rule in the circles of those persons who have to apply it and therefore leads to ineffectiveness. Thus, in § 6 of the Hague Convention II of 1899, and in § 5 of the Hague Convention IV of 1907, there is the recognition that the provisions adopted attempted to mitigate the evils of war "as far as military requirements permit".

4.3.6.2   A principle of discretionary jurisdiction

Second, for certain authors, military necessity is additionally a principle of the law of armed conflicts encompassing the whole domain of belligerent sovereignty of a party to the conflict, in other words, the domain of its discretionary jurisdiction. The law of armed conflicts has, according to this view, limited the freedom of a belligerent party to adopt some course of conduct only by explicit prohibitive rules. When there are no such rules, there remains the freedom to act in order to try to overpower the enemy. This domain of freedom to act would be positively contained in and expressed through the notion of military necessity. It must, however, be emphasized that under modern IHL this domain of freedom has been limited by so many general principles and rules that it has lost much of its past consistency. We may also recall the principles of humanity (including the Martens Clause) and of limitation.

4.3.6.3   A dual principle of limitation and extension

Third, on the operational legal level, the principle has a double head of Janis, looking and pulling in two different directions.

On the one hand, the principle operates as a *limit* to the amount of permitted violence. Any form of violence excessive to the war aim is unnecessary and therefore prohibited. The aim of war is not to destroy as much as possible; it is to overpower the enemy in order to impose one's own will. Thus, what is necessary to achieve this limited aim, if compatible with the rules of IHL, is allowed; all destruction going beyond this limited aim is prohibited. The Preamble of the 1868 Petersburg Declaration expresses this limitation in clear words:

> "That the only legitimate object which States should endeavour to accomplish during war is to weaken the military forces of the enemy; That for this purpose it is sufficient to disable the greatest possible number of men; That this object would be exceeded by the employment of arms which uselessly aggravate the sufferings of disabled men. . .".

This principle of military necessity operating as a constraint on the use of lawful violence has the following main effects in the law of armed conflicts: (1) any act of violence which is useless from the military standpoint (vengeance, will of destruction, and so on) is prohibited; (2) if there are different military options to achieve a certain goal, but some have a greater degree of destructiveness or impact on civilians, the choice should go towards the less destructive means.[9] Imperative necessity means that there is no equally effective lawful military means, involving less damage or suffering, which would be sufficient to achieve the legitimate end. This centripetal function of military necessity operates as an additional level of restraint. It prohibits acts which are not otherwise illegal, when they are not necessary for the achievement of legitimate goals. Consequently, to the specific restraints contained in the detailed rules of IHL one general restraint is added by virtue of a GPL, in other words, by a *lex generalis*, which will render unlawful the action to the extent it is not militarily necessary. It is not sufficient that the action is compatible with specific IHL rules to be lawful; it must also comply with the general constraint of military necessity.

On the other hand, the principle operates as an *exemption from the respect for rules of IHL*, and here its action is to extend the range of legally permissible violence. The function of the principle is here centripetal: a belligerent may take liberties with the applicable IHL. The danger is to render IHL less effective, to invite a masking of violations of rules and to risk a spiralling down by similar action of the other side. However, no IHL can provide prohibitions for all situations which may occur in practice. There must remain a certain flexibility in context. It may be in order to prohibit the destruction of private (civilian)

---

9 See article 57, § 3, AP I.

property during warfare, but it springs to reason that the prohibition can hardly be absolute. There are circumstances, which cannot be exhaustively enumerated in advance, where the destruction of such property becomes necessary from the military standpoint. The prohibition has here to yield to military necessity. Thus, for example, if the only route through which a series of tanks may pass to join a military operation means dynamiting some private buildings, the prohibition of destruction gives way to the necessity described.

Contrary to the old laws of war, it is now accepted that military necessity cannot be invoked generally in order to put aside any rule of IHL in case of necessity. Thus, for example, it would no longer be possible to argue that prisoners of war could be killed on capture if it were impossible for the forces of the detaining power to keep them under control (in such a case, under the current law, the prisoners would have to be released).[10] The faculty to argue for an exemption from a rule of IHL on the basis of military necessity exists under the law as it stands only when that rule of IHL refers itself expressly to the circumstance precluding wrongfulness of military necessity. Thus, article 23, letter g, of the Hague Regulations of 1907 reads: "[It is forbidden] to destroy or seize the enemy's property, unless such destruction or seizure be imperatively demanded by the necessities of war". Allowance can also be made through clauses allowing for flexible interpretations, such as "Prisoners of war shall be evacuated, as soon as possible. . .".[11] Or else, it can be implicit in requirements to weigh up military advantages against collateral damage.[12] In particular, it is not possible to invoke the "state of necessity" under article 25 of the International Law Commission (ILC) Articles on the Responsibility of States for Internationally Wrongful Acts (2001), applicable in the law of peace, for excusing violations of IHL. IHL has its own, in this sense self-contained, regime of exemptions for necessity. The reason for the speciality of this branch of the law lies in the fact that IHL is in itself a law of emergency or necessity:[13] it contemplates application in the very special situation of warfare, and considerations of military necessity are already factored

---

10 For the nineteenth century, see the debate in C. Calvo, *Le droit international théorique et pratique*, vol. IV, 5th edn, Paris, 1896, p. 197; P. Pradier-Fodéré, *Traité de droit international public européen et américain*, vol. VII, Paris, 1897, pp. 72ff.

11 Article 19, § 1, Geneva Convention III.

12 Article 51, § 5, letter b, AP I.

13 "In short these rules and customs of warfare are designed specifically for all phases of war. They comprise the law for such emergency": *Krupp* case (1948), US Military Tribunal: M. Whiteman, *Digest of International Law*, vol. 10, Washington, 1968, p. 302.

in its drafting. It would be odd to allow a general plea of necessity to take liberties with rules which are precisely designed for a state of necessity like armed conflict; the necessity is here already situated in the primary rule, it should therefore not be re-factored into the level of secondary rules. The result would otherwise simply be that IHL would cease to be binding on the belligerents, since it would be possible to argue for non-application of any rule of IHL on the basis of subjective discretion. Thus, the US Military Tribunal in the *Hostages Trial* (*In re List*) (1948), rightly affirmed: "Military necessity or expediency do not justify a violation of positive rules [. . .] Articles 46, 47 and 50 of the Hague Regulations of 1907 make no such exceptions to its enforcement. The rights of the innocent population therein set forth must be respected even if military necessity or expediency decree otherwise".[14] In the *Rauter* case (1948), the Special Criminal Court of Holland could say that: "The laws of war purporting to lay down what actions are prohibited in warfare would be useless if the belligerents were allowed to deviate from them on the ground of a state of necessity".[15] Or else, the Judge Advocate, in the *Von Lewiski* case (1949), recalled the following to the Judges of the US Military Tribunal: "Once the usages of war have assumed the status of laws they cannot be overridden by necessity, except in those special cases where the law itself makes provision for that eventuality".[16]

4.3.6.4   *A principle for both international armed conflict and non-international armed conflict*

Fourth, the principle of military necessity in the sense described applies to IAC and NIAC. If the domain of freedom of the belligerents may be somewhat greater in NIAC, there remains the limitation of military necessity and also the allowance made for exemption from certain IHL rules in certain circumstances, Thus, article 17, § 1, of AP II, relating to the prohibition of forced movement of civilians, makes an exception for the "security of the civilians" and for "imperative military reasons". There is, therefore, a perfectly analogous functioning of the principle in IAC and NIAC: the limitation and the permission limbs operate in both types of armed conflict. However, since there are few specific treaty rules applicable to NIAC, the exemption clause of military necessity will more often than not have to be considered under CIL,

---

14 *Annual Digest and Reports of Public International Law Cases* (*ILR*), vol. 15, 1948, p. 647.

15 *Ibid.*, vol. 16, 1949, p. 533.

16 *Ibid.*, p. 512.

THE MAIN PRINCIPLES OF INTERNATIONAL HUMANITARIAN LAW 87

construed in analogy to the parallel provisions applicable in IAC. In other words, when an IAC provision is held to be of customary nature and to apply in both types of armed conflict, an eventual military necessity clause contained in it will be considered as being part and parcel of the customary rule applicable in both types of armed conflict, unless there is evidence to the contrary. The presumption is for the customary nature of the provision in all its parts, in other words, in its peculiar equilibrium.

4.3.6.5 An operational principle

Fifth, the military necessity argument has other operational functions. Thus, it is possible to argue that a provision on which the military necessity exception is engrafted thereby also makes allowance for military reprisals in case of breach. The violation itself could be considered as creating a military necessity, allowing a proportionate response. Why should the norm be able to stand an exemption for military reasons, but not for a response to previous violations? The clause relative to military necessity here becomes an indicator as to the still available domain of armed reprisals under modern IHL. It is manifest that some strict interpretation should here prevail, in view of common article 1 of the Geneva Conventions. Moreover, it may be recalled that the provisions on the protection of persons under the Geneva Law do not contain exception clauses for military necessity and therefore would also not allow reprisals under the argument presented here.

Further, the military necessity clauses could also serve in the context of interpretation of IHL, and in particular in a sort of "hierarchical" construction of that branch of the law. These clauses allow three layers of IHL to be vested with different degrees of legal importance. At the top of the "hierarchy" are the provisions not allowing for any exemption by military necessity, especially the humanitarian provisions of the Geneva Law for the protection of persons. In an intermediate position follow the rules permitting an exemption for imperative military necessity. An example of this is article 55, § 3, of Geneva Convention IV, concerning the supply of food and medical items in occupied territories. At the lowest level come the provisions allowing for an exemption for any type of simple military necessity or need. Article 15 of the Hague Regulations of 1907 is an example of such a provision, relating to facilities accorded by the belligerents to relief societies for prisoners of war. This reconstruction of IHL can serve at least for interpretation purposes. It can also supply arguments for the determination of the precise scope of *jus cogens* in IHL,[17] a notion further connected with articles 6/6/6/7 and 7/7/7/8 of Geneva Conventions I–IV. It must be stressed that even provisions with a military necessity clause can form a peremptory norm. Indeed, a derogation of this norm would be allowed only for certain precise purposes, linked to the interpretation of the necessity clause; conversely, any derogation for other purposes would be forbidden. The result is a sort of partial or functional *jus cogens*. Overall, it would thus be possible to determine four main positions in this regard: (1) IHL forming *jus dispositivum*, to be found, for example, in some administrative provisions of the Hague Regulations of 1907 (for example, article 52 or article 55) or in special agreements concluded by the belligerents; (2) IHL forming a soft form of *jus cogens*, where derogation is allowed, but is allowed only for legal acts relating to military necessity; (3) IHL forming a stronger *jus cogens*, where derogation is permitted only for legal acts relating to imperative military necessity; (4) IHL forming an absolute *jus cogens*, where no derogation is allowed, whatever its aim. The majority of modern IHL provisions are in this last category.

The question of admissible derogation gains particular momentum with regard to normative action of the UN Security Council (UNSC). It seems legally admissible to state that the Security Council of the UN could derogate in a necessary and proportionate way from a provision of IHL when this provision makes allowance for military necessity. It is perhaps also possible to give a slightly more generous interpretation of the scope of such a derogatory space for action deemed to be in the general interest of the "international community".[18] The point arises especially in the context of post conflict nation building concurring with the rules of the law of occupation. Apart from the fact that administrative rules on occupation, such as the one on usufruct contained in article 55 of the Hague Regulations, are *jus dispositivum* and can be put aside by the Security Council, there would be a further mass manoeuvring through the military necessity exceptions.

---

17 On this point, see for example, R. Nieto-Navia, "International Peremptory Norms (Jus Cogens) and International Humanitarian Law", in L. C. Vorah, F. Pocar, Y. Featherstone, O. Fourmy, C. Graham, J. Hocking and N. Robson (eds), *Man's Inhumanity to Man, Essays in Honour of Antonio Cassese*, The Hague/London/New York, 2003, pp. 595ff.

18 See S. Vité, "L'applicabilité du droit international de l'occupation militaire aux activités des organisations internationales", *International Review of the Red Cross*, vol. 86, 2004, pp. 24ff.

4.3.6.6   *A principle of necessity under* jus ad bellum?

Sixth, can the military necessity under IHL be influenced by the principle of necessity under *jus ad bellum*? It is clear that only military action covered by the principle of self-defence, Security Council authorization or a government invitation, eventually as limited by the further principles of necessity and proportionality, is lawful under *jus ad bellum* law. Must therefore all military action with its military necessities *in bello* conform to that general limitation under *jus ad bellum* to be lawful at all? Does the same apply to action on behalf of an authorization of the UNSC? Would military action outside the four corners of the mandate entail that the whole action is unlawful and no military necessity *in bello* could be claimed? It has been argued that such a contamination of *jus in bello* by *jus ad bellum* must be resisted on this plane as it must be resisted on other planes. Indeed, if the necessity under *jus ad bellum* was applied as stated under *jus in bello*, the result would be that the aggressor would be placed on a better footing than the State acting in self-defence. The former is not subjected to limitations as regard necessity and proportionality, but the second, under self-defence or Security Council authorization, is so limited. Therefore, we would instil in the body of IHL a reverse inequality of the belligerents, favouring the aggressor and unfavourable towards the aggressed, favouring the State targeted by sanctions and unfavourable towards the State acting on behalf of the Security Council.

The correct legal answer to this conundrum is once more to keep *jus ad bellum* and *jus in bello* issues distinct. It is obvious that limitations coming from the former influence the strategic level of military planning. It must, however, also be accepted that operational military planning must remain entirely under the guise of IHL, and therefore the lawfulness of a military action or attack must be measured only under *jus in bello* requirements. But the distinction is not always easy to draw in this area of the law. The following example will illustrate the point.

Military necessity aspects have been put in operation in different contexts. In the *Wall* opinion of the ICJ (2004),[19] the issue at stake was the construction of the Israeli wall in the Palestinian occupied territories (it must be emphasized that the point was not whether Israel had a right to construct a wall to protect itself, but whether it had a right to construct such a wall in the occupied territory rather than on its internationally

---

19 ICJ, *Reports*, 2004-I, pp. 192–4, §§ 135ff.

recognized boundary). The Court ruled that certain provisions – such as article 49, § 6, of Geneva Convention IV on colonization of occupied territories – do not contain exception clauses for military necessity and that therefore no exemption can apply on this ground. The Court then went on to analyse provisions containing a saving clause for military necessity, such as article 53 of Geneva Convention IV, relative to destruction of objects. The clause here requires that the destruction is rendered "absolutely necessary by military operations". The interpretation of such a clause must therefore be strict. According to the Court, these conditions are not met with regard to the state of evidence and also as to the fact that the wall is constructed within occupied territory. The destructions do not seem absolutely necessary with regard to the military operations, nor do they seem proportionate.

These rulings of the Court allow the following remarks. First, when the exception is for "military operations", a broad interpretation is allowed, so that the military necessity exception can also be invoked in occupied territories after the general close of military operations.[20] Indeed, there are still sporadic military operations in occupied territories. This shows that even with military necessity exception clauses a narrow interpretation need not prevail on all issues. Second, the Court took account of the route chosen for the wall and its infringement of a number of human rights of the Palestinian populations – and ruled that these infringements could not be justified by military exigencies.[21] A territorial and human rights issue here has its effect on the *jus in bello* assessment. It is not entirely clear what the relation of this argument is to the one discussing the lack of conclusive evidence for the necessity invoked (in advisory proceedings, there is no strict presentation of evidence accompanied by the burden of proof). But the argument may be taken to mean that even if conclusive evidence as to military necessity would have been established, it could not have justified that particular course of the wall – since it would have been possible to construct it on the internationally recognized boundary. The fact that certain settlements would then not have been protected is probably regarded as irrelevant by the ICJ, since that would imply that Israel profits from its own wrong. It had no right to install those settlements there in the first place, and cannot now invoke this state of affairs to benefit from constructing a wall inside the occupied territory. In sum, the military necessity is here strongly intermingled with extra-

---

20 *Ibid.*, p. 192, § 135.
21 *Ibid.*, p. 193, § 137.

military considerations analogous to *jus ad bellum* issues. They could hardly be separated clearly here, since the whole opinion of the ICJ was decisively coloured, not so much by the fact that there was a wall, but by its route. And it is only logical that this fact had its impact on all issues in the opinion, including the military necessity limb. Compare the rulings of Israeli courts on the same issue to the rulings of the ICJ.[22] The Israeli courts differed from the ICJ not so much on the particular tools of analysis: even the municipal courts found certain sections of the wall to be contrary to principles of necessity and proportionality. The greatest difference lay in the fact that the municipal court took it as a non-revisable political question that a wall was constructed, that it was necessary to have it for public security and that it was constructed in occupied territory. The issue on which they ruled was only if this or that part of the wall did prove or did not prove disproportionate when weighed against the rights of the inhabitants of the occupied territory.

4.3.6.7   *A principle operating in criminal international law*

Seventh, numerous examples of military necessity put into operation can be found in the branch of criminal international law. In the ICTY cases, the notion of military necessity features frequently. Thus, in the context of "wanton destruction of villages, or devastation not justified by military necessity", the exception is directly contained in the text of the offence. The ICTY checks that there is no military necessity for the destruction as such, and also that the collateral civilian damages are nor excessive with regard to that military necessity.[23] Military necessity may also excuse indirect attacks on civilian persons and civilian objects, under the limb of (non-excessive) collateral damage.[24] Such attacks will at least not be considered as a war crime. In IHL, the question would rather turn on the existence of a sufficient military *advantage* to compensate the civilian losses. But it can be said that if there is a sufficient advantage of this type, there may also be a military necessity for the purposes of criminal international law (even if the word is here taken in a much broader sense than in IHL). This difference of meaning has the merit of recalling that legal notions are relative to the branch of the law in which they are applied, and may even

---

22 See the site of the Israeli Supreme Court: http://elyon1.court.gov.il/eng/verdict/framesetSrch. html. In particular, see the *Beit Sourik Village Council* case (2004), in M. Sassoli, A. Bouvier and A. Quintin, *How Does Law protect in War?*, vol. II, 3rd edn, Geneva, 2011, pp. 1000ff.

23 See for example, the *Martic* case (Trial Chamber, 2007), §§ 89ff, 90, 93.

24 *Kordic* case (Appeals Chamber, 2004), § 54.

depend on the legal provision in which they have been inserted. There is no legal rule that a similar concept must have the same legal meaning throughout the legal branches. The aim of the regulation, as well as the systematic context, indeed does often differ and thus explains a difference in legal meaning. The military necessity test will also apply in the context of other offences than war crimes, for example, for crimes against humanity, persecution and forcible transfer.[25]

The standard of review of the ICTY with regard to military necessity is rather demanding. The same can be said for the post World War II jurisprudence.[26] The plea was accepted in the *High Command Trial* in the context of a scorched earth policy/spoliation by General Rendulic, retreating from Norway on the advance of the Red Army.[27] The fact that he erred on the exact urgency of the action (because he believed the Soviets nearer than they actually were) was not influential: it was an excusable error of fact. The Tribunal acknowledged that a retreat under arduous conditions, where quick decisions have to be taken, might give rise to the defence of military necessity more easily than other situations. The same ruling was applied with regard to destruction of property (article 23, letter g, of the Hague Regulations 1907) in the *Hostages Trial*.[28] In most cases, however, the plea of necessity was rejected. This jurisprudential stance is based on the conception that exonerations from the law (in particular for a "law of necessity" like IHL) have to be interpreted strictly. Moreover, exceptions tend to be generally strictly interpreted: *exceptiones sunt strictae interpretationis*. A broad and generous admission of liberties with regard to IHL duties would quickly lead to the wholesale breakdown of a branch of the legal order which is already implanted on arid and dangerous soil. This conception has been rightly translated by the criminal judges into the relevant rules of international criminal law, which has therefore here displayed a truly serving function with regard to IHL.

---

25 *Blagojevic and Jokic* (Trial Chamber, 2005), § 597.

26 United Nations War Crimes Commission, *Law Reports of Trials of War Criminals*, vol. XV, London, 1949, pp. 175–6.

27 *Ibid.*, vol. XII, London, 1949, pp. 123–6.

28 *Ibid.*, vol. VIII, London, 1949, pp. 66–9.

5 Applicability issues: finding a way out of the quagmire

5.1 The problem stated

With the shift from the old laws of war to the modern IHL, in other words, from belligerent issues of conduct of hostilities to the central core of protection of persons, the issue of applicability of the law has become all the more important. If a proper protection of the victims of war during armed conflict is to be secured, the application of the law should be regulated at once in an objective, clear and certain manner. Complications, differing thresholds, ambiguities inviting quibbling and quixotic arguments, and the like, decisively weaken the protective aim of humanitarian law. This is all the graver since IHL consists of minimum humanitarian protections, of an absolute nature, which should never be abandoned. Unfortunately, the actual state of the law, especially in NIAC, does not live up to these expectations or necessities. In all too many cases, there is too much room for argument as to whether there is an armed conflict and whether IHL applies at all. True, with the shift from the laws of war to IHL the subjective trigger has been abandoned in favour of an objective trigger (see Chapter 1): when there is an armed conflict defined as an issue of fact, the application of the law automatically follows. In the old laws of war, the issue was obscured by the subjective trigger of the state of war (which flowed from a legal act of will by at least one belligerent) or by the recognition of belligerency (which again flowed from such a legal act of will). However, this victory of the modern law proved to some extent Pyrrhic. The trigger was now objective (existence of an armed conflict as a fact). But since the definition of the armed conflict gave rise to uncertainties, and its application to the facts of a particular case augmented the uncertainties, the subjectivity again invited itself on that plane: is there an armed conflict to which IHL applies? The issue has been particularly arduous in the context of NIAC, where the propensity of the local government and its allies to deny an armed conflict (and thus to avoid granting some belligerent status to the rebels) is particularly high.

We must therefore consider two points in this chapter. The first question is to what legal facts does IHL attach the legal consequences of its application? This is the issue of "applicability" of the law. We will limit this question to issues of the material scope of applicability, in particular to the definition of the armed conflict as the typical situation triggering the application of IHL. There are also other issues of applicability, namely personal (to whom does IHL apply?), temporal (when does IHL apply?) and spatial (where does IHL apply?). The last two issues are closely linked (but not identical) with the material scope of application, since the general answer to the temporal question is that IHL apples from the beginning to the end of the armed conflict, and the general answer to the spatial question is that IHL applies wherever acts and omissions linked to the armed conflict take place. Second, we will have to see how modern IHL can find ways out of the quagmire of a law relating to applicability issues, which is too complicated and leads to gaps and uncertainties, to the detriment of the protected persons.

5.2   The material applicability of international armed conflict

When does IHL in IAC apply? What are the legal facts triggering its application? There are five situations to which IHL in IAC applies: (1) peacetime; (2) armed conflict; (3) declared war; (4) territories occupied without armed resistance; (5) wars of national liberation. In the first category, peacetime, only some rules of IHL apply. In all the other categories all the rules of IHL in IAC apply, subject to the ratification or accession of the different treaties, since these only apply to the States parties. The fifth category applies to all parties to AP I, not having entered a reservation on article 1, § 4. It is, however, doubtful if that category reflects CIL, in view of the great resistance it provoked at the time of its adoption. The question is not anymore very relevant today, when the time of decolonization wars has passed. Categories 1–4 have their seat in common article 2 of the Geneva Conventions I–IV, defining the material scope of application of the Geneva Conventions. The criteria it contains reflect CIL criteria for the applicability of IHL in IAC. Moreover, these customary criteria, applicable since 1949, are taken to have overridden, as *lex posterior* of a general character, the conditions of applicability of older IHL conventions, which, according to their wording or implicitly, were applicable in a situation of "war". Since 1949, these older conventions are taken to be applicable under the same conditions as the Geneva Conventions, under their article 2, by virtue of the new customary rule, by which, through subsequent practice, older rules have been abrogated and replaced.[1]

Common article 2, §§ 1 and 2, of the Geneva Conventions reads:

> § 1. In addition to the provisions which shall be implemented in peacetime, the present Convention shall apply to all cases of declared war or of any other armed conflict which may arise between two or more of the High Contracting Parties, even if the state of war is not recognized by one of them.
>
> § 2. The Convention shall also apply to all cases of partial or total occupation of the territory of a High Contracting Party, even if the said occupation meets with no armed resistance.

All the mentioned triggers are independent from one another and thus alternatives. Apart from the peacetime limb, the three other triggers all lead to the application of the whole body of IHL in IAC. There is thus no legal interest in trying to come under one rather than the other trigger, since no different legal consequences flow. Politically, there may be an obvious interest in avoiding entering into a "declaration of war" – but from the vantage point of IHL, this makes no difference. As we shall see, one of the main aims of the triggers is not to leave any land uncharted, in other words, not to leave open any gap which could result in a loss of protection for the persons likely to benefit from the application of IHL. A short analysis of these triggers is in point. We will, however, omit the last trigger (wars of national liberation: articles 1, § 4, and 96 of AP I) which are not very relevant in today's practice.

5.2.1 Peacetime

There are certain provisions of IHL which by their wording or by their object and purpose (and thus by interpretation) must be applicable immediately on the entry into force of the convention containing them, for any State bound by the convention. Thus, it would make no sense to say that the duty to disseminate IHL,[2] and to train the armed forces in IHL,[3] commences only when an armed conflict erupts; at that moment

---

1 See also for example, article 154, Geneva Convention IV, priority is given to the new notions of the Geneva Conventions, which displace the older notions of the Regulations.

2 On dissemination at large, in civil society, see S. Tawil, "International Humanitarian Law and Basic Education", *International Review of the Red Cross*, vol. 82, 2000, pp. 581ff.

3 See article 1 of the Hague Regulations or articles 47/48/127/144 of the Geneva Conventions I–IV; articles 83, 87, AP I, and article 19, AP II.

it would clearly be too late. In the same way, when a provision asks the States parties to try to separate as much as feasibly possible military objectives from areas of concentration of civilians, in order to avoid heavy collateral civilian damages in case of armed conflict, this duty extends to the planning of territory in peacetime.[4] Further, when IHL requires or allows the parties to a convention to set up sanitary services and to provide for sanitary (hospital) zones for the event of an armed conflict, this duty or power must perforce be performed (or be able to be exercised) already with the entry into force of the convention. Thus, article 14 of Geneva Convention IV, concerning hospital and safety zones, is formulated: "In time of peace, the High Contracting Parties, ... may establish ... hospital and safety zones". These provisions, among others, show that it is conceptually wrong to hold that the law of peace and the law of armed conflicts are mutually exclusive. They indeed do overlap in many respects. First, IHL already applies in part in peacetime, as we have seen. Second, HRL, which comes from the peacetime law, extends its application to times of emergency, including armed conflict (subject to the faculty of limitations for public interest and of suspension of certain rights, called wrongly "derogation"). Third, all legal provisions of the law of peace not incompatible with the state of armed conflict remain in force. Thus, for example, to the extent there are still embassies of the belligerents on their respective territories, the diplomatic law applies. The diplomatic personnel enjoy the diplomatic inviolability, privileges and immunities, and the premises enjoy their inviolability. The old maxim according to which *inter bellum et pacem nihil est medium*[5] (there is nothing common to peace and war) is thus not applicable any more – if it ever was. However, the provisions of IHL applicable in peacetime are reduced in number; the bulk of IHL provisions apply only under one of the other triggers.

5.2.2   Armed conflict

Article 2 of the Geneva Conventions stipulates that IHL shall also apply in case of "any other armed conflict", adding this category to the one on "declared war". However, it is warranted to start with the armed conflict, since it is the ordinary trigger of IHL application. Conversely,

---

4 Article 58, AP I. The provision opens by the wording "The Parties to the conflict shall . . .", but it is understood that some obligations in this effect already arise in peacetime: see Y. Sandoz, C. Swinarski and B. Zimmermann (eds), *Commentary on the Additional Protocols of 8 June 1977 to the Geneva Conventions of 12 August 1949*, Geneva, 1987, p. 692, no. 2244.

5 Cicero, *Philippica*, VIII, I, 4; Grotius, *De iure belli ac pacis* (1625), lib. III, cap. XXI, 1.

"declared war" has faded away in international practice. The term "any other" shows that armed conflict was seen by the drafters of the Geneva Conventions as a residual category, a catch-up concept whose function was to fill any gap in applicability which would have led to a loss of protection. The concept of "armed conflict" makes reference to a pure fact, to which the legal order attaches certain determined consequences, namely the application of IHL rules. This pure fact is the one of "hostilities". When there are actual hostilities between armed forces of two, or more than two, different States taking place somewhere out there, this fact is sufficient to trigger the application of IHL. The qualification of these hostilities as a "war", as a "police action", as a "peacekeeping operation", as an "armed reprisal", or any other legal category, is irrelevant. This is what was meant by the perhaps somewhat naïve term "pure" fact. Any time there are hostilities there is a need to apply IHL for the protection of those involved. Exactly this will happen every time there are such hostilities. Therefore, the legal qualification of these hostilities must be irrelevant, since no distinct legal consequence shall flow from it. The recourse to the concept of "armed conflict" was due especially to the intention of escaping from the strictures of the concept of "war"[6] (see also below). Contrary to what is generally believed, the term "war" does not refer to a fact. According to traditional doctrine, there is a war in the legal sense only when at least one of the parties to the conflict intends to create a State of war (*animus belligerandi*). This will is normally expressed through a declaration of war. If the belligerents want to avoid a state of war by not intending to create one, there are hostilities, but there is no war in the legal sense. The war is thus not a simple fact; it is rather a legal situation, flowing from a legal act. It is an expression of intention creating certain legal consequences. There are different reasons for why a State could want to avoid creating a state of war: first, to avoid applying the laws of war (before 1949, when there was a subjective trigger for application); second to avoid involving Parliament in the military operation; third to avoid neutrality duties with regard to third States and so on. In the time of the League of Nations there was a frequent occurrence of such forcible military interventions short of war.[7] This created a gap in the application of the laws of war: a State could circumvent these laws by simply avoiding creating a state of war. The category of the "armed

---

6 On the traditional concept of war, see for example, L. Kotzsch, *The Concept of War in Contemporary History and International Law*, Geneva, 1956.

7 On this issue, see A. E. Hindmarsh, *Force in Peace, Force Short of War in International Relations*, Cambridge, 1933.

conflict" in common article 2 had the aim to ensure the application of IHL in any case of armed conflict (fact of hostilities), independent of the legal label and of a legal act of discretionary will. The point here is not to leave gaps in protection.

There are certain aspects of "armed conflict" which fall to be further discussed.

5.2.2.1   Armed forces of States

First, the actors confronting each other must be armed forces of States. The question of how a State organizes itself is a question of domestic jurisdiction and of domestic law. A State may use paramilitary or even police forces for military tasks. It can globally or effectively control armed bands, which then become its organs or agents under articles 4 or 8 of the ILC Articles on the Responsibility of States for Internationally Wrongful Acts (2001). If State armed forces confront armed groups not controlled by a State, the armed conflict is not international in nature. The law of NIAC will apply. Thus, if some angry peasants take up their arms and make a punitive expedition across the national boundary, and they are involved in some fighting with armed forces of the foreign State, this is not an armed conflict in the sense of article 2, Geneva Conventions or related CIL. At best, it could only be a NIAC, but it will hardly fulfil the criteria of organization and intensity applicable there. It is not always clear, as a point of fact, whether armed forces are controlled by a State. This is true for armed bands operating abroad. Consider also the situation in the Ukraine in March 2014, where in the first days some paramilitary units acted in Crimea without any clarity as to whether these were local pro-Russian units or Russian armed forces.

5.2.2.2   No criterion of intensity

Second, there is no criterion of intensity for an IAC. The notion is indeed only functional. Any time there is hostile action between armed forces of States, IHL shall apply. A border incident is an "armed conflict" in the sense of the Geneva Conventions. There is no reason to say that the first injured soldier shall not be cared for under Geneva Convention I, simply because he or she is for the moment only one, and thus the armed conflict is not yet sufficiently intense. By the same token, the weapons used by the military forces must conform to IHL requirements from the time of the first shot. The perspective is functional: if a situation of hostility between armed forces triggers the need for application of some IHL rule, then IHL shall apply. For example, if there are some injured or sick persons, if there is a prisoner of war, if there is fighting (means and methods of warfare), and so on, IHL rules are relevant and shall apply. The capturing of some military personnel outside the context of any actual armed hostilities again makes necessary the application of IHL (even low-level). The term "hostilities" thus refers to "hostile action"; it does not necessarily refer to armed fighting. We come here to the fringes of low-level application of IHL. From the point of view of IHL this is, however, not truly problematic. If there is a small border incident, the application of IHL rules will remain extremely low-level; but application will be secured. However, politically it may be very difficult for the States involved to say that they have been in an "armed conflict", even if it lasted only for a few minutes. Consider a Greek minister of defence appearing in front of the press and saying that after one of the incidents on the island of Imia during the 1990s, Greece and Turkey had been in an "armed conflict". Responsible diplomacy will rightly try to downplay such incidents and will not have recourse to apparently martial vocabulary. The proper qualification of a situation under IHL and the political possibilities are here incompatible. The application of IHL will in such cases be secured in fact, while the concerned States do not admit that there has been an "armed conflict".

5.2.2.3   "Attacks" launched by mistake

Third, there remains the issue of military low-level "attacks" launched by mistake. In 1968, Swiss armed forces, during an exercise, fired some canon bullets into the territory of Liechtenstein by mistake.[8] Swiss armed forces entered more than once into Italian territory by mistake, when they lost their way in the mountains because of bad weather conditions. Is that an armed conflict, in the sense of what we have just said? Or is the lack of hostile intent by the purported attacker a relevant criterion to be taken into account? Now, the answer to the last question is clear: belligerent or hostile intent (as a subjective criterion) is irrelevant to the existence of an armed conflict. This is fairly clear when one considers the aim of the law of 1949, which is not to leave any gaps in protection and to privilege objective triggers. If belligerent intent were relevant, we would turn back to the concept of "war" or some related concept, where the application of the law turns on subjective – and

---

8 See *Annuaire suisse de droit international*, vol. 26, 1969/1970, p. 158.

often uncertain – considerations. In most of the situations mentioned above, there will be no armed conflict for the reason that there are no hostilities *between* two or more States. Liechtenstein or Italy will not mistake the situation and think that they face a military attack. In both situations there was, moreover, no damage of a belligerent nature: no injured soldier, no prisoners, and so on. (the canon bullets in the first example came down in a forest). The relationship remains thus entirely under the law of peace, with the duty to make reparation for damages caused (for example, to the forest) or to offer excuses (for the violation of territorial sovereignty). However, if incidents described above, taking place between friendly States, will not trigger an armed conflict, the same incidents happening in other parts of the world may lead to an armed conflict. If India fired canon bullets into the territory of Pakistan, this might ignite an armed conflict, in view of the vivid tensions between the two countries. In order to avoid such escalation, it would be wise to immediately communicate to the other party that the shots were accidental and apologize. The overall result is that such situations will not normally lead to an armed conflict, but occasionally they may do so.

5.2.3   Declared war

This traditional trigger has been maintained in the Geneva Conventions mainly because there may be "wars" without "armed conflict", in other words, wars without actual hostilities. But even if a declaration of war is followed by hostilities, the category of the "declared war" remains relevant for the time period between the declaration and the beginning of the hostilities. IHL already applies during this time-span. Moreover, there are declarations of war not followed by any hostility, such as a series of declarations of war on the Axis powers (or on Germany) by Central and Latin American countries during World War II. Such a declaration was a condition for being invited to the San Francisco Conference on International Organization (UN).[9] The "declared war" thus again closes a gap in the law, by ensuring that IHL is applied even if there are no actual hostilities. To what extent can IHL be relevant in such a situation? To be sure, Hague Law relating to means and methods of warfare will not apply, since there is no warfare. Conversely, Geneva Law will find its place: in most cases there will be "enemy" civilians on the territory of the belligerents, who have to be protected in

---

9 U. Fastenrath, "Article 3", in B. Simma, D. E. Khan, G. Nolte and A. Paulus (eds), *The Charter of the United Nations, A Commentary*, vol. I, 3rd edn, Oxford, 2012, p. 336.

their persons and property under Geneva Convention IV. It may lastly be added that the question whether the declaration of war is lawful under *jus ad bellum* (self-defence or authorization by the UNSC) or not (aggression) is entirely irrelevant under *jus in bello*. The issue of separation of *jus ad bellum* and *jus in bello* has already been touched upon.

5.2.4 Territory occupied without armed resistance

According to § 2 of common article 2 of the Geneva Conventions, IHL (notably the law of occupation) shall also apply where a territory is occupied, totally or partially, when this occupation meets with no armed resistance. The text of the Convention says "even" if the occupation meets with no armed resistance. This wording does not imply that occupation obtained in the course of an armed conflict shall also be covered by § 2; it is rather covered by § 1 of article 2, as an incident of the armed conflict. The meaning of the word "even" is to make clear that IHL/occupation law shall *also* apply if the occupation does not flow from an armed conflict, in other words, hostilities. As we will see, there is some legal relevance to this distinction as to whether § 1 or § 2 is applicable to an occupation. The overall aim of § 2 is again to fill a protection gap. If provision was not made for the particular situation it envisages, occupations not following an armed conflict or a declaration of war, and yet belligerent and hostile, could be held not to be subject to the application of IHL. Consider for example the invasion of Denmark by Germany in 1940 (where Denmark renounced a hopeless resistance) or a hypothetical invasion of Costa Rica (which has no armed forces, supposing that no other State exercises collective self-defence on its behalf). Paragraph 2 thus now extends to this situation of "pacific coercive occupation". Other situations are also covered. Thus, the IMT at Nuremberg considered that the German "protectorate" over Bohemia and Moravia was covered by the rules of belligerent occupation under the Hague Regulations of 1907.[10] Furthermore, all the situations of deployment of troops on foreign territory where the local sovereign has not given its consent are included; as are the situations where the consent to the presence of foreign troops was initially given, but withdrawn at a certain moment. This latter situation occurred in the case of Namibia (with regard to South African forces)

---

10 *Trial of the Major War Criminals before the International Military Tribunal*, Nuremberg, 1946, vol. 22, p. 497.

after 1966[11] and more recently in the case of the Democratic Republic of Congo (with regard to Ugandan troops) after 1998.[12] A hostile occupation without armed resistance has also taken place recently in the Crimea (2014).

Another difficulty arises with the wording of § 2. In § 1 it is stated that the Geneva Conventions shall apply to declared war or armed conflict "which may arise between two or more of the High Contracting Parties"; in § 2 it is written that the Convention shall also apply to occupation of the territory "of a High Contracting Party". In principle, the issue here is only one of the law of treaties: the Convention thus regulates its applicability and addresses itself only to the States that have ratified or acceded to it. Conversely, by virtue of the *pacta tertiis* rule, it does not purport to regulate situations concerning non-parties. It is understood that CIL has no such limitation, since there are no States parties to it. Thus, it applies to all belligerent States and other belligerent entities. However, the wording of § 2 has been taken to mean that if the status of a territory is controversial, it cannot be said that it appertains to a "High Contracting Party", and that thus the Convention does not apply. This argument was made by Israel with regard to the occupied Palestinian territories.[13] All other national and international actors, including the ICRC,[14] the ICJ[15] and other international tribunals[16] have rightly rejected this position. It runs afoul of two cardinal considerations under IHL. First, it is based on confusion between *jus ad bellum* and *jus in bello* issues. IHL is attached only to the fact of occupying a territory which was formerly effectively held by another party. The question of title to territory is alien to its application. Notice that if it were otherwise, it would be sufficient to claim that a territory in reality belonged to you in order not to apply occupation law when invading and occupying. Kuwait would not have been occupied territory in 1991. In short words, IHL is attached only to the effectiveness of possession. As soon as the military forces of a

---

11 See UNGA Res. 2372 (XXII), 1968; Res. 2403 (XXIII), 1968; Res. 2871 (XXVI), 1971, where, in § 8, respect of Geneva Convention IV is demanded.

12 *Armed Activities* case (*DRC v. Uganda*), ICJ, *Reports*, 2005, pp. 196ff, §§ 42ff.

13 See M. Shamgar, "The Observance of International Law in the Administered Territories", *Israel Yearbook of Human Rights*, vol. 1, 1971, pp. 262ff.

14 See R. Kolb and S. Vité, *Le droit de l'occupation militaire*, Brussels, 2009, p. 83. See also the *Wall* opinion, ICJ, *Reports*, 2004-I, pp. 175–6, § 97.

15 *Wall* opinion, ICJ, *Reports*, 2004-I, pp. 173ff, §§ 90ff.

16 With regard to boundary arguments made by Eritrea: see Eritrea/Ethiopia Claims Commission, *Central Front, Ethiopia's Claim* 2 (2004), *RIAA*, vol. 26, p. 170, § 29, and p. 183, §§ 77–8.

State displace armed forces, effectively holding in a stable way a part of a territory, by invading it, this triggers the application of the law of occupation. Second, it is squarely contrary to the legislative aim of § 2. This paragraph was not inserted in the convention in order to open up gaps, but rather to close gaps. It was made for ensuring the greatest amount of effective protection. The interpretation presented above runs directly against this clear legislative aim and cannot therefore be countenanced. If a territory is under the control of a State not party to the Geneva Conventions, then these conventions will not apply, but the customary rules of the law of occupation will be applicable. These rules are essentially the same as the conventional ones. By reason of these sterile controversies over the personal scope of application of § 2, a certain prevalence has been given to § 1. This is correct also from the systematic point of view, § 2 being a residual clause with respect to § 1. If a territory is occupied as a consequence of an armed conflict (such as the Palestinian territories, through the conflict of 1967), § 1 is applicable since the territory was not occupied without resistance.[17] Paragraph 2 is therefore confined to a subsidiary position, ruling only on the occupation of territory where there has been no declaration of war or armed conflict at all.

5.2.5   Conclusion

Overall, it can be said that the application of IHL in IAC is regulated in a quite flexible and broad way. The polar star in the matter is the trigger of "armed conflict" as the fact of hostilities. Hostilities are interpreted broadly on two accounts: there is no requirement of a certain intensity; the interpretation is largely functional, in other words, IHL shall apply any time the situation on the ground touches upon one of the regulations of this branch of the law (for example, by the existence of an injured person, or the use of certain weapons). The humanitarian aim of modern IHL is here very visible: the scope of application is voluntarily quite extended, so that the actual or potential victims of war may be adequately protected. The main aim of the law is to eliminate any gap in protection. This effort culminates in common article 2 of the Geneva Conventions. Through this careful regulation, there are few situations where the application of the law is doubtful or denied. In general, States are much more ready to accept the application of IHL rules with regard to inter-State situations, when reciprocity interests also militate in the direction of a broad application of the law, than they are to apply such

---

17 This is also the ruling of the ICJ: *Wall* opinion, ICJ, *Reports*, 2004-I, pp. 174–5, §§ 93, 95.

rules in NIAC. Doubts do arise mainly at the lowers edges of "armed conflict", when the "hostilities" are limited to sporadic incidents or to the simple unfriendly taking into custody of foreign military personnel. In such situations, the way out of potential difficulties has to be sought through direct contacts between the concerned States and their agreement on the application of the relevant legal rules.

5.3   The material applicability of non-international armed conflict

The situation in regard to NIAC is much more intricate. This is the case on many levels.

First, States are much less inclined to accept international regulation and control by third parties of highly sensitive internal affairs, when a government is struggling for its survival against elements it considers criminal. The result of this more than lukewarm attitude is that the functional and broad approach under IHL in IAC is abandoned in favour of an approach requiring a certain intensity of conflict and a certain degree of organization of the rebels before the threshold of armed conflict is reached. Thus, quantitative criteria are imported into the law. Such criteria are prone to endless discussion, each actor being able to interpret them differently with regard to the facts at hand. The local government and its allies will deny the existence of an armed conflict; other States, sympathetic to the rebels, will admit the armed conflict much more quickly; and actors such as the ICRC will be situated somewhere in between. What can be said is that there is no sufficient legal certainty in such a situation. Different positions can be taken according to different interests. But even if it were assumed that any actor considered the question in perfect good faith, the evaluation would remain difficult: when exactly did the NIAC in Syria (since 2011/2012) start? Generally speaking, the distinction between internal disturbances and armed conflict remains somewhat uncertain. Frequently, there is a gradual escalation of internal disturbances and no hard and fast line of division, which could be taken lock, stock and barrel. From the point of view of the law, this creates a sort of qualification gap. The fact, on which the application of almost the whole body of the law depends, is not clearly determined. From the point of view of the political interests of the States, this confused situation is welcome. It allows them to argue in each case according to their shifting interests, without any significant legal constraints.

Second, questions arise in the context of the definition of belligerents. In IAC, things are clear: armed forces of States confront each other. In NIAC, the pivotal entity is the "non-State armed group", sometime called rebels.[18] When these groups fight for secession of a part of the territory or for seizing the power in the State, in other words, when they fight for political ends, the application of IHL in NIAC does not pose insurmountable problems. But what if the armed groups are criminal bands acting mainly for private ends? The situation of the drug cartels in Mexico springs to mind, as do a series of armed conflicts in African failed or quasi-failed States. In the Mexican case, the ICRC still holds that there is no armed conflict, but rather that there prevails criminality requiring police action. In the African conflicts there was often the conclusion that there was an armed conflict. However, it must be understood that such criminal bands often do not have any tangible interest in respecting IHL; quite to the contrary, their policy can be precisely to violate it (for example, by abductions). How far is IHL the proper law to be applied? There are difficult problems here, at the outer edges of IHL in NIAC.

Third, contrary to IHL in IAC, where there is only one type or, better, one notion of "international armed conflict" to which all the rules of that body of law apply, in IHL in NIAC there are two distinct thresholds for "armed conflict", to which partially different sets of rules apply. On the one hand, there is common article 3 of the Geneva Conventions I–IV, with a lower threshold of applicability; on the other hand, there is AP II, with a higher threshold of applicability. The rules contained in AP II can be applied as conventional law only under the higher threshold conditions spelled out in article 1 of that Protocol. The position under CIL, conversely, is far from clear. This further complicates the position.

Fourth, a civil war is not necessarily a NIAC in all its parts. If there is foreign intervention of a certain type, the conflict can be partially internationalized, in other words, the law of IHL in IAC applying to certain of its situations, while the law of IHL in NIAC applies to other situations within it. These are so-called "mixed armed conflicts", or "internationalized NIACs". The picture is thus further complicated. These aspects now need to be disentangled by legal analysis.

---

18 For an analysis, see Z. Daboné, *Le droit international public relative aux groupes armés non étatiques*, Geneva/Zurich/Basel, 2012.

5.3.1 Lower threshold of application

The division line for the applicability of IHL in NIAC on the lower part runs between the existence of "internal disturbances and tensions" on the one hand, and the existence of an "armed conflict" on the other. Article 1, § 2, of AP II reads: "This Protocol shall not apply to situations of internal disturbances and tensions, such as riots, isolated and sporadic acts of violence and other acts of a similar nature, as not being armed conflicts".[19] This provision is taken to codify a principle of CIL of armed conflicts. It is therefore also applicable in the context of common article 3 of the Geneva Conventions I–IV. Three remarks may be made on this divide. First, it is unnecessary to define internal disturbances and tensions (IDT). If the term "armed conflict" (for NIAC) is defined, then all situations not falling under this definition of armed conflict are *a contrario* situations of IDT. The advantage of such a one-sided definition is that no loophole is left. If a situation "X" is not an armed conflict, it is automatically an internal disturbance or tension. If, conversely, the two terms were positively defined, there could be discussion as to a situation "Y", which seems to satisfy neither the criteria of one nor the criteria of the other. There would then be the need for a further legal rule expressly stipulating that in such a case the situation "Y" shall be considered as an internal disturbance and tension or as an armed conflict, by virtue of a legal fiction. This would at once be a more complicated legal regulation and would also invite biased interpretations in order to come under the cover of the meta-rule mentioned. Second, the situations expressly mentioned in article 1, § 2, of AP II are purely illustrative: riots, sporadic acts of violence, and so on. These terms have no specific legal meaning but are solely descriptive. Generally speaking, there is a distinction between "disturbances" and "tensions". The first term refers to situations characterized by a higher level of violence; the second conversely applies to situations of a lower level of violence. Disturbances are riots, spontaneous uprisings of populations, looting, and so on. Tensions are situations characterized for example, by large-scale arrests and a number of "political prisoners", the existence of inhumane conditions of detention and ill-treatment on a large scale, disappearances, emergency legislation, and so on. In other words, the first term refers to actual violence and the second more markedly to structural violence. Third, if there are IDT, IHL will not apply. But

---

19 On this provision, see Y. Sandoz, C. Swinarski and B. Zimmermann (eds), *Commentary on the Additional Protocols of 8 June 1977 to the Geneva Conventions of 12 August 1949*, Geneva, 1987, pp. 1354–6.

that does not mean that no international law norms will apply. It stands to reason that HRL will continue to apply in such situations, subject to possible limitations for public interest or even under the so-called "derogation" clauses[20] (better: suspension clauses). It is also known that the ICRC has a legal right of initiative to offer its services in such situations, subject to the acceptance by the State concerned.[21] Overall, it is therefore necessary to define the term "armed conflict". This definition will mark the lower end of applicability of IHL in NIAC.

5.3.2   System of international humanitarian law with respect to armed conflict (NIAC)

Contrary to the law of IAC, there is no single type of NIAC; instead, there are three types: first, common article 3 of the Geneva Conventions, NIAC; second, AP II, NIAC; third, mixed armed conflicts, partially IAC and partially NIAC. The latter type of armed conflict is not truly an additional legal type. It is simply an armed conflict in which IHL in IAC applies to some legal relationships while IHL in NIAC applies to others. The IHL in NIAC applying in such a situation is either a common article 3, NIAC or an AP II, NIAC. The distinction between article 3 and AP II, NIAC lies in the fact that AP II, NIAC is more restrictively defined than article 3, NIAC. This means that some additional requirements must be met for an article 3, NIAC to be also an AP II, NIAC. However, AP II, NIAC requires all the elements already necessary for an article 3, NIAC; it just adds two further elements. This has as a first consequence that all AP II, NIAC are automatically article 3, NIAC. But the reverse is not true: only some article 3, NIAC are also AP II, NIAC. There would in any case be no armed conflict, being neither article 3 nor AP II, except IAC. This has then as a second consequence that the lower threshold IDT is delimited by article 3, NIAC. The sequence is: IDT – article 3, NIAC – AP II, NIAC, in growing order of legal requirements. Article 3, NIAC is the residual category of NIAC: all NIAC not specifically qualified fall under article 3; some NIAC also fall under AP II. As for other conventions of IHL extending application of their regime to NIAC, and as to CIL of NIAC, the legal presumption is that such norms apply to article 3, NIAC, unless the norm expressly says that it is applicable only under the conditions of AP II.

---

20 See for example, article 4 of the Civil and Political Rights Covenant of 1966: M. Nowak, *UN Covenant on Civil and Political Rights, Commentary*, 2nd edn, Kehl/Strasburg/Arlington, 2005, pp. 83ff.

21 Statutes of the International Red Cross, article VI.

5.3.3   Common article 3, NIAC

Article 3 of the Geneva Conventions I–IV is less than prolix on the conditions of its application. It limits itself to a negative definition, stipulating that the rules it contains shall be applicable in "the case of armed conflict not of an international character". This negative definition has one merit and one deficiency. It has the merit of formatting a residual category: all armed conflicts not being IAC, automatically fall under article 3; there is no gap or loophole. Thus, for example, an armed conflict between governmental forces and rebels across a national boundary, not being IAC (because it does not take place between States) is automatically an article 3, NIAC. (We have seen earlier that the term "occurring on the territory of a High Contracting Party" raises an issue of applicability of the Geneva Conventions on account of ratification or accession to the Convention and not an issue of a type of armed conflict not covered by the provision – in other words, the limitation is *ratione personae* not *ratione materiae*: see Chapter 2). Conversely, this definition has the disadvantage of not making explicit what an armed conflict for its purposes actually is. But this is necessary, as we have seen, since the opposite term of IDT is also legally undefined. With the absence of a positive definition on both sides and solely negative definitions it is impossible to define a boundary. This is the reason why a special committee of the ICRC reflected on the issue in the 1950s, and since then article 3, NIAC is defined essentially by two cumulative aspects.[22]

First, there is the need for a *minimum of organization* of the non-State armed groups. The point is that these persons must be organized in some military way, as a relatively disciplined group of persons, subjected to a responsible command and thus capable of respecting rules of armed conflict. The discipline and organization must not reach the levels of a well-organized State army. The point is just that the rebels appear to be able to carry out orders and respect rules of warfare. This cannot be expected from unorganized looters or rioters, and hence the application of IHL would be illusory there. This latter situation remains in the realm of IDT. This criterion may pose problems in two sets of situations. First, when

---

22 *Rapport de la Commission d'experts chargés d'examiner la question de l'application des principes humanitaires en cas de troubles intérieurs*, Geneva, 3–8 August 1955, Publication no. 480, Geneva, 1955, pp. 6–7; *Rapport de la Commission d'experts chargée d'examiner la question de l'aide aux victimes des conflits internes*, RICR, 1963, pp. 78–9.

the armed groups are very loosely organized, in unstructured armed conflicts on the territory of weak or failed States. The borderline of a reasonable application of IHL is here somewhere reached and then overstepped. Second, when armed groups are very organized but essentially pursuing criminal aims (for example, drug cartels in Mexico). The military organization of such groups has up to this day been denied.

Second, there is the need for a *minimum of intensity* of the armed conflict. It must give rise to an open fight, involving a distinctive segment of social forces, in other words, armed hostilities reaching the threshold of a collective social fight. The number of victims must be of a certain quantity and the rule of thumb is that police forces are not enough to respond to the situation, military forces of the State being required. The gist of the matter is that if fighting takes place as is typical for "warfare", the intensity criterion is satisfied. These criteria have been further refined in the case-law of the ICTY, as we shall see. Contrary to the requirement of the "organization" of the rebels, which makes sense under IHL, for it describes a minimum condition of its capacity to be applied, the requirement of "intensity" is essentially political in nature. States do not want to apply IHL rules in internal conflict, where they fight against what they consider criminal elements, unless the fighting has taken such proportions that it becomes unreasonable to resist such application. Moreover, there is also a practical justification for the intensity rule. NIAC normally evolve gradually: there is first some civil unrest, then the tensions augment, and as time passes some armed groups emerge. It does not seem unreasonable to reserve the application of IHL to the latter phase of escalation. There remains, however, the fact that there is no principled reason why the conflict should be "protracted" (in time) or have provoked a significant number of victims before some IHL protective provisions are allowed to apply. When such arguments are made, this is essentially due to political resistance.

These two criteria of customary IHL have been refined in the jurisprudence of international bodies. This jurisprudence also expressed on a third criterion, whose role has never been clear, namely that of the "protractedness" of the armed conflict. Two examples of this case-law may be given here. The first rightly softens the wrong idea that the armed conflict must have lasted a certain amount of time. The second spells out in more detail criteria for the intensity and organization requirements.

5.3.3.1   Protractedness in the case-law

In the *Abella* (*La Tablada*) case (1997),[23] the Inter-American Commission of Human Rights considered the isolated attack of an armed group on a military base, without a context of generalized armed violence. However, this attack, lasting roughly two days (30 hours), had been of great intensity, and carried out with proper military means by an organized group. The Commission therefore opined for the existence of a NIAC and not merely for the existence of an IDT. Article 3 of the Geneva Conventions was applicable to this NIAC. This position of the Commission shows that the NIAC under article 3 need not be protracted in time. Organization and intensity may exceptionally also be short-term events. Conversely, the ICTY gave the following definition of armed conflict: "[An armed conflict exists] whenever there is a resort to armed force between States or protracted armed violence between governmental authorities and organized armed groups or between such groups within a State".[24] Later, however, the ICTY engaged in a progressive downgrading of the "protracted" criterion. In the *Haradinaj* case (Trial Chamber, 2008), the Tribunal expressed significantly on the issue.[25] It stated that since the *Tadic* decision of 1995, the protracted criterion referred more to the "intensity" of the conflict than to a concept of duration (for NIAC).[26] Here the Tribunal indulged in a process of alignment of its jurisprudence to the usual concepts of IHL. When the criterion of "protraction" was first used, it was considered as a departure from the classical IHL expression. Indeed, the criterion is not mentioned in the relevant conventions, in particular common article 3 of the Geneva Conventions I–IV or AP II. There was, therefore, a debate over the true scope of the new formula of the ICTY.[27] In particular, if the protracted criterion meant that a conflict had to last a certain amount of time, this would have amounted to a supplementary condition for the application of IHL and would thus have produced certain gaps in protection. Furthermore, the interpretive question with regard to the relation of protraction and intensity would appear. To what extent

---

23 See M. Sassòli, A. Bouvier and A. Quintin, *How Does Law Protect in War?*, vol. III, 3rd edn, Geneva, 2011, pp. 1639ff.

24 *Tadic* (Appeals Chamber, 1995), § 70.

25 At §§ 39ff.

26 § 49. The *Boskoski* Trial Chamber seems, however, to hold that the protracted criterion imports a time-element into the equation: TC, 2008, § 186.

27 See M. Sassòli and J. Grignon, "Les limites du droit international pénal et de la justice pénale dans la mise en œuvre du droit international humanitaire", in A. Biad and P. Tavernier (eds), *Le droit international humanitaire face aux défis du XXIe siècle*, Brussels, 2012, pp. 144–6.

could the one be autonomous from the other? Would the protraction criterion operate retroactively? In other words, would the armed conflict be taken retroactively to have existed since the first day of armed clashes, but only after a certain time had passed? This might suggest that a certain amount of time would have to elapse in order to know where we stand; and from the point of view of the actors, time would have to pass before they could know what obligations are imposed on them. This is at odds with the protective aim of IHL. It is also at odds with the notions of international criminal law. If an actor in the conflict could not be sure that the situation would turn out to be an armed conflict, he or she could claim the lack of a criminally relevant *mens rea*, or at least an excusable error of fact. Difficult notions of excusable mistake and non-excusable mistake would arise. We may now consider that the time for these doubts and interrogations has passed.

5.3.3.2   *Intensity and organization in the case-law*

The *Boskoski* case (Trial Chamber, 2008) is the ripest and most developed judicial expression of the ICTY on this issue. The facts of the case were particularly delicate. They concerned the situation in Macedonia (FYROM). The situation was described as one of subversion, instability and terrorism. Was there a NIAC? The Trial Chamber emphasized that the formal label given to the facts was not decisive. A situation of "terrorism" could be an armed conflict. That was shown by many instances of State practice, for example, Peru, US (Al-Qaeda), Israel (Palestine), and so on. The UN Commission of Inquiry had been of the same opinion for the situation in Lebanon (2006).[28] Conversely, isolated acts of terrorism fail to reach the threshold of required intensity.[29] The Tribunal then turned to the questions of intensity and organization. The list of the factors accounting for "organization" and "intensity" draws on the whole previous case-law and is the most complete.

For the *intensity*, the following factors were mentioned:[30]

> Various indicative factors have been taken into account by Trial Chambers to assess the "intensity" of the conflict. These include the seriousness of attacks and whether there has been an increase in armed clashes, the spread of clashes over territory and over a period of time, any increase in

---

28 §§ 180ff, 188.

29 § 190.

30 § 177, footnotes omitted.

the number of government forces and mobilisation and the distribution of weapons among both parties to the conflict, as well as whether the conflict has attracted the attention of the United Nations Security Council, and whether any resolutions on the matter have been passed. Trial Chambers have also taken into account in this respect the number of civilians forced to flee from the combat zones; the type of weapons used, in particular the use of heavy weapons, and other military equipment, such as tanks and other heavy vehicles; the blocking or besieging of towns and the heavy shelling of these towns; the extent of destruction and the number of casualties caused by shelling or fighting; the quantity of troops and units deployed; existence and change of front lines between the parties; the occupation of territory, and towns and villages; the deployment of government forces to the crisis area; the closure of roads; cease fire orders and agreements, and the attempt of representatives from international organisations to broker and enforce cease fire agreements.

For the *organization* requirement, the Trial Chamber stressed that the group must have a hierarchical structure and its leadership (chain of command) must be vested with the requisite authority to exert authority over its members.[31] Certain groups, as they existed in Somalia in 1993, were, for example, too anarchical to stand this test.[32] On the other hand, the warring groups do not need to be as organized as the armed forces of a State; nor do they need to control a part of the territory in order to be able to carry out sustained and concerted military operations, as required by article 1 of AP II.[33] The Trial Chamber then turned to the factors showing the existence of a sufficient degree of organization. The list is as follows:[34]

> 199. Trial Chambers have taken into account a number of factors when assessing the organization of an armed group. These fall into five broad groups. In the first group are those factors signaling the presence of a command structure, such as the establishment of a general staff or high command, which appoints and gives directions to commanders, disseminates internal regulations, organises the weapons supply, authorises military action, assigns tasks to individuals in the organisation, and issues political statements and communiqués, and which is informed by the operational units of all developments within the unit's area of responsibility.

---

31 § 195.
32 § 196.
33 § 197.
34 §§ 199–203, footnotes omitted.

Also included in this group are factors such as the existence of internal regulations setting out the organisation and structure of the armed group; the assignment of an official spokesperson; the communication through communiqués reporting military actions and operations undertaken by the armed group; the existence of headquarters; internal regulations establishing ranks of servicemen and defining duties of commanders and deputy commanders of a unit, company, platoon or squad, creating a chain of military hierarchy between the various levels of commanders; and the dissemination of internal regulations to the soldiers and operational units.

200. Secondly, factors indicating that the group could carry out operations in an organized manner have been considered, such as the group's ability to determine a unified military strategy and to conduct large scale military operations, the capacity to control territory, whether there is territorial division into zones of responsibility in which the respective commanders are responsible for the establishment of Brigades and other units and appoint commanding officers for such units; the capacity of operational units to coordinate their actions, and the effective dissemination of written and oral orders and decisions.

201. In the third group are factors indicating a level of logistics have been taken into account, such as the ability to recruit new members; the providing of military training; the organized supply of military weapons; the supply and use of uniforms; and the existence of communications equipment for linking headquarters with units or between units.

202. In a fourth group, factors relevant to determining whether an armed group possessed a level of discipline and the ability to implement the basic obligations of Common Article 3 have been considered, such as the establishment of disciplinary rules and mechanisms; proper training; and the existence of internal regulations and whether these are effectively disseminated to members.

203. A fifth group includes those factors indicating that the armed group was able to speak with one voice, such as its capacity to act on behalf of its members in political negotiations with representatives of international organisations and foreign countries; and its ability to negotiate and conclude agreements such as cease fire or peace accords.

The conclusion of the Trial Chamber was that there was a NIAC in FYROM in August 2001.[35]

---

35 § 292.

Overall, it can be said that the criteria of intensity and organization are gradual rather than categorical. Therefore, they will give room for argument in many situations. As we have already stressed, the criteria do not ensure legal certainty as to the applicability of IHL in article 3, NIAC. This may be seen as a deficiency of these rules, but it must be added that this is what the legislators of the Geneva Conventions intended and continue to want.

5.3.4   AP II, NIAC

AP II contains a greater number of protective provisions for NIAC, but it links their applicability to a higher threshold. It requires two additional conditions to the ones spelled out in article 3: first, that the rebels control a part of the territory; and second that the hostile relationships considered are those between the governmental forces and the rebel (or dissident State army) forces, to the exclusion of the hostile relationships between rebel forces or between rebel forces and dissident forces. Thus, article 1, § 1, of AP II reads:

> This Protocol, which develops and supplements Article 3 common to the Geneva Conventions of 12 August 1949 without modifying its existing conditions or application, shall apply to all armed conflicts which are not covered by Article 1 of the Protocol Additional to the Geneva Conventions of 12 August 1949, and relating to the Protection of Victims of International Armed Conflicts (Protocol I) and which take place in the territory of a High Contracting Party between its armed forces and dissident armed forces or other organized armed groups which, under responsible command, exercise such control over a part of its territory as to enable them to carry out sustained and concerted military operations and to implement this Protocol.[36]

In short, AP II applies only to NIAC of a certain quality (territorial control, sustained military operations) and of a certain type (governmental forces versus rebel forces). If a NIAC does not fulfil these conditions, it is to be qualified automatically as an article 3, NIAC. With its criterion of territorial control, AP II reproduces an objective version of the old condition for a recognition of belligerency (there, too, the territorial control of the rebels was required before a third State or the local government could recognize the rebels as belligerents and apply the

---

36 On this provision, see Y. Sandoz, C. Swinarski and B. Zimmermann (eds), *Commentary on the Additional Protocols of 8 June 1977 to the Geneva Conventions of 12 August 1949*, Geneva, 1987, pp. 1350ff.

laws of war, including neutrality). The territorial control must not be non-negligible or substantial. But it must allow for sustained military operations and also for the ability to carry out the duties under the Protocol: for example, to provide the persons whose liberty have been restricted with fundamental guarantees according to article 5 of AP II. The core of the matter is thus the "ability to implement the Protocol". It was considered that only some armed groups were in a position to apply the demanding provisions of AP II (when compared with article 3), and this fact was taken as justifying the higher threshold. To be sure, there were also political reasons for the higher threshold, many States being more than reticent to extend their obligations under NIAC. The gist of the matter is thus to ask functionally whether a rebel movement is able to perform the rights and mainly the duties under the Protocol, and if there is a minimum territorial control. The territorial control may be minimal and the ability to conduct sustained military operations may be taken for granted as a legal fiction if there is such territorial control (*de facto* government). It must be added that the customary rules for NIAC do not reproduce this higher threshold under AP II; nor do the conventions which extend their scope of application to any type of armed conflict. Moreover, the Rome Statute of the ICC (1998), in its article 8, § 2, letter f, defines a series of war crimes representing breaches of AP II provisions but drops any reference to the threshold of applicability under article 1, § 1, of AP II. It thereby aligns the applicability of those war crimes on the conditions of application of NIAC under article 3. This state of affairs has as an effect a certain degree of legal uncertainty: under CIL, provisions apply at the lower article 3 threshold; in conventional law, under AP II, they apply at a higher threshold. The conflict between both could be solved by recourse to the *lex specialis* rule: the parties to AP II, in their mutual dealings, would be subjected to the higher threshold of AP II; their relations to States not bound and the relations among States not bound by AP II would remain under the more liberal criteria of CIL. The paradoxical result would be that there might be an incentive to become a party to AP II, in order to evade the lower threshold of CIL, at least in dealings *inter se*. A different legal conclusion could be reached only if more recent CIL was taken to override older conventional law, in other words, as a subsequent modification of it: *lex posterior derogat legi priori*. But it is not obvious that later general international law derogates from earlier special international law. Overall, there is a certain degree of legal uncertainty here, which must again be overcome, if necessary, by special agreement between the concerned parties. We will come back to the issue of special agreements.

5.4   Mixed armed conflicts

Mixed armed conflicts are more precisely "internationalized NIACs" or conversely "deinternationalized IACs".[37] In other words, such conflicts are at their root NIAC or IAC, in which certain belligerent relationships belong to the other category, in other words, a NIAC with certain IAC relationships or an IAC with certain NIAC relationships. Internationalization or deinternationalization can operate for the conflict as a whole or only partially. There are thus four possible relationships: (1) NIAC/IAC, as a whole; (2) NIAC/IAC, partially; (3) IAC/NIAC, as a whole; (4) IAC/NIAC, partially. Examples of each category may be briefly given. For category (1), the classical example is the old-fashioned recognition of belligerency. By this recognition, the civil war was completely internationalized, so that the laws of war applied to it, in the relations between the belligerents and the recognizing State (if that State was a third State) or between the belligerents (if the recognition emanated from the local government). An example fitting better into the modern practice would be that of successful secession. The armed conflict starts as a NIAC and at some point in time becomes an IAC, if the secessionist forces have succeeded in establishing a new State and that new State is recognized internationally (there remains, however, a doubt as to what extent the original home State is bound to apply IHL in IAC if it does not on its part recognize the new entity). For category (2), the classical example is that of foreign intervention. One part of the conflict remains NIAC, another is IAC. The Libyan intervention in 2011 is a case in point: in parallel, there were an IAC (NATO States versus Libya) and a NIAC (Libyan government versus rebels). For category (3), the transformation of occupational forces into invited forces is the classical example. If a State occupies a territory IHL in IAC applies. When the local population has voted for the installation of a government being sufficiently independent from the occupier, and that new government issues an invitation for the foreign forces to remain, belligerent occupation is transformed into peaceful occupation. To the extent there are still skirmishes or local fighting against armed bands, these are now exclusively covered by NIAC. This was said to be the case for the US in Iraq after 2004. For category (4), the classical example is again that of occupation. If there is such

---

37 For a thorough discussion of such issues, see M. Milanovic and V. Hadzi-Vidanovic, "A Taxonomy of Armed Conflict", in N. D. White and C. Henderson (eds), *Research Handbook on International Conflict and Security Law: Jus ad Bellum, Jus in Bello and Jus post Bellum*, Cheltenham, 2013, pp. 256ff.

occupation, the relationship between the occupational forces and the local insurgents is covered by IHL in IAC (to the extent the rebels pretend to fight as resistance movements for the cause of the local sovereign). To the extent, however, that local governmental forces develop and also fight against some rebels in that territory, the conflict becomes at least partially a NIAC (to the extent the local forces are not globally controlled by the occupier). It must be recalled that some sporadic fighting is not incompatible with the existence of an occupied territory. Category (4) is certainly the most difficult to see realized on the ground.

The most frequent occurrence is that a NIAC is at least partially internationalized. This occurs normally through foreign military intervention in a civil war. Another way by which this may occur is by the sending of troops under the – at least partial – command of an international organization, such as peacekeeping forces of the UN. Such forces, true, are not sent to take part in an armed conflict. But they can be entangled in such a conflict, as the old precedent of the Congo in the 1960s shows. There is much uncertainty as to the law applicable between such UN forces (or forces of regional organizations) and local factions. The Bulletin of the Secretary General of 1999,[38] laying down rules for such forces, is frankly inspired by the law of IHL in IAC. There are further good arguments for applying in this case the law of IAC, and not of NIAC. The latter applies to relationships between State and non-State actors, or between non-State actors, but not necessarily to relationships where an international organization is a party. There is no good argument to hold the UN accountable for less than the higher standards of IHL in IAC when engaged in an armed conflict, especially in view of its own human rights standards.[39] However, it must be admitted that this position also creates some problems; for example, by the fact that if IAC law applies, rebels captured by the organization are prisoners of war. This may not be unwelcome, since the reciprocity will then be guaranteed and UN forces captured will also be able to enjoy that status, in law and probably also in fact. But it has as a consequence that such rebels could not be handed over to the local State, at least if there is no guarantee that it will treat them as prisoners of war (by virtue of article 12 of Geneva Convention III). Moreover, will the rebel

---

38 On this Bulletin, see D. Shraga, "The Secretary-General's Bulletin on the Observance by UN Forces of International Humanitarian Law: A Decade Later", *Israel Yearbook on Human Rights*, vol. 39, 2009, pp. 357ff.

39 And see also articles 55–6 of the UN Charter.

groups be able to implement the provisions of Geneva Convention III? There is also the fact that international practice is, to say the least, not very clear on the point and that several contributing States, notably the US, claimed during the Somalian operation in 1992 to apply IHL in NIAC to such situations. We may not pursue the point further here, but we may recall that the present author has written a study on this point.[40]

We may thus revert back to the issue of foreign intervention. The intervention relevant for the purposes of partially internationalizing the armed conflict is the sending of military troops or personnel to the territory where the NIAC takes place, or that of performing military action in that territory, for example, by bombing. The delivery of arms and logistic support is not enough. This support raises only issues pertaining to the law of peace, namely non-intervention in internal affairs. The sending of so-called "volunteers", when steered by a State, is also covered. The NIAC is not internationalized as a whole in such a situation. As the case-law of the ICJ shows in the *Nicaragua* case (1986), the conflict is split into a series of specific bilateral relationships.[41] The gist of the matter is that whenever State forces confront State forces there is an IAC; whenever State forces confront non-State armed groups or such groups confront each other, there is a NIAC. As we will see, the confrontation of State forces may not only occur directly, but also constructively. Moreover, the setting we will now expound is often very complicated. Especially in a NIAC where there is intense foreign intervention by more than one State, it would be easier but not necessarily practically possible to apply one single set of legal rules. *Ex lege*, this cannot be done. Once more, the only possibility for getting out of the quagmire is to conclude special agreements in order to expand and unify the applicable rules. There are seven types of possible relationships here.

1. *State forces versus rebels* (within one territory) → IHL in NIAC.
2. *State forces of an intervening State (on behalf of the local government) versus rebels* → IHL in NIAC. Notice that the crossing of a boundary is not material; what is material is that State forces confront non-State forces. The rationale for this rule is that States would be reluctant to follow an invitation by the local govern-

---

40 R. Kolb, *Droit humanitaire et opérations de paix internationales*, 2nd edn, Basel/Brussels, 2006.

41 ICJ, *Reports*, 1986, p. 114, § 219.

ment to come to its help if they were put in a worse position than that government by having to apply IHL in IAC rather than only IHL in NIAC. Therefore, State practice does not countenance an application of IHL in IAC.

3. *State forces (local government) versus State forces of an intervening State (on behalf of the rebels)* → IHL in IAC.

4. *State forces of an intervening State (on behalf of the government of the local sovereign) versus State forces of another intervening State (on behalf of a rebel group)* → IHL in IAC.

5. *State forces versus rebels (situated across its national boundary)* → IHL in NIAC. Notice again that the crossing of the boundary is not material.

6. *State forces versus rebels (controlled by a foreign government)* → IHL in IAC. If the rebels are at least global, or all the more if they are effectively controlled, by a foreign State, then they appear as an organ or agent of that foreign State, which acts *longa manu* through such groups. Legally speaking, it is then two States confronting each other through a proxy. Effective control is not necessary for internationalizing the conflict (but is necessary for State responsibility issues). Effective control is roughly speaking "order" control: I can impart orders and I am obeyed: if I say do this, it is done; if I say abstain from doing this, the abstention is carried out. I operate through a remote control. Global control is less stringent. This overall control test was precisely described by the *Gotovina* Tribunal (ICTY): "This test [of overall control] is satisfied where, *inter alia*, a State has a role in organizing, coordinating or planning the military actions of the organized armed group and that State finances, trains, equips or provides operational support to that group".[42] It has been added that for an overall control to be established it is not sufficient to equip and to finance, but that there must also be the coordination and the planning of the military operations.[43] Conversely, it is not necessary that the third State make specific orders or issue specific instructions.[44] Roughly speaking, overall control means that without foreign military (not only logistic) support, the group could not subsist.

7. *Rebel forces versus rebel forces* → IHL in NIAC, and more precisely only article 3, NIAC, not AP II, NIAC, but also all rules of CIL applicable to NIAC.

---

42 *Gotovina* (Trial Chamber, 2011), § 1675.
43 *Prlic* (Trial Chamber, 2013), § 86.
44 *J. Stanisic* (Trial Chamber, 2013), § 954.

The reader will easily recognize real scenarios behind all these situations. Thus, situation (1) is that of any classical NIAC, for example, the Syrian civil war (2011–present). Scenarios (2), (3) and (4) were fulfilled in the Vietnam War (1964–1973). Scenario (5) was present in the Israel/Hezbollah-Lebanon armed conflict of 2006. Scenario (6) was realized, for example, in the Bosnian War (1992–1995). Scenario (7) has had applications in Colombia or in the Democratic Republic of Congo. The most remarkable result of this bilateralization of relationships is that the applicable law splits into multiple sets of particular law. This effect is further accentuated by the law of treaties: the split would not only be on the lines just presented, but also on the fact as to whether any particular State involved in the conflict has ratified or acceded to any particular convention, for example, AP I. The overall result is thus a considerable, if not excessive, complexification of the applicable law. This complexity runs counter to the main aim of modern IHL, which is to secure a maximal and consistent protection during times of armed conflict. But it has to be taken as the correct expression of the current legal regulation.

5.5   The way out of the quagmire

We have encountered a series of situations where the complexity or the gradual nature of the legal categories allows for considerable uncertainty in the applicability of IHL, to the detriment of protected persons. Thus, we have seen that sometimes an IAC, at its lower end, can be disputed. Sometimes an occupation can be considered remaining aloof from the application of Geneva Convention IV, on the basis of arguments concerning the status of the territory and the fact of having ratified a certain convention. There are a number of treaty gaps: this or that State may not have ratified or acceded to this or that convention, and the position in CIL may be disputed. Most importantly, we have seen that the beginning of application of NIAC is gradual and uncertain. The applicable customary law may be in doubt, especially with regard to provisions contained in AP II: when does the higher threshold of article 1, § 1, of AP II apply and when does it not? Can this threshold be circumvented by applying CIL? How are the rebels to be bound to a certain convention of IHL when they did not ratify it (ratification and accession of IHL conventions is only open to States)? What about the multiple and intricate legal relationships in case of foreign intervention, which may render the law uncertain. Thus, for example, it may be unclear whether a State globally controls a rebel faction: the information will not always be available, since such support is made undercover. What if claims differ in this respect: one belligerent claiming that such control exists and that IHL in IAC should apply; the other claiming that it does not exist and that IHL in NIAC should apply? What if an international organization participates in the conflict through troops under its partial (strategic) command? We have seen that the legal position as to the law applicable in this context is unclear. UN troops would be bound to apply the rules in the Bulletin, but since that Bulletin covers only some rules, the question remains as to all the other rules. If a movement of national liberation should still exist and fight, what about a belligerent relation with a State not having ratified AP I and having always resisted the allegation according to which decolonizing armed conflicts are IAC? Can we say that the customary rule treating such conflicts as IAC is established? And what if the stubborn State still resists? What should be done, further, with the many gaps in NIAC? Could the States not accept some further obligations, going beyond the little that is applicable *ex lege* (at least on a conventional basis)? What is to be done when it is unclear and disputed whether a belligerent occupation has started (for example, with regard to a previous invasion phase) or whether it is terminated (for example, by invitation of a local government, or possibly by a resolution of the UNSC[45]). What if occupation law does not formally continue, since there is no (constant) physical presence on the territory anymore, but a foreign power still exercises a large degree of control over a territory by "blockading" its border (for example, Gaza)? These are quite different situations (among others) where the application of the law can be in doubt and therefore in jeopardy. What can be done to improve the application of IHL to the benefit of the protected persons, and thus in its very spirit?

The answer to that last question lies on two planes. First, on the legal plane, nothing specific can be done. The law is as it is; a belligerent is entitled to have it applied as it stands *de lege lata* – even if that may have unfortunate consequences. A legal operator cannot just reinvent the law he or she holds to be better or more just, since he or she would be arrogating to him or herself the powers of a legislator. Obviously, this does not mean that such a person may not employ him or herself for a change of the law though the appropriate legislative channels.

---

45 On that issue, in the context of Iraq (2004), see R. Kolb, "Occupation in Iraq since 2003 and the Powers of the UN Security Council", *International Review of the Red Cross*, vol. 90, 2008, pp. 29ff.

Second, on the level of political negotiation, confidence-building and goodwill, and hence the conclusion of special agreements (in other words, the creation of new particular law between the belligerents) almost all is possible. The formal applicability of IHL may here be bracketed out; the question of recognition of the rebels or other status questions may be cast to the rear; practical issues of protection and reciprocity interests may conversely enter the limelight. Thus, the belligerents may be approached and asked whether they would be ready to accept, on an *ad hoc* basis, and in full reciprocity, certain obligations which are not applicable *ex lege*, or whose application *ex lege* is disputed. In this way, what we here called a "way out of the quagmire" could be found. Practical issues take the precedence over ideological battles; specially tailored regimes for the particular situations can replace general regimes posing problems. The fact is that such special agreements have most often been concluded.[46] Thus, for example, in the Spanish Civil War (1936–1939), where IHL could not be applied because it was not an IAC, the ICRC obtained that many rules were accepted between the Burgos and Madrid forces, such as the treatment of prisoners at least as favourably as prisoners of war.[47] Since then, the flow of special agreements has not decreased. A famous special agreement is that of the parties to the Bosnian War (1992–1995),[48] where there was an acceptance to apply the main IHL conventions, such as the Geneva Conventions and AP I. Another telling example is the Israel–Arab War of 1973,[49] where the belligerents accepted to apply the rules on the protection of the civilian populations against the effects of hostilities on the basis of the Draft of the ICRC, which would later lead to articles 48ff of AP I. The general legal basis for such special agreements are articles 6/6/6/7 of the Geneva Conventions I–IV.

There are two types of special agreements. First, those whereby the parties agree on the modalities to carry out an obligation under legally applicable IHL; for example, the practical way to repatriate heavily injured prisoners of war under articles 110–111 of Geneva Convention

---

46 See the list in F. Bugnion, *Le Comité international de la Croix-Rouge et la protection des victimes de la guerre*, Geneva, 1994, pp. 1205ff.

47 *Ibid.*, pp. 307ff.

48 This agreement has been useful to the ICTY: *Tadic* (Appeals Chamber, 1995), § 73; *Blaskic* (Trial Chamber, 2000), § 172. For the text of the special agreement and further relevant documents, see M. Sassoli, A. Bouvier and A. Quintin, *How Does Law Protect in War?*, vol. III, 3rd edn, Geneva, 2011, pp. 1713ff.

49 F. Bugnion, *Le Comité international de la Croix-Rouge et la protection des victimes de la guerre*, Geneva, 1994, p. 849.

III. Such agreements are largely declaratory: they carry out existing obligations. Second, special agreements which are meant to close gaps or to remove uncertainties in the applicable law; for example, an agreement to apply provisions of AP I even if the State has not ratified that convention. Such agreements are constitutive: they create new legal obligations. These latter agreements are the ones whereby uncertainties and gaps in the law can be removed. It is certainly not ideal that the applicable law can sometimes be weakened or even brushed aside by replacing it with particular regimes, *à géométrie variable*. However, this is the best that can sometimes be achieved. Since IHL is mainly a practical branch of the law, where the obtaining of protection is the paramount aim, the way by which we may reach it is, after all, secondary. It may be added to the foregoing, that articles 6/6/6/7 of Geneva Conventions I–IV, according to their text, prohibit any special agreement that "adversely affect the situation of protected persons". In other words, the rights of the protected persons may be increased through such agreements but cannot be diminished. The application of this rule is not always easy,[50] but its gist cannot give rise to doubt. Overall, we may thus say that the practical "way out of the quagmire" is generally the way of the special agreement. This may not be satisfactory; but, at the end of the day, *quod fieri non debet, factum valet*. And the fact is here not devoid of its own value.

---

50 For a closer discussion of the issues raised, see R. Kolb, "Jus cogens, intangibilité, intransgressibilité, dérogation positive et négative", *RGDIP*, vol. 109, 2005, pp. 305ff.

6 Combatants and civilians: a sometimes difficult divide

6.1 General aspects

The divide between combatants and civilians is crucial in IHL. It is crucial for purposes of Hague and Geneva Law. In the Hague Law (means and methods of warfare), the distinction is pivotal for the application of one of the most fundamental principles of that branch of the law, namely the principle of distinction. The obligation of belligerents to distinguish between civilian persons and objects on the one hand, and military objectives (persons and objects) on the other, and to directly attack only the latter at the exclusion of the former, turns, as far as persons are concerned, on the present distinction. To the extent the clarity of the distinction is reduced, the targeting is rendered more difficult, and ultimately the protection of civilians will be jeopardized. In the Geneva Law (protection of persons), the distinction is essential because the protective regimes of the two categories of persons are different. For combatants, there is a distinct protection under Geneva Law only when they are *hors de combat* and in the control of the adverse party, mainly by injury, sickness, being shipwrecked or surrender. For civilians, there is a larger degree of protection, provided they do not actively participate in hostilities. Geneva Conventions I–III organize the protection of combatants; the one for civilians is Geneva Convention IV. It may be added to the foregoing that the distinction exists only in IAC. In NIAC, there are no combatants under IHL. Thus, strictly speaking, there remain only different categories of civilians, enjoying varying degrees of protection according to their involvement or not in the armed conflict.

The difficulty with the distinction is that it has at all times been only relative and has come constantly under stress by different sets of events. In the nineteenth century, the question as to the distinction arose mainly in the context of the different views between military powers and States with small or no armies. The former argued that the distinction had to remain strict and clear, according to the best military tradition: only members of the State armed forces could be considered combatants; the civilians had to remain completely aloof from any combat action. The smaller States held that some room had to be left for "patriotic warfare". Not disposing of strong State armies, these States needed some spontaneous support by their citizens in case of invasion. They were thus inclined to accept some degree of civilian involvement in armed conflict, allowing civilians to revert to combatant status under certain defined conditions. The debate raged at the Brussels Conference of 1874; a compromise was eventually reached only in The Hague in 1899.[1]

In the twentieth century, the greatest stress came from the development of asymmetric warfare and recourse to guerrilla tactics (or even terrorism).[2] Guerrillas could not fulfil the traditional stringent requirements for a civilian to be transformed into a combatant. Thus, they were either to be considered as unprivileged fighters, or some degree of reform of the law had to be attempted to encompass them as combatants. The first branch of this alternative holds all the more true when it comes to "terrorism". The position of the US after 11 September 2001 is emblematic in this regard. In a so-called "war" of a State against persons labelled as terrorists, IHL was partly set aside and, in particular, combatant status was not easily recognized on such "outlawed" persons.[3] Stress on the distinction also came from a tendency to enrol the whole society, including its civil components, in the war effort.[4] The effect of this inclusive approach has been a tendency towards total warfare with a concomitant tendency to target civilian assets, since they also contribute to the war effort to some extent. In recent times, an additional stress was put on the distinction between civilian and combatant by the development of private military companies. Their personnel are civilian, but they engage in the conflict in varying degrees.[5] The overall result of such increasingly fuzzy borders of the traditional categories is a loss of certainty in cardinal IHL concepts, without which the system of IHL can hardly function properly. Thus, the targeting is

---

1 R. Buss, *Der Kombattantenstatus – Die kriegsgeschichtliche Entwicklung eines Rechtsbegriffs und seine Ausgestaltung in Verträgen des 19. und 20. Jahrhunderts*, Bochum, 1992.

2 M. Veuthey, *Guérilla et droit humanitaire*, Geneva, 1983.

3 See for example, E. Crawford, *The Treatment of Combatants and Insurgents under the Law of Armed Conflict*, Oxford, 2010; K. Dörmann, "The Legal Situation of 'Unlawful/Unprivileged Combatants'", *International Review of the Red Cross*, vol. 85, 2003, pp. 45ff.

4 H. A. Smith, *The Crisis in the Law of Nations*, London, 1947, pp. 67ff.

5 See for example, F. Francioni and N. Ronzitti (eds), *War by Contract*, Oxford, 2011; E. Gillard, "Business Goes to War", *International Review of the Red Cross*, vol. 88, 2006, pp. 525ff.

cast into increasing difficulty in the numerous situations where civilians are not clearly distinguished from combatants. The protection of persons is jeopardized when civilians increasingly participate directly or even indirectly in hostilities. As a result, a belligerent will look at adverse civilians with a growing suspicion and a temptation to take collectively harsh measures against them. This contributes to weakening, dismantling or spiralling down essential protections under IHL.

6.2   Who enjoys the privilege/status of the combatant?

The combatant enjoys a series of privileges under IHL. On the one hand, true, he or she can be targeted at any time, not only when in active combat, but also, for example, while sleeping in the casern. This can hardly be seen as a privilege. However, on the other hand, the combatant is privileged in a number of regards. First, he or she cannot be criminally prosecuted for the acts of violence committed, if these acts conformed to applicable IHL (so-called combatant immunity). Second, once captured by the enemy, the combatant has the right to be treated as prisoner of war, with all the rights and duties attached to that status. Third, the combatant, as prisoner of war, cannot lose that privileged status up to the time he or she is released or repatriated. The rule is "once prisoner of war, always prisoner of war", up to the time of release. Hence, a prisoner of war cannot lose his or her status and his or her conventional rights by transfer from one belligerent to another or by transfer to a neutral State.[6] The State transferring the prisoner must make sure that the State receiving him or her will grant the prisoner all the guarantees under Geneva Convention III. According to the text of article 12, § 2, of Geneva Convention III, the receiving State must have ratified Geneva Convention III. But if it has not ratified or acceded to that convention, a transfer should be accepted, under a teleological interpretation of that provision, if the third State has accepted by a special agreement to apply Geneva Convention III to that prisoner. Lastly, as we have seen, there is another function the notion of combatant displays in the IHL system, namely in the context of the principle of distinction and targeting.

To begin with legal analysis, we must keenly notice that modern IHL knows only of two mutually exclusive legal categories of persons. There are combatants on the one hand and civilians on the other; *tertium*

---

6 See article 12, § 2, Geneva Convention III and article 111, Geneva Convention III.

non datur.[7] Article 50, § 1, of AP I thus defines the civilian as a "non-combatant": all persons not being combatants are automatically civilians. There is legally no other category and neither is there a gap. This completeness of the system is crucial: it secures that there is no legal black hole and that each person under some protective regime of IHL. The category of "unlawful combatants" may have its standing under the municipal law of a State, where it can produce certain legal consequences.[8] Under IHL, this is a misnomer: an "unlawful combatant" is simply no combatant at all. Indeed, under IHL, a combatant is by definition a lawful combatant; if he or she is not lawful, in other words, does not fulfil the conditions for being a combatant, he or she is not a combatant and does not enjoy the privileges of the combatant. Such a person is then automatically a civilian. However, this does not mean that such a person enjoys the same protection as a "peaceful" civilian. First, when actively participating in hostilities, he or she may be targeted. Second, he or she was not entitled to participate in these hostilities and thus does not enjoy the immunity of the combatant. This means that he or she may be prosecuted for all acts of violence committed, and may in principle even face the death penalty. Third, such civilians may fall under the "loss of some protections" clause enshrined in article 5 of Geneva Convention IV, for example when they engage in sabotage action or in hostilities. The fact that an "unlawful combatant" is a civilian does not, therefore, have the consequence that this civilian will enjoy the same protections as the bulk of "peaceful" civilians. The status of civilian under IHL is consequently not linked with the fact of being peaceful, doing no harm, not participating in hostilities. Combatants and civilians may indeed both participate in hostilities, the former by right, the second in fact. If the latter engage in hostilities, they will lose some protections ordinarily granted to civilians under IHL; but they will not lose civilian status. This is part of the systematic construction of IHL. And, as can be seen, it leads to no absurd or unrealistic result.

Who is entitled to combatant status? The regulation of that matter was first achieved in article 1 of the Hague Regulations (1899/1907) and later repeated in article 4 of Geneva Convention III (in the latter case for determining who is entitled to prisoner of war status). There

---

7 This is a basic tenet of IHL, confirmed by the ICTY: *Brdjanin* case (Trial Chamber, 2004), § 125.
8 The term was first used by a US Military Tribunal in World War II, in the context of saboteurs: see the *Ex parte Quirin* case (1942), US Supreme Court, in M. Sassoli, A. Bouvier and A. Quintin, *How Does Law Protect in War?*, vol. II, 3rd edn, Geneva, 2011, pp. 881ff.

is some difference in the two issues, in other words, who is a combatant and who is a prisoner of war. If the bulk of prisoners of war are captured combatants, there are two categories of persons entitled either to prisoner of war status or to a treatment not less favourable than that of prisoner of war, while not being combatants. First, certain civilian persons closely following the army are entitled to prisoner of war status if captured. The reason for that particular regulation is that the adverse belligerent, having captured them, is interested in keeping them captive and not releasing them, since these persons perform tasks useful to the adverse army. Releasing such persons would be making harm on itself. Thus, under article 4, A, § 4, of Geneva Convention III, certain persons who accompany the armed forces without actually being members thereof, such as civilian members of military aircraft crews, war correspondents, supply contractors, members of labour units or of services responsible for the welfare of the armed forces, are prisoners of war if and when retained. By virtue of article 67, § 2, of AP I, the same is true for personnel of the civil defence. Civilian members of aircraft contribute to the working of the military aircraft; war correspondents may retain sensitive information, and so on. They may thus be captured and detained, but must then be granted prisoner of war status. Second, there are two categories of persons being integrated into the armed forces and yet not becoming prisoners of war if captured. If detained by an adverse belligerent, they must, however, be treated at least as favourably as prisoners of war. These persons are the medical and religious personnel of the army (article 33, § 1, of Geneva Convention III). Such persons are not considered prisoners of war for the reason that the prisoners of war have to be released in principle only at the end of the armed conflict. Conversely, medical and religious personnel can be kept in adverse detention only as long as needed to take care of the prisoners of their own nationality detained by the enemy. It is sensible to keep a doctor of the adverse medical services of the army to take care of the prisoners of his own nationality in a prisoner of war camp: he or she will speak the language of the prisoners; know their culture, preferences and needs; enjoy a greater degree of trust of the prisoners, and so on. However, if medical or religious personnel are in excess of what is needed to take care of the prisoners of their own nationality, they *must* be released.[9] This is why these persons are not considered prisoners of war. If they were so considered, a special category of prisoners of war to be released before the end of the armed conflict would

---

9 Article 33, § 1 and § 3, Geneva Convention III.

have to exist. Apart from these two special categories, all the other prisoners of war are combatants who have been captured.

There are three categories of persons entitled to and enjoying combatant status.[10] These three categories, stemming initially from article 1 of the Hague Regulations, are the result of a delicate compromise between the military powers, fully accepting only the first of these categories, and smaller States (such as Belgium or Switzerland), insisting on categories two and three. The first category is the classical one of members of the armed forces. Categories two and three pour some degree of civilian participation into the armed conflict. They allow transforming certain civilians into combatants when a series of conditions is met. Roughly speaking, combatants are thus the members of the armed forces plus two special categories of civilians having changed their initial status.

6.2.1 Members of the armed forces of a State

The first category is that of the members of the armed forces of a State.[11] Who is such a member depends on the municipal law of the State concerned. The State will define in its legislation how its army is organized, what persons form part of it and for what time. It may include paramilitary units within the army,[12] or provide that certain police forces may also have military duties in times of armed conflicts (*gendarmerie* in France or Belgium, *carabinieri* in Italy). Other police forces or trained groups could also be incorporated into the army on an *ad hoc* basis. In such a case, there must be a notification of that fact to the adverse belligerent. From the point of view of international law, certain forces are considered to be part of the army of the State when they in fact perform military functions for the State (*de facto* military organs). There is an analogy here with articles 4 and 8 of the ILC Articles on the Responsibility of States for Internationally Wrongful Acts (2001). Another important point to notice is that all the members of the armed forces are by definition combatants,[13] whether they

---

10 A good contribution on this issue can be found in K. Ipsen, "Kombattanten und Kriegsgefangene", in H. Schöttler and B. Hoffmann (eds), *Die Genfer Zusatzprotokolle, Kommentare und Analysen*, Bonn, 1993, pp. 136ff; and K. Ipsen, "Combatants and Non-Combatants", in D. Fleck (ed.), *The Handbook of International Humanitarian Law*, 2nd edn, Oxford, 2008, pp. 79ff.

11 Article 4, A, § 1, Geneva Convention III.

12 According to article 43, § 3, AP I with a duty of notification to the adverse party.

13 Article 43, § 2, AP I.

actually have a fighting mission or not, whether they actually have a weapon or not, and so on. Subject to the special status of medical and religious personnel discussed above, all military personnel of the army are thus by definition combatants. Take as an example the present author's own position in the Swiss army. He is in the legal section (more precisely: law of armed conflicts), in the branch of military justice. He has no weapon (though he could ask for one). If there is an armed conflict involving Switzerland, and he is called in the army, he would be a combatant. The essential point is that every member of the army could be used for combative functions. For example, the present author could be given a weapon and called to fight. That is enough for considering that a person is a combatant, and if captured a prisoner of war. Lastly, it is important to stress that the non-recognition of a State or of its government has no bearing whatsoever on combatant status. It is not possible for a State to argue that since it has not recognized another belligerent, that belligerent and its members are non-existent for it, and that there are thus no adverse combatants. Article 4, A, § 3, of Geneva Convention III and related CIL are very clear on this point. If it were otherwise, there would be a significant gap in IHL, all the more since armed conflicts occur with some frequency in the context of States generally hostile to each other, or not recognizing each other. Once more, modern IHL attempts through the mentioned regulation to close a dangerous protection gap.

6.2.2   Levy in mass *(levée en masse)*

This is a traditional category for transforming civilians into combatants. Today, it is not much relevant, but it is not completely outmoded either. This category denotes the strong link between a State, its territory and its population. According to article 4, A, § 6, of Geneva Convention III, the inhabitants of a territory who spontaneously take up arms on the approach (invasion) of the enemy, in order to defend that territory against the invasion forces, are thus considered combatants. There are only two specific conditions for claiming combatant status under levy in mass: (1) the arms must be carried openly, in other words, visibly; and (2) the law of armed conflicts must be respected. Nowhere else in IHL is a transformation of a civilian into a combatant possible on such relaxed conditions. This reflects the urgency of the situation and the necessity to be ready for swift action, if levy in mass is to make sense at all. The open carrying of the arms has the aim of allowing for a distinction between peaceful civilians, not participating in the conflict, and non-peaceful civilians, participating in the conflict, and thus being targetable. Since there is no requirement of a fixed and distinctive sign, the open carrying of the arms is the only requirement for securing distinction. Condition 2 requires that the participant to a levy in mass behaves like a soldier, if he or she wants to reap the advantages normally reserved to a soldier. However, this criterion raises some difficulties to which we will return when we discuss the third category, in other words, resistance movements. The transformation of civilians into combatants under levy in mass can occur only in a narrow time-window: during the invasion phase, in other words, in the first contact of the local population with invading forces. Article 4, A, § 6 indeed limits the levy in mass phase to "non-occupied territory", in other words, to the phase of movement of the invading army.[14] The reason for this restriction is an expression of the principle of necessity: IHL can accept the transformation of civilians into combatants under the quite light conditions of levy in mass only if there is no time to organize more thoroughly, by engaging into armed units with distinctive signs. In occupied territory, there is such time; thus, a civilian cannot claim combatant status under the lighter conditions of the levy in mass. Conversely, at the moment of first contact by invasion, there is no time to organize into armed units. Here, but only here, the law concedes to single civilians the right spontaneously to take up arms for "patriotic warfare". If on the first contact with the enemy there should be enough time to organize into more traditional armed units, the special privilege of the levy in mass shall not be available. But there are difficult problems of evidence here. The same rationale is true for the term "spontaneous": if the civilians do not take up arms spontaneously, but are organized by the State, it should be expected that the State is able to conform to the more stringent traditional criteria, in particular with the providing of a uniform or at least a distinctive sign. So long as this ordinary organization into armed units is possible, it has to be done; levy in mass is not available and cannot be used to circumvent the stricter requirements. This is the basis of article 2 of the Hague Regulations. In short, the authorization under levy in mass is subsidiary, as a true right of necessity. Overall, it can therefore be said that levy in mass supposes the following requirements: (1) spontaneous taking up of arms; (2) no time to organize into armed forces, militias or resistance movements; (3) in territory that is not occupied; (4) the open carrying of arms; (5) respect for applicable IHL.

---

14 This is the reason why in the Franco–Prussian War, the Prussians declared certain parts of France occupied territory by simple paper proclamation (in other words, without actual presence), in order to try to disallow levy in mass in these areas. See P. Pradier-Fodéré, *Traité de droit international public européen et américain*, vol. VII, Paris, 1906, pp. 646–7.

6.2.3 Militias, volunteer corps and movements of resistance

Under article 4, A, § 2, of Geneva Convention III, civilians can also be transformed into combatants when they affiliate to certain paramilitary movements, notably to resistance movements, volunteer corps or other militias in occupied territory. This important provision reads as follows:

> Members of other militias and members of other volunteer corps, including those of organized resistance movements, belonging to a Party to the conflict and operating in or outside their own territory, even if this territory is occupied, provided that such militias or volunteer corps, including such organized resistance movements, fulfil the following conditions:
> (a) that of being commanded by a person responsible for his subordinates;
> (b) that of having a fixed distinctive sign recognizable at a distance;
> (c) that of carrying arms openly;
> (d) that of conducting their operations in accordance with the laws and customs of war.

In the Hague Regulations, this regime was foreseen for militias and volunteers; in 1949, it was extended to resistance movements, taking account of the experience of World War II. There are five conditions for such a transformation to lead to combatant status. First, the armed groups must be "belonging to a Party to the conflict". The armed group does thus not act in its own name, but for the cause of a State. This is already required by the fact that an IAC and not a NIAC is at issue. This "appurtenance" or "allegiance" criterion is satisfied if the group fights for the cause of the sovereign ousted from the occupied territory and/or if there is some link or recognition by its authorities in exile (if such exist) with the resistance movement at stake. This link does not need to be formal, as it had to be in the past; a factual link is sufficient; for example by the character of the military operation, showing clearly for what party to the conflict the group is acting.[15] The aim of the criterion, apart from maintaining a relationship to IAC, is to ascertain that only armed groups fighting for the political cause of the sovereign come within the realm of IHL and not, for example, a criminal band acting for private ends. It is not all rare that

---

15 J. Pictet (ed.), *Commentary III, Geneva Convention relative to the Treatment of Prisoners of War*, Geneva, ICRC, 1960, p. 57. See also K. Del Mar, "The Requirement of 'Belonging' under International Humanitarian Law", *EJIL*, vol. 21, 2010, pp. 105ff.

such criminal bands come into being in a territory where the ordinary administrative structures have disappeared. Second, the groups must be "commanded by a person responsible for his subordinates". The group must therefore present a military structure; there must be a certain degree of military discipline; there must be a chain of orders, followed by the subordinates. From the systematic point of view, this condition reflects the necessity of a capacity to respect IHL norms: it is only when there is an armed group with some military discipline that the commander can secure the respect of rules of armed conflict. This requirement is clearly of a collective nature: the group as such must possess such a disciplinary structure. If a single member of the group does not behave in a disciplined way, the members of the group do not thereby lose their combatant status. Third, the members of the armed group must have "a fixed distinctive sign recognizable at a distance". This sign takes the place of the uniform. The requirement is linked with the principle of distinction: the adverse belligerent must be able to distinguish at any time peaceful civilians from civilians having transformed into combatants. The sign must be "fixed". It cannot be worn at certain moments and put aside at other moments, lest the principle of distinction and also that of loyalty be breached. A notification of the sign is not necessary; it must simply be visible at a distance. What that exactly entails is context-related. A simple armband may be insufficient, because it would not be sufficiently visible and also, perhaps, too easy to remove (unless it is, for example, glued upon the clothes). But if it is big enough and in a vivid colour, the opposite may be true. The condition of the fixed and distinctive sign is individual: only a member of the group conforming individually to this requirement can claim combatant status. The fact that other members of the group do conform to that condition is not sufficient. Fourth, there is the requirement of "carrying the arms openly". This requirement stems again from the principle of distinction, but goes further. For distinction, it is sufficient to have a fixed and distinctive sign. The open carrying of arms is thought additionally to put the members of such groups on the same footing as the members of the army. The point is one of equality: if you want to be treated as a combatant, behave as a combatant. The open carrying of arms does not, however, mean that the arms must be carried visibly, ostensibly or manifestly. Again, a member of the group must fulfil this requirement on an individual basis in order to be able to claim combatant status. Fifth, there is the requirement of "conducting their operations in accordance with the laws and customs of war". This requirement stems from the conception that to come within the reach of IHL and benefit from its rules (as a combatant), the price to pay is to respect these rules: he who has the advantages must also bear the charges. It is moreover a requirement thought to incentivize respect for IHL: in order to be able to claim combatant status under it, IHL has to be respected in the first place. Finally, this condition expresses the principle of reciprocity: the members of the regular armed forces have to respect IHL; therefore, so should the members of armed groups (equality of belligerents). There is, however, some doubt as to the collective or individual character of this requirement. The common understanding is that the condition applies on an individual basis.[16] But there is some room for the opposite argument, since the text of the convention contains the collective word "their" (conducting *their* operations . . .). The dominant view seems to have been that every member had to fulfil this requirement on an individual basis – this was apparently the understanding at the revision Conference of 1977 leading to the abolishment of this quite strict criterion.

Overall, as can be seen, there are many and quite strict criteria for coming within the reach of this provision. When compared with levy in mass, the conditions have been tightened, since here there is more time to organize and the urgency has disappeared. These strict criteria reflect the traditional mistrust of the legislator of IHL with regard to civilians aiming at becoming combatants. The traditional ideal of IHL is that civilians shall remain pacific and be protected, while combatants shall be incorporated in the armed forces of a State and possess a combatant privilege. In the conditions of the twentieth century, this strict and simple divide could not, however, be maintained unaltered. Some intermingling of civilians and combatants has become unavoidable. IHL is at pains to maintain as neatly as possible the distinction, according to what is possible in the circumstances.

6.3   The reform through Additional Protocol I

After 1949, there has been one major development, which continues to expand up to this day: the increase in frequency of asymmetric wars. Wars of national liberation (decolonization) have been of this type; "War on Terror" is a more recent layer of asymmetry. The specific problem with such warfare is that the weaker party will avoid open military confrontation, inspired by old-fashioned ideals of loyalty. It

---

16 Y. Sandoz, C. Swinarski and B. Zimmermann (eds), *Commentary on the Additional Protocols of 8 June 1977 to the Geneva Conventions of 12 August 1949*, Geneva, 1987, pp. 525–6.

could not stand such a direct confrontation, where it would be bound to be immediately defeated. David can win against Goliath only by recourse to imagination, not by direct man-to-man fighting. Hence, the notoriously weaker party will have recourse to guerrilla tactics. This means that its fighters will hide amidst the civilian population or in the countryside; they will come out from there at the last moment to hit at the adverse forces and then run away; and they will mix up with the civilian population or hide in the countryside as quickly as possible after their strike. The stronger party will obviously not appreciate such tactics, which it is bound to feel are disloyal or even terroristic. The main question then arises as to combatant status. Assuming that there is an IAC, can members of the stronger party be combatants, according to the strict conditions under article 4 of Geneva Convention II, and article 1, Hague Regulations of 1907? The answer is certainly positive, since those persons will in most cases be regular members of the armed forces of their State of origin. Can the members of the armed groups of the weaker party (still in IAC) be combatants under the same conditions? The answer is almost always negative, since they will not fulfil the traditional requirements. Members of such groups will not be able to wear fixed and distinctive signs, visible at distance, and carry their arms openly all the time, without being immediately arrested or shot down by the adverse forces. In other words, only armed groups controlling a part of the territory, but not weaker asymmetric parties to the conflict, can fulfil the traditional conditions. Moreover, there will be an argument that guerrillas did not respect the law of armed conflicts, for example by not carrying fixed signs and open arms. Hence, under the latter heading as under the former ones, their members will not be successful in claiming combatant status. The net result of the foregoing is that one party to the conflict will always be able to claim combatant and prisoner of war status for its members, while the other party will never be in a position to reciprocate. This leads to sheer and utter inequality of the two belligerent parties with regard to IHL. In turn, this inequality has as a consequence the practical demise of this body of the law. IHL cannot work on the basis of inequality. No belligerent will accept an obligation to provide rights and guarantees which it does not enjoy itself, in other words, when it is treated as outlawed. The main point is thus as to how the law on combatant status can be reformed so as to limit this inequality and allow some practical functioning of IHL. If no solution is found, the risk is to render IHL irrelevant for one of the most frequent types of armed conflicts of modern times, namely asymmetric warfare. This would be opening a significant protection gap, contrary to the main aim of IHL, which is to secure the application of its rules in all actually existing armed conflicts. The point is thus not to legalize guerrillas or, worse, to legitimize them; even the less is it to pave the way to terrorism. The point is to reintroduce some balance into the law of armed conflicts in the context of asymmetric warfare, in order to keep the law alive rather than having it crumble. *Ut res magis valeat quam pereat*: it is better to keep things alive rather than have them perish.

What reform of the law could be thought of? The main point was to somewhat relax the criteria of article 4, A, § 2, of Geneva Convention III. Notice that the aim was not to relax the traditional criteria in a general fashion. These criteria should continue to apply in most situations. However, when a belligerent could not respect these criteria in the context of a particular situation (asymmetric warfare), it could, as a sort of necessity regulation, fall back on a more relaxed regime. The three traditional criteria posing problems in our context were the following: the fixed and distinctive sign; the open carrying of arms; the non-respect for IHL. The other criteria were not felt as being problematic; they did not need to be reformed. The conditions under the Geneva Convention III continue thus to be applicable, to the extent they have not been modified by AP I (for the parties to AP I).[17] First, the requirement of respect for IHL has been abandoned.[18] The point was not to say that armed groups should not respect IHL anymore[19] – quite to the contrary. Violations of the law continue to lead to criminal responsibility, notably under the grave breaches regime. The point was only to say that the respect of the law of armed conflicts was no longer a condition for claiming and obtaining combatant status. Even if a member of an armed group was said to have violated IHL, he or she could not be deprived of combatant status (but could be prosecuted for war crimes, if such crimes had been committed or were considered to have been committed). The main reason for this reform is a point of equality and of practicability. A regular member of the armed forces never loses his or her status as combatant, notwithstanding any number of violations of IHL he or she may have committed. It was considered that members of armed groups should be put in the same position. Moreover, there was an issue of practicability: it was all too

---

17 Article 96, § 1, AP I. On the wars of national liberation, see G. Abi-Saab, "Wars of National Liberation in the Geneva Conventions and Protocols", *RCADI*, vol. 165, 1979-IV, pp. 353ff; H. A. Wilson, *International Law and the Use of Force by National Liberation Movements*, Oxford, 1988, pp. 149ff.

18 Article 44, § 2, AP I.

19 Quite on the contrary, as the text of article 44, § 2, AP I shows.

easy for a belligerent to pretend that a member of an armed group had not respected IHL in order to deny him or her combatant status. Since there is no regular and impartial court to control such an allegation, the temptation to adduce such a violation is all too great. Much of the usefulness of granting combatant status under IHL is thereby rendered nugatory. Second, the requirement of a fixed and distinctive sign has been completely abandoned. The distinction from civilians is now secured only by the open carrying of arms. The drafters of the Protocol have taken account of the practical impossibility of guerrillas securing such visibility. Third, the arms have to be openly carried, but only during a narrower time-window. Article 44, § 3, of AP I, one of the most controversial provisions of that instrument, controls here. It reads as follows:

> In order to promote the protection of the civilian population from the effects of hostilities, combatants are obliged to distinguish themselves from the civilian population while they are engaged in an attack or in a military operation preparatory to an attack. Recognizing, however, that there are situations in armed conflicts where, owing to the nature of the hostilities an armed combatant cannot so distinguish himself, he shall retain his status as a combatant, provided that, in such situations, he carries his arms openly:
> (a)   during each military engagement, and
> (b)   during such time as he is visible to the adversary while he is engaged in a military deployment preceding the launching of an attack in which he is to participate.
> Acts which comply with the requirements of this paragraph shall not be considered as perfidious within the meaning of Article 37, paragraph 1 (c).

This provision makes clear that the general rules are set aside only in situations in "armed conflicts where, owing to the nature of the hostilities an armed combatant cannot so distinguish himself", in other words, in guerrilla situations. In all other situations, the traditional rules prevail. The exception of § 3 is a "necessity exception"; if it is not possible to respect the rules, an exception is accepted. However, the exception is not based on the general saving clause of military necessity. The impossibility must stem from the "nature of the hostilities". This open-ended term was preferred to the one used by the Rapporteur, referring explicitly to wars of national liberation and occupied territories.[20] However, it is manifestly to those two situations that the provision is

---

20 See Y. Sandoz, C. Swinarski and B. Zimmermann (eds), *Commentary on the Additional Protocols of 8 June 1977 to the Geneva Conventions of 12 August 1949*, Geneva, 1987, p. 529.

addressed. There, guerrilla warfare has occurred in practice. Moreover, as an exception, the rule of § 3 is subjected to a narrow interpretation: *exceptiones sunt strictae interpretationis*. Further, as can be seen, the time-frame for a distinction from the civilians has been narrowed. The arms must be borne openly – and thus a distinction with regard to civilians secured – only between the deployment on the last position from where the attack is to be launched and the attack itself (up to its termination), while the fighter is exposed to the visibility (normal eyesight) of the adverse party.[21] Letter b is typically concerned with guerrilla attacks and not with defensive action. It is therefore a special rule for a particular circumstance, within the exception relating to the "nature of the hostilities". There has been much discussion about the outer edges of this timeframe. It is clear that the deployment does not start when the fighter leaves his home or from an assembly point for fighters. If he or she had to carry the arms openly since that moment, guerrilla warfare would be *de facto* or even *de jure* prohibited, and the whole aim of the provision defeated. The correct interpretation seems to be that the arms have to be carried openly from the *last* position, from where the attack has to be launched. The formula of § 3 is not, however, entirely precise in this regard. It was the result of a compromise between very distant positions of different delegations. The interpretation favoured here is thus not generally accepted. However, two further aspects seem clear. First, there is a nexus between the place of deployment and the visibility criterion. The arms must be carried openly only for such time as the fighter is "visible to the adversary". The criterion is formulated objectively, independent of the knowledge of the fighter. However, the obligation makes sense only if compared with what the fighter knew or ought to have known. Thus, *a contrario*, if the fighter is not visible to the adverse party, he need not carry the arms openly at that moment. This is particularly relevant for ambushes, when the fighters are hidden. It will, however, be rare that such fighters do not carry the arms openly, like a soldier would do, in an ambush situation. Indeed, in such situations these arms have to be used most quickly at any moment the adverse party passes nearby. Second, the visibility criterion applies to the view of a naked healthy eye, not improved by technical devices, such as spectacles or satellite screening. If the latter were allowed, virtually everything would become visible and the criterion would lose any sense. At the other end of the timeframe, it seems clear that the fighter may cease to carry arms openly as soon as the military engagement (hostilities) is terminated, including the time of flight from the place of engage-

---

21 *Ibid.*, pp. 533ff.

ment. This is part and parcel of guerrilla tactics. In conclusion, it must be stressed that § 3 is not CIL. It remains today the most controversial provision of AP I, for reasons which will be exposed in due course.

If a fighter does not comply with these requirements[22] (which regrettably are not as clear as they should be, in particular with regard to the deployment issue), the sanction is laid out in § 4.[23] This paragraph again contains a very controversial provision. It is made up of two interrelated layers: if a fighter does not comply with the relaxed conditions under § 3, he or she loses the right to prisoner of war status – but retains the right to be treated at least as favourably. The situations covered by this double rule vary: for example, a fighter respects the conditions of § 3, but only in a context where this paragraph does not apply (outside a guerrilla context as previously defined); or a fighter does not carry the arms openly at the place of last deployment, while exposed to the visibility of the adverse party; or the fighter does not carry the arms openly during the military engagement. The reason for the double rule is to further the domain of reciprocity between the belligerents and to secure a proper regime of protection. It was thought that the prisoner of war regime is not a holiday club regime; that it rather expresses a minimum of humane treatment, which should in substance be guaranteed to anyone. Moreover, the better the treatment of a fighter on the one side, the greater the hope that the other party will also be inspired by generosity; or vice versa, the greater the harshness on one side, the greater the risk of reciprocation on the other.

As for the legal consequences of this regime, two aspects may be mentioned. First, the captured unruly fighter may be subjected to criminal prosecution on a broader basis than if he or she was a prisoner of war. Since he or she is not such a prisoner, he or she does not come to enjoy the privilege of the combatant. Thus, he or she can be prosecuted not only for war crimes or offences unrelated with the armed conflict, but also for acts of violence committed while being underprivileged (in other words, not fulfilling the conditions of the combatant). In simpler words, such a fighter is a civilian directly participating in hostilities, who can be criminally prosecuted for doing so. He or she must, however, be materially treated like a prisoner of war, for example, enjoying the protections during trial as set out in articles 82ff of Geneva Convention

---

22 If there is a doubt on this issue, see article 45, § 1, AP I.
23 See Y. Sandoz, C. Swinarski and B. Zimmermann (eds), *Commentary on the Additional Protocols of 8 June 1977 to the Geneva Conventions of 12 August 1949*, Geneva, 1987, pp. 537–9.

III, and article 75 of AP I. Second, there remains a doubt as to the scope of the equivalence of protection under § 4. The prisoner shall be given "protection equivalent to . . .". This clearly extends to all material protection provisions, such as the ones on hygiene, adequate food, labour conditions, contact with the outside world, and so on. However, there are also some provisions under Geneva Convention III which are linked with the military status of a combatant, for example, the right to wear the uniform.[24] Are these provisions also covered by the equivalence criterion? A strict interpretation could suggest that these provisions are not covered. However, if some provisions of Geneva Convention III are singled out from the equivalence, there might be quibbling and consequently legal uncertainty as to which provisions are indeed inextricably linked with combatant status and which are not. A belligerent will be well advised not to insist on such differences, which after all concern only details. Having been contested since the time of its adoption, it is not possible to affirm that the provision contained in § 4 reflects CIL; but it binds the parties to AP I in their dealings *inter se*.

Is the provision excessive? Does it lead to a loss of incentive to respect the conditions for being a combatant, since the treatment as prisoner of war is still secured? In regard to the rationale mentioned above, the provision does not seem to be excessive; it is at best generous, and has its own policy motivation. Moreover, there is still an incentive to respect the rules for becoming a combatant, since the scope of a possible criminal prosecution in case of capture is considerably different in the two situations. This is a marked difference with the law of NIAC, where absent any combatant status no such incentive exists. Finally, it has to be noted that the rule was also adopted for a realistic purpose, not to disincentivize rendition. If the guerillas knew that they could not hope for correct treatment after surrender, they would rather continue to fight, to the detriment of the adverse party. The rule is therefore not only a generous one, it is also one that is in the interests of the adverse belligerent.

This reform of the Protocol was thought to be a realistic adaptation to modern conditions of asymmetric warfare. However, it has been accused in certain quarters, notably in the US and Israel, as opening the door to terrorist activities.[25] This criticism is exaggerated.

---

24 Article 40, Geneva Convention III.
25 See the overview and sound criticism in G. H. Aldrich, "Why the US of America Should Ratify Additional Protocol I", in A. Delissen and G. Tanja (eds), *Humanitarian Law of Armed Conflict, Challenges Ahead, Essays in Honour of F. Kalshoven*, Dordrecht/Boston/London, 1991, pp. 127ff.

First, AP I applies only in IAC, not in NIAC. This restriction in fact limits the scope of its provisions to situations of guerrilla warfare in occupied territories (and, in the past, wars of national liberation). It can hardly be said that this scope is excessive, even if it may disturb States which regularly occupy territories. Second, the armed group claiming combatant status for its fighters must be linked to a State or people whose right to self-determination is recognized. The affiliation criterion under the chapeau of article 4, A, § 2, of Geneva Convention III ("belonging to") continues to apply. Not every armed group, or even criminal group, is within the reach of IHL. Third, IHL remains binding on these groups and its fighters. Terror used against the civilian population is expressly prohibited.[26] The principle of distinction remains binding.[27] Thus, indiscriminate attacks, for example, by bombing marketplaces, are prohibited and may still be qualified as terrorism. AP I neither condones them nor regularizes them. Fourth, if a fighter does not respect the applicable rules of IHL, he or she may possibly be able to claim combatant status, but that does not liberate him or her from criminal prosecution for war crimes or other offences, and sometimes even from the death penalty. It can hardly be said that such regulation is too lenient. The gist of the problem is political: States which regularly occupy foreign territories do not like guerrilla fighters launching hostile action against their military forces. That was true of the Germans during World War II and it remains true for occupying States today. The labels "freedom fighter" and "terrorist" is particularly moveable in such a context. The point is not that one or the other of these States may be more justified than the other, that one of the causes may be better than the other – this is undisputed, but pertains to *jus ad bellum*. Consequently, the distinction according to the justice of the cause pertains to *jus ad bellum* and should not infiltrate *jus in bello*.

It may be added to the foregoing that AP I also regulates the status of some particular categories of persons. First, there is the spy (article 46 of AP I). The status of a spy turns essentially on whether he or she performed his or her activities while in uniform or not. The gist of the distinction is rooted once again in the principle of distinction and secondarily in the principle of loyalty. Thus, it must be noted that, according to article 46, § 1, even a regular member of the armed forces is not entitled to prisoner of war status when engaged in spying without his or her uniform (in other words, under false pretences). This is

---

26 Article 51, § 2, AP I.

27 Article 48, AP I.

one of the rare examples where the primary and secondary status of combatant and prisoner of war differ. Such a member of the armed forces remains combatant, precisely as a member of such forces. But he or she is not entitled to prisoner of war status. Second, there is the mercenary (article 47 of AP I), a category that has regained some prominence in the context of private military security companies.[28] The provision contained in article 47 of AP I is so narrowly defined as to be largely inapplicable. It will in most cases be impossible to prove subjective criteria such as the fact that the person has been specially recruited to fight in an armed conflict (at least in the context of private security companies) or that he or she "is motivated to take part in the hostilities essentially by the desire for private gain and, in fact, is promised, by or on behalf of a Party to the conflict, material compensation substantially in excess of that promised or paid to combatants of similar ranks and functions in the armed forces of that Party". Moreover, if a person is incorporated into the army, at whatever level, he or she automatically ceases to be a mercenary. It can hardly be said that this provision stands out as a great legislative success.

6.4   Civilians directly participating in hostilities

There is a category of persons participating in the conflict as fighters and yet who are not combatants. These are civilians "directly participating in hostilities". Such civilians are not legally entitled to participate in the hostilities. They just participate in fact. These civilians do not, therefore, enjoy the combatant privilege: if captured, they can be tried for all acts of violence they have committed as "unprivileged" fighters. Moreover, they can be attacked during their military engagement. The category of civilians directly participating in hostilities shows that in IHL a civilian is not necessarily peaceful, or innocent as is sometimes said (innocent comes from *in-nocentes*, in other words, those who commit no harmful acts). The category of civilians participating directly (sometimes the word is actively) in hostilities stems from the two Additional Protocols, and is thus applicable in IAC and NIAC. For IAC, it is contained in article 51, § 3, of AP I; for NIAC, reference must be made to article 13, § 3, of AP II. There are thus two categories of civilians: the ones participating directly in hostilities;

---

28 On the issue as to the extent to which such persons can be considered mercenaries, see for example, H. Krieger, "Der privatisierte Krieg: Private Militärunternehmen im bewaffneten Konflikt", *Archiv des Völkerrechts*, vol. 44, 2006, pp. 169ff.

and the others, remaining peaceful (including those who participate indirectly in hostilities or in the war effort). The legal regime of both is not identical, since the former may at certain moments be targeted while the latter may never be the object of a direct attack. They may only face not excessive collateral losses in the context of an attack on a military objective.[29] The question arises when exactly a civilian participates directly in hostilities. The issue is of greatest importance in the context of modern warfare, including the "War on Terror", where an increasing number of civilians pour into the fighting and the distinction between combatants and civilians becomes blurred. Notwithstanding its importance, the Protocols do not clarify the concept. This is the reason why the ICRC issued a Guideline on the question.[30] It is today the main interpretive reference on the notion of direct participation in hostilities (with its common acronym: DPH). This is not the place to engage in a lengthy analysis of all the subtleties of the notion. The main lines of it will be presented, and one difficult case, the "War on Terror" and drone warfare will then be discussed as an illustration.

As to the substance of DPH, two main aspects must be emphasized, one with relation to the persons covered, the other with relation to the subject matter at stake.

6.4.1 Persons covered

First, there is a distinction made by the ICRC for two *categories of civilians* directly participating in hostilities.[31] The first category concerns the civilian sporadically participating in hostilities. This is the farmer by day and fighter by night paradigm. Such civilians lose protection only during their military activity, but retain it during their civilian life. In the farmer's case, protection against attacks by day, loss of protection by night, when engaged. This is the principle of the "revolving door". The person passes from one status to the other, from protection to non-protection and then again to protection. The rationale for this

---

29 Article 51, § 5, letter b, AP I.

30 ICRC and N. Melzer, "Interpretive Guidance on the Notion of Direct Participation in Hostilities under International Humanitarian Law", *International Review of the Red Cross*, vol. 90, 2008, pp. 991ff. On this notion in general, see the abundant literature indicated in M. Sassoli, A. Bouvier and A. Quintin, *How Does Law Protect in War*, vol. I, 3rd edn, Geneva, 2011, pp. 262ff, 264–5.

31 ICRC and N. Melzer, "Interpretive Guidance on the Notion of Direct Participation in Hostilities under International Humanitarian Law", *International Review of the Red Cross*, vol. 90, 2008, pp. 1007, 1034ff.

rule is that the danger of collateral civilian damage is too high, as is also the danger of erroneous attacks, if it were possible to target such a person at all times. To be sure, it is possible to arrest the person at all times and to try him or her for unlawful participation in the armed conflict. However, it is not possible to drop a bomb on such a person, or to effectuate a targeted killing, during the phase of non-participation in the hostilities. The reasons for the rule are the fear of excessive collateral damage to civilian persons and objects; and the danger of abuses in his or her phase of civilian life, since nothing proves that the person targeted was really engaging in armed conflict. The criticism levied against this rule by military circles is that it creates an inequality between regular soldiers and civilians directly participating in hostilities. The former can constantly be targeted, the latter only at certain moments. Moreover, it is said that the revolving door allows abuses by constantly shifting and leapfrogging from one status to the other, thereby jeopardizing the principle of distinction. These criticisms are certainly warranted. But the question is one of balance. In view of the eminent dangers for peaceful civilians if the revolving door principle was given up, the current position is still the better solution than a general licence to attack. It must also be stressed that the comparison of the regular members of the armed forces and the sporadically fighting civilian, under the guise of a purported equality, is at best misleading. The two categories of persons are not in the same situation, since the former is affiliated to the army, which warrants a continuous combat function, while the latter is precisely only a sporadic participant.

The second type of civilian is the one who becomes a member of an organized armed group and remains enrolled there. He or she is cast in a so-called "continuous combat function", like a regular member of an armed force. As long as that civilian remains affiliated or enrolled in the armed group, and thus displays a continuous combat function, he or she can be targeted at any time, for example, while sleeping, as could a regular soldier of the army. The criticism against this rule comes from humanitarian circles. It is claimed that this rule will allow targeted killing; that great problems of evidence arise as to whether a person is enrolled in the armed group and as to whether he or she is still a part of it (at least outside the context of actual military operations); that there is a great risk of unleashing attacks on persons who are peaceful civilians or only sporadic participants, and so on. Again, these criticisms are true, but there has to be a certain balance between fully organized armed groups and State forces, if IHL is to work realistically. A better balance than that proposed by the ICRC is apparently not forthcoming.

6.4.2 Subject matter

Second, there is the question *what acts constitute a DPH?*[32] Only specific acts may lead to DPH, not the status of a person or a simple intention to act. The specific act must meet three cumulative criteria:[33]

1. the act must be likely to adversely affect the military operations or military capacity of a party to an armed conflict or, alternatively, to inflict death, injury, or destruction on persons or objects protected against direct attack (threshold of harm);
2. there must be a direct causal link between the act and the harm likely to result either from that act, or from a coordinated military operation of which that act constitutes an integral part (direct causation);
3. the act must be specifically designed to directly cause the required threshold of harm in support of a party to the conflict and to the detriment of another (belligerent nexus).

Each of these criteria needs some commentary.

The *threshold of harm* requirement defines the acts accounting for a direct participation. Such acts are those adversely affecting the military operations or military capacity of a party to the conflict, for example, killing, capturing, destroying, sabotaging, clearing mines of the adversary, computer network attacks, and so on. To these must be added the acts causing death, injury or destruction even in the absence of military harm, in other words, attacks on civilians. The relevant acts under DPH are thus broader than the term attack under article 49, § 1, of AP I, meaning acts of violence against the adversary, whether in offence or in defence (unless civilians are included in the term "adversary").

The *direct causation* requirement stems from the condition of "direct", not merely "indirect", participation in hostilities, as contained in the provisions of AP I and AP II quoted above. The gist of the matter is that the harm at stake must be caused in one single causal step. However, in complex military operations, this includes conduct that causes harm only in conjunction with other acts. It is thus sufficient that the relevant acts are part of an operation directly causing the harm. Temporal or geographic proximity is not required. Thus, for example, delayed

---

32 *Ibid.*, pp. 1012ff.
33 *Ibid.*, pp. 995–6.

weapon systems are covered. The direct causation is also satisfied by the truck driver driving ammunition to the frontline, or by voluntary human shields, depending on the circumstances.

The *belligerent nexus* requirement has the aim of eliminating from the concept of DPH, action not linked to the armed conflict, for example, criminal activities. The acts performed must therefore be specifically designed to cause harm in support of one party to the conflict and to the detriment of the other. The test is objective and not subjective: the objective purpose of the act is relevant, not any hidden intention. The mental state of the actor could only be relevant in extreme cases, for example, when somebody ignores that he or she is transporting a bomb, or in cases of physical coercion for involuntary human shields (but that may not be recognizable by the adverse party and is then not relevant to it). The nexus criterion has the main function of excluding violence not linked to the armed conflict. This is violence situated in the realm of law enforcement; for example, crimes, flows of refugees blocking roads, riot suppression measures, and so on. There is here no support for the cause of one of the belligerents. The criterion can admittedly be difficult to apply in some cases. The assessment must be careful and the presumption always favourable to peaceful civilian status.

As for the temporal beginning and end of DPH,[34] the concept includes preparatory measures as well as deployment and return from the location of the action. Preparatory measures include only military measures for a specific act and constituting an integral part of it. However, no temporal or geographical proximity is needed for these preparatory acts in regard to the action of execution. Loading bombs on an airplane is sufficient. The fact that the place where these bombs will be dropped is remote has no relevance. Preparatory measures for unspecified attacks do not fall under these categories; for example, the build-up of a general capacity for attack. Deployment and return are an integral part of the act in question. Assessments must be made case-by-case. Overall, it is particularly important not to over-stretch the stage of preparatory measures. Otherwise, the danger looms large that a great number of civilians will be targeted under the general umbrella of DPH.

The Interpretive Guidance of the ICRC is far from perfect, as any other guidance would also have been far from ideal. It is hardly possible

---

34 *Ibid.*, pp. 1031ff.

to square the circle. IHL is not designed for a direct participation of civilians in hostilities. Such participation remains to some extent necessarily an erratic block within its system and its proper equilibrium. However, since IHL is there to regulate a reality on the ground, we have to make the best of the fact that in modern armed conflicts civilians tend to participate in many guises. Previously, this happened under the sole banner of patriotic warfare, today it occurs under the flag of a great series of causes, some less noble than others, as the issue of terrorism shows. The effort of the ICRC has levied criticism to which the ICRC has responded;[35] the debate will continue. This is not the place to enter into the details of the current debate. However, we may test the issue in one particularly salient context, namely the so-called "War on Terror".

6.5   International humanitarian law, "War on Terror" and drones

The War on Terror issue raises problems of *jus ad bellum, jus in bello* and HRL. We may here focus only on the *jus in bello* limb, and mention in passing some HRL concerns, without going into *jus ad bellum* aspects at all (when is the use of force on foreign territory lawful?). With regard to IHL, the problems arise on different planes. They tend to weaken or hamper the functioning of some fundamental rules of this body of law. We may consider these problems in their full complexion, not limiting ourselves to the sole issue of the combatant or civilian, which is the core of this chapter.

6.5.1   Existence of an "armed conflict"

First, there is the issue of the *existence of an "armed conflict"*. In order to invoke the bulk of IHL rules – allowing a more generous recourse to killing than the rules applicable in peacetime – there must be an armed conflict. Such a conflict supposes belligerent parties, in other words, States or armed groups, both identifiable and placed under a responsible command. Shadowy terrorist networks are not usually a belligerent party; they have no rights and should not have the rights of a belligerent; they are and remain a criminal

---

35 N. Melzer, "Keeping the Balance between Military Necessity and Humanity: A Response to Four Critiques of the ICRC's Interpretive Guidance on the Notion of Direct Participation in Hostilities", *Journal of International Law and Politics*, vol. 42, 2010, pp. 831ff.

organization.[36] However, in certain cases the fight of a State against a non-State group may form a NIAC. NIAC supposes fighting taking place against groups having a certain degree of organization and possessing certain intensity.[37] If it is accepted that varying terrorist groups can or even do fulfil such criteria (which is not obvious), the consequence seems to be that the battlefield (and the application of IHL) becomes spatially unlimited. There would be an "armed conflict" between the US and an unlimited number of groups, involving an unlimited number of States. We would arguably already find ourselves in World War III, the US being entitled to use belligerent lethal force on the territory of an undefined number of States. Moreover, the terrorist groups would have been upgraded into belligerents. True, their members are not vested with combatant privilege, in other words, the right to use force against military targets. The persons composing these groups had no right to use force, and they are still subjected to various criminal codes of the States on whose territory they operate and of the victim States. But there remains the fact that they would be entitled to claim some undefined degree of "equality" between the belligerent parties in regard to the applicable law and to negotiate on their claims.

Taking the case of the drones used in Pakistan, the US considers itself as a party to a NIAC against the Taliban and their associates. The US has flown a great number of attacks on Taliban positions. But the number of attacks of the terrorist groups against the US and its allies has remained extremely low. Would such a low-intensity conflict suffice to qualify as a NIAC under common article 3 of the Geneva Conventions, or even to AP II? Is Al-Qaeda sufficiently organized, or is it just a loose network, a sum of loose affiliations? As we have seen, the ICTY has interpreted the criteria for the existence of a NIAC in an extensive way in the context of events in Macedonia (FYROM) in 2001,[38] but there remain doubts

---

36 On the issue of the War on Terror, see for example, L. Condorelli and Y. Naqvi, "The War against Terrorism and Jus in Bello: Are the Geneva Conventions Out of Date?", in A. Bianchi (ed.), *Enforcing International Law Norms against Terrorism*, Oxford, 2004, pp. 25ff; M. E. O'Connell, *International Law and the "Global War on Terror"*, Paris, 2007; M. Sassoli, "Use and Abuse of the Laws of War in the 'War on Terrorism'", *Law and Inequality: A Journal of Theory and Practice*, vol. 22, 2004, pp. 195ff.

37 See for example, the jurisprudence of the ICTY: *Limaj* (Trial Chamber, 2005), §§ 83ff; *Mrksic* (Trial Chamber, 2007), §§ 405ff; *Haradinaj* (Trial Chamber, 2008), §§ 37ff; *Boskoski* (Trial Chamber, 2008), §§ 175ff.

38 ICTY, *Boskoski* case (Trial Chamber, 2008), §§ 173ff.

in our context.[39] The situation could, however, also be considered from another perspective. The US possibly acts (on invitation?) in the context of another NIAC fought between the Pakistan forces and the Taliban groups on its territory. This conflict would certainly fulfil the conditions of organization and intensity; and it would even satisfy the condition of a territorial control of the rebels, as required by article 1, § 1, of AP II for the applicability of that Protocol.

Overall, there is a loss of certainty. Traditionally, the law of armed conflicts applies in a set of well-defined and well-tailored situations of belligerency, between well-determined belligerent parties. The "War on Terror" implies a significant loss of such focus. There is consequently a growing pressure for the development of new rules of IHL, tailored to the specific situations of fuzzy military engagements, a new law straddling law enforcement and conduct of hostilities. This is the gist of the US argument that the Geneva Conventions are out of date. Indeed, not all rights and duties of belligerents under common article 3 and AP II, or other customary rules, would fit such situations of low intensity and the low organization of the "terrorist" forces. Nor would IHL really fit the "criminal law" background of most of these situations. This is precisely the reason why new rules would have to be devised. However, this would split IHL into a potentially high number of context-related rules, here for fighting terrorism (drones), there for fighting drug trafficking (Mexico), still other for territories not actually occupied but only controlled from the air or the outside, and so on. IHL is already quite complex in its taxonomy.[40] To add further categories will over-stretch it and lead to its increasing ineffectiveness.

It seems that IHL is perfectly equipped to deal with situations of true belligerency – but that the "War on Terror" is largely not an issue of IHL at all. This is not true in situations of actual belligerent fighting, the best example being the battlefield between the US and the Taliban in Afghanistan between 2001 and 2002. When the war against terrorism comes down to a concrete hostile encounter between concrete belligerents, it is fully adequate to apply it.

---

39 N. Lubell, "The War (?) against Al-Qaeda", in E. Wilmshurst (ed.), *International Law and the Classification of Conflicts*, Oxford, 2012, p. 436. See also N. Lubell, *Extraterritorial Use of Force Against Non-State Actors*, Oxford, 2010, pp. 112ff.

40 M. Milanovic and V. Hadzi-Vidanovic, "A Taxonomy of Armed Conflict", in N. D. White and C. Henderson (eds), *Research Handbook on International Conflict and Security Law: Jus ad Bellum, Jus in Bello and Jus post Bellum*, Cheltenham, 2013, pp. 256ff.

6.5.2   Distinction in the targeting

Second, there is the issue of *distinction in the targeting*. The problems posed here are not inherent problems with unmanned vehicles, but rather concern the actual use of drones by the US. It is generally recognized that as an instrument of war among others, drones are neutral. They can be used to increase the accuracy of military strikes, since it will be possible to eliminate some physical stress of the pilot on the spot, wait for the best moment to attack, take the necessary time to verify all the parameters (due to the long flying capacity of the engines),[41] and so on. Conversely, drones can also be used in such a way as to pose problems with regard to targeting, especially if the targeting process does not live up to the conditions posed under IHL (especially under articles 50–58 of AP I, or article 13 of AP II and related CIL). The danger is central pillars of IHL that are too loose, and to prepare the terrain for still less stringent requirements in targeting. Thus, it is known that fully autonomous unmanned vehicles (not guided by a human being) are now being developed. Such engines, it is said, will, at least in certain situations, not have the necessary time to comply with a full proportionality assessment. Such an assessment is, however, required by article 51, § 5, letter b, of AP I, in the context of IAC; moreover, the proportionality rule is applicable also in NIAC as a customary rule for all types of armed conflict.[42] The result would be that technical reasons could lead to a dropping, or to a significant restriction, of a central requirement of IHL.

In Pakistan, the greatest problem is that of the "signature strikes". Drone attacks are classified into two categories: personality strikes and signature strikes. The former target specified persons, known to be affiliated to a terror or insurgent group, such as Al-Qaeda or the Taliban. Conversely, signature strikes target persons on the basis of an analysis of their displacements on the territory, and further on the basis of a bundle of suspect behaviours, such as, for example, the bearing of arms. Roughly 90 per cent of drone attacks are signature strikes.[43] It stands to reason that the criteria used for signature strikes

---

41 See M. W. Lewis, "Drones and the Boundaries of the Battlefield", *Texas International Law Journal*, vol. 47, 2012, p. 297. See also UN Doc. A/68/389, Promotion and Protection of Human Rights and Fundamental Freedoms while Countering Terrorism, p. 23.

42 See J. M. Henckaerts and L. Doswald-Beck, *Customary International Humanitarian Law*, vol. I, Cambridge, 2005, pp. 46ff.

43 K. J. Heller, "One Hell of a Killing Machine", *Journal of International Criminal Justice*, vol. 11, 2013, pp. 89ff, 90.

are inherently imprecise. To be travelling in an area controlled by the Taliban bearing weapons (a signature used by the US[44]) can hardly be squared with the targeting requirements of IHL. It ignores contextual and cultural realities, for example, the fact that in the tribal Afghan societies bearing arms is not necessarily a sign of terrorist or insurgent action. The same can be said for some forms of traditional use of arms in wedding ceremonies (and there have been more than one US attack in the context of such ceremonies).

In a NIAC (which is here relevant), the proper targeting under IHL must rest on the distinction between "fighters" and civilians, or, more precisely, between civilians participating directly in hostilities and civilians not so participating in hostilities,[45] on the legal basis of article 13 of AP II. The issue of targeting turns on the notion of direct participation. Such a "direct participation", as may be recalled, exists in two situations. First, in case of a "continuous combat function", when an individual is "affiliated" to an armed group, and as long as he or she remains a member of this group. He or she can then be targeted as a combatant without any temporal limitation; for example, also when he or she is sleeping. Alternatively, second, when there is a sporadic participation in the conflict, on the basis of the "revolving door" principle. According to this principle, the person participating can be targeted for the time-span he or she is effectively participating in hostilities by committing acts "likely to adversely affect the military operations or military capacity of a party to an armed conflict". The criteria of threshold of harm, direct causation and belligerent nexus already mentioned, are applicable to both categories of participation, continuous and sporadic. Members of an armed group will regularly fulfil them, whereas they have to be tested in a more precise way for sporadic participation in an armed conflict.

Problems with the categorizations of the ICRC Study in our specific context are the following. First, there remain persons who can be targeted throughout (continuous combat fighters and members of the armed forces), while others cannot always be targeted (sporadic fighters), creating some inequality of belligerents. But that is unavoidable and is based on sound reasons; after all, only those who fight continuously should be targetable continuously; moreover, the principle

---

44 *Ibid.*, p. 98.
45 On this notion in our context, see N. Lubell, *Extraterritorial Use of Force Against Non-State Actors*, Oxford, 2010, pp.135ff.

of equality of belligerents applies only in a very limited way to NIAC. Second, there remains the problem of proof of "continuous combat function" and that of possible abuses in this context. But this problem is also unavoidable. International law, including IHL, must, at the end of the day, rely on a degree of good faith on the part of the involved States. Third, as can be seen, drone strikes, especially those based on signatures, cannot be rendered compatible with the principles on targeting. Persons are hit on the sole basis of varying degrees of suspicion, and not on the basis of reliable evidence as to the "direct participation in hostilities". Therefore, purportedly applicable IHL categories are rendered inapplicable and even nugatory. It must, however, be noted once more that the problem lies not in the action by drones itself; it is rather the particular use of drones for signature strikes which has shattering consequences for the application of IHL. The odd result of such practices is the targeting, in other words, the death and injury, of a series of persons who are not "fighters" but "innocent civilians" – precisely what IHL tries to avoid as much as possible. It is not improbable that such action will trigger a great thirst for revenge and will increase enrolment in the terrorist groups. The strategy would then be self-defeating. There is ample evidence to show that for every terrorist or civilian killed, the terrorist groups are able to enrol a still greater number of new volunteers.

6.5.3   Principle of proportionality

There remain the principles linked to the preparation and carrying out of attacks, especially the principle of *proportionality*.[46] The rule is that an attack shall not be launched if it may be expected to cause incidental loss of civilian life, injury to civilians, damage to civilian objects, or a combination thereof, which would be excessive in relation to the concrete and direct military advantage anticipated. This rule is contained in article 51, § 5, letter b, of AP I for IACs, and is valid also for NIAC on the basis of CIL, perhaps in the latter category in a slightly more loose complexion (as inferred from article 13 of AP II and State practice). Contrary to the wording used, the rule is not really one of proportionality, but rather the prohibition of disproportion. The armed forces may attack only military objectives; but those at least they must be free in principle to always attack; otherwise, a belligerent could not attack anything. A restriction on the ability to target military objectives is consequently provided only for the case of a clear "excess" in the collateral civilian losses as compared to the military advantage gained.

---

46 See generally in our context *ibid.*, pp. 155ff.

In the context of drones, it is difficult to reach clear-cut opinions. Signature strikes do not in themselves raise problems of proportionality, but rather problems of directly attacking persons who are not "fighters". The issue is one of the proper selection of the military objective in the first place, not the collateral damage a lawful attack on a military objective may produce. However, a signature strike (or a personality strike) targeting a civilian not participating directly in hostilities or a "fighter" can also produce collateral effects on other "innocent" civilians. Then the issue of proportionality arises. Conversely, as such, drones may be used for precise if not surgical targeting; in this sense, they could lead to an improvement in the implementation of the proportionality requirement. Precise information on the issue of proportionality is rather scarce. However, it seems that in Pakistan a significant number of "innocent" civilians have been killed or injured in the drone attacks. It is impossible from the outside to assess whether the principle of proportionality has thereby been violated, since that would require a mastery of the particular facts. What was the military advantage pursued (which depends on the importance of the person targeted)? What have been the measures for a proper preparation of the attack in order to minimize collateral losses? How many persons could be expected to be collaterally hit, and how gravely? On the general plane, apart from a particular operation, what is the overall quota of collateral damages? And so on.

6.5.4   Human rights law

For the sake of completeness, we may add related issues of HRL, especially with regard to targeted killing or extra-judicial killings, and their relation to the right to life.[47] There are further issues related to torture, ill-treatment, abductions and *habeas corpus*, but these do not concern drones and may thus be laid to rest for the present purposes. The tendency of the US is to argue for a *lex specialis* approach, giving precedence to IHL over HRL,[48] because of its greater licence to kill. Further, the argument of the US is against extraterritorial application of HRL. However, this narrow approach is rejected by a unanimous body of international jurisprudence and is indeed unsound.[49] To the extent

---

47 On the issue of targeted killings, see mainly N. Melzer, *Targeted Killings in International Law*, Oxford, 2008. In our context, N. Lubell, *Extraterritorial Use of Force Against Non-State Actors*, Oxford, 2010, pp. 169ff.

48 The meaning of this approach is that in case of a conflict between a norm of international HRL and a norm of IHL in the context of targeting persons the norm of IHL should prevail.

49 R. K. Goldman, "Extraterritorial Application of the Human Rights to Life and Personal Liberty, including Habeas Corpus, during Situations of Armed Conflict", in G. Gaggioli and R. Kolb

that HRL is applicable – and in fact and law it is – the use of drones may lead to an unprecedented weakening of one of the cornerstone rights under these instruments, namely the right to life. Manifestly, under HRL, this right is not absolutely protected. Exceptions are recognized, precisely such as killing in wartime. The right goes fundamentally to the prohibition of arbitrary killing. Extra-judicial killings will often be so qualified. These are killings without due process of law. They involve the heaviest sanction possible, namely the death penalty, without any judicial review. To be sure, not every extra-judicial killing would be unlawful. But most of them will be incompatible with the right to life.[50] In what situations could an extra-judicial killing be compatible with HRL?

In order to remain within the bounds of HRL, drone killings must be "in accordance with the law", not "arbitrary" and respect the principles of "necessity" and "proportionality". It is not always clear whether the drone attacks flown comply with domestic US law. The question remains whether there are some secret legal instructions covering such action, but these would hardly qualify as a legal basis under HRL, if only because of their lack of publicity. A lethal attack could avoid being arbitrary if it was shown that it took place against a fighter under IHL rules (*lex specialis*).[51] However, as many of these attacks do not comply with IHL requirements (for example, the signature strikes discussed above), there is hardly a chance that an international human rights monitoring body would accept such a plea, divesting it of its own jurisdiction. The greatest problems arise under the requirements of necessity and proportionality. Under HRL, these are quite strict criteria.[52] It must be shown that there was no lesser force-option available; that arrest was prepared and attempted; that proper training and equipping of the acting forces in view of lesser options than death were organized, and so on. These are quite exacting requirements in extra-territorial counter-insurgency operations. At the end of the day, the requirements of necessity and proportionality risk being fulfilled only

---

(eds), *Research Handbook on Human Rights and Humanitarian Law*, Cheltenham, 2013, pp. 104ff.

50 See for example, UNGA, "Report of the Special Rapporteur on Extrajudicial, Summary or Arbitrary Executions: Study on Targeted Killings" (P. Alston), Doc. A/HCR/14/24/Add.6.

51 On this issue, see N. Lubell, *Extraterritorial Use of Force Against Non-State Actors*, Oxford, 2010, pp. 236ff. See also M. Milanovic, "Norm Conflicts, International Humanitarian Law, and Human Rights Law", in O. Ben-Naftaly (ed.), *International Humanitarian Law and International Human Rights Law*, Oxford, 2011, pp. 95ff.

52 The famous *McCann v. UK* case of the ECtHR (1995), Ser. A, No. 324.

when there is an imminent threat by the targeted person. The easiest option to get out of that "quagmire" is to play the card of *lex specialis*, in other words, of a priority of IHL in the context of a particular operation. This could be the case for drone attacks complying with the rules of IHL. Indeed, such a priority could be an incentive to comply with IHL rules. However, the incentive is quite remote in view of the fact that there is no international human rights court with compulsory jurisdiction or enforcement powers.

As can be seen, the "War on Terror" raises several issues in the context of IHL and HRL, some of them relate to the definition of combatants and some to the notion of DPH. The latter has become of the essence in the context of modern warfare, and in particular in the context of many asymmetric NIACs confronting a State and armed groups.

7   Targeting: a context-related legal set of rules

The targeting issues are situated in the heart of the principles of limitation[1] and of distinction.[2] It is one of the most central issues of modern IHL, and lies at the centre of the Hague Law.[3] It is also one of the most interesting chapters of IHL, since it contains few hard and fast rules to be applied lock, stock and barrel. The matter is too open-ended and context-related to be limited by a series of strict provisions. Rather, the rules indicate general criteria which have to be assessed in the concrete contexts of circumstances. This imports a great degree of flexibility and purpose-orientation into the law. There is room for legal creativity and for juridical assessment, which makes the matter lively and always renewed. In this sense, the targeting issues are the opposite of the law of Geneva Convention I, where there are a series of technical rules on the organization of sanitary services and the care to be provided to protected persons.

7.1   The prohibition of attack on civilian objects

The core provision in this context is contained in article 52 of AP I. Paragraph 1 of this article reads: "Civilian objects shall not be the object of attack or of reprisals. Civilian objects are all objects which are not military objectives as defined in paragraph 2". Paragraph 2 adds the definition of the military objective, in other words, defines which objects may be attacked:

---

1 Article 22 of the Hague Regulations 1907 and article 35, § 1, AP I: "In any armed conflict, the right of the Parties to the conflict to choose methods and means of warfare is not unlimited".

2 Article 48, AP I: "In order to ensure respect for and protection of the civilian population and civilian objects, the Parties to the conflict shall at all times distinguish between the civilian population and combatants and between civilian objects and military objectives and accordingly shall direct their operations only against military objectives".

3 On targeting, see the very stimulating and thorough analysis by I. Henderson, *The Contemporary Law of Targeting*, Leiden/Boston, 2009.

Attacks shall be limited strictly to military objectives. In so far as objects are concerned, military objectives are limited to those objects which by their nature, location, purpose or use make an effective contribution to military action and whose total or partial destruction, capture or neutralization, in the circumstances ruling at the time, offers a definite military advantage.

Paragraph 3 supplements the two foregoing rules with a legal presumption: "In case of doubt whether an object which is normally dedicated to civilian purposes, such as a place of worship, a house or other dwelling or a school, is being used to make an effective contribution to military action, it shall be presumed not to be so used". We may comment on these provisions by a series of remarks.

First, the definition of the civilian object, which is protected against the attack, is cast in negative terms. An object is civilian if it is not a military objective. One could have expected that IHL would positively define the objects protected and leave as a residual category those which may be attacked, in order to stress the scope of the protection. In reality, the opposite course has been chosen. This negative legal technique enlarges the scope of protection. As soon as an object does not fulfil the conditions of a military objective, it thereby automatically becomes an object protected against attack, at least in those circumstances. The narrower explicit category gives a power to attack and destroy; the larger residual category prohibits attack and destruction. By the opposite way of defining protected objects, the larger residual category would have been the one designing the objects open to attack. In short, the scope of allowable attacks would have been larger. Moreover, the negative definition is a legal technique often used in IHL. It ensures that there is no gap: if an object does not fall into one category, it then automatically falls into the other; if an object is not military, it is civilian. If both categories, the military and the civilian, were positively defined, problems of interpretation would arise. Objects could exist which would fit the conditions of neither category. These objects could then fall in a legal black hole. At the least they would produce difficulties of interpretation and hence legal uncertainty. The negative definition avoids these problems. As already suggested, this is a frequently used technique in IHL. We find it for the definition of civilian persons (all those who are not combatants)[4] or for the definition of common article 3, NIAC (armed conflicts not of an international character).[5]

---

4 Article 50, § 1, AP I.
5 Common article 3, Geneva Conventions I–IV.

Second, if civilian objects are not positively defined, the military objectives must be so defined. It would be circular to affirm that military objectives are all those which are not civilian, while saying at the same time that civilian objects are all those which are not military. The positive definition of military objectives can theoretically occur in two ways. Either there is a list of such objectives; or there is a contextual definition. In the latter case, the law would expound the general criteria on account of which a decision as to the character of the object can be taken in the concrete circumstances. The belligerent is here vested with a power of appreciation or concretization according to the facts at hand. The first approach, enumerating the objects, has never been attempted in its pure form. Some listed items were sometimes explicitly designed in some legal texts,[6] but the list was never thought to be exhaustive. Thus, the list indicated certain military objectives but had to concede that other objects could also be military objectives, so that some additional general criteria to define such objects remained necessary.

Third, the list approach has some important shortcomings. In the first place, a list will necessarily be incomplete. No legislator will be omniscient and able to think of all the possible objects having a military utility. Even if there could be such a heavenly legislator, it would hardly be possible to imagine future objects. In sum, the list would constantly contain loopholes and would have to be continuously revised. Moreover, such a long list would hardly be handy. If an interpreter had to go through lists containing hundreds of items for checking whether there is the object he or she is looking for – how convenient would that be? In the second place, as we have already seen, since the list could never be exhaustive, it would still be necessary to define some general residual criteria by which to add other objects. But if such criteria are defined, the gist of the matter would turn to the criteria. There might arise questions as to whether the listed items fulfil these criteria or not in the particular circumstances, so that a doubt about the relationship of the listed items with regard to the criteria could arise. However, there are even more essential reasons why such a list approach is unhelpful. In the third place, the idea that some object can always by attacked, since it would be inherently a military objective, is conceptually wrong. An object may render military services; but if

---

6 See article 24 of the Hague Rules on Aerial Warfare (1923), which was not a binding convention, or article 8 of the Hague Convention on the Protection of Cultural Objects During Armed Conflict (1954).

there is no military advantage in its attack or neutralization, it is *not* a military objective and cannot be attacked. This is most visible in historical military objects. Abstractly, these are military objects; yet they no longer make any military contribution and there is no advantage in attacking them. The list-definition is thus too broad. It conveys the idea that the listed objects can always be attacked, which is wrong. General criteria of a restrictive nature would remain necessary. Therefore, the criteria are of the essence, while the list is not. In the fourth place, the list approach is inexact on another account. Any object whatsoever can serve for military action and become a military objective. Thus, the list would have to include all the objects of the earth – and thus become useless. Take as an example a tree. This is normally a civilian object. But it could be used militarily, for example, by putting weapons on it. If it then makes a military contribution and there is a military advantage in attack, this becomes contextually a military objective. Note that this remains true even if the weapons are temporarily removed, if it can be expected that the tree will continue to serve as a deposit of arms in the future. Nevertheless, it would be nonsensical to put a tree on the list of military objectives. Rather, the criteria by which a tree could become a military objective would have to be indicated. This means once again that the criteria, and not the list, are controlling.

Fourth, the contemporary law on targeting is based completely on the contextual or criteria approach (see the text of article 52, § 2, of AP I). Any examples of items which are typically military objectives are avoided, in order not to convey the wrong idea. It must be appreciated that this approach is narrower than the list approach. The listing of an item conveys the idea that it can be attacked; the criteria force the attacker to check for any object whatsoever if in the circumstances it concretely fulfils the conditions for attack.

Fifth, the two main and exhaustive criteria mentioned in article 52, § 2, are the "military contribution" and the "military advantage". Military objective equals contribution plus advantage. The test as to the two criteria is radically case-by-case oriented, in full context and in the concrete circumstances. The law requires from the operator that he or she apply the criteria to the facts at hand. The law thus does not define the concrete military objectives; it defines the criteria by which these military objectives will be determined in the single case. As a consequence the matter is very relative. An object may be a military objective in this context but not in another (since, for example, the military advantage can vary); it can be a military objective now but not in one hour (again, for example, if the military advantage has faded away). It may also remain a military objective but attack may be allowed at a certain moment and not in another, according to the proportionality equation at different moments. For example a school-class is just passing near the objective, and expected collateral damage would rise too high if the objective was attacked now – but perhaps not in ten minutes. It may also be noticed that when an objective is not a military objective anymore (even if that is only temporary), according to the law it becomes a civilian object. A military item, if not liable to be attacked now, is legally for that time a civilian object. This is an effect of the negative definition, expounded above. This shows the specialty of the definition of legal terms, which may vary from the common use of terminology. Lastly, it must be stressed that the "contribution" and the "advantage" are cumulative requirements: there must be a military contribution *and* an advantage in destroying or neutralizing the object. The wording of article 52, § 2, is very clear on that issue. It would thus be wrong to argue that if a military advantage exists in attacking the object, there must perforce be a military contribution (it would here flow automatically out of the advantage). There may be some military advantage to attack pre-emptively some port installation or other devices, but absent a military contribution, such items are not military objectives. Any other answer would considerably broaden the scope of possible attacks. There is some degree of disagreement as to whether the two elements must be simultaneously fulfilled, or whether there can be some temporal sequence here.[7] If a military advantage fulfils the strict conditions under article 52, § 2, there is no reason why it could not occur in the future with regard to the timing of the attack – so long as it remains definite and certain, not speculative. The example often made in this context is the attack on a computer system that diminishes planning capabilities in the immediate future. The advantage must not flow directly from the destruction or neutralization of the object. It can also relate to the deception on where the true attack will take place. One may mention, for example, the Allied attacks on Pas de Calais in 1944, in order to cover the Normandy Operation. The two criteria fall now to be analysed separately.

Sixth, what is a *"military contribution"*? The precise definition of that element in AP I is "objects which by their nature, location, purpose or use make an effective contribution to military action". There are various elements here. First, "contribution" means that an object renders

---

7 See I. Henderson, *The Contemporary Law of Targeting*, Leiden/Boston, 2009, pp. 51–3.

services (has a usefulness) to the concrete conduct of military operations, in attack and defence, and not merely to the general war effort.
The selling of oil resources "contributes" to the war effort, since it
realizes cash flow allowing this effort to be sustained. Yet, this is not
a military contribution: it is not directly linked to the performance of
military operations. Second, the contribution must be "effective". This
word is meant to exclude any potential, hypothetical or speculative
contribution. May a contribution be considered or expected only if it
is not speculative? The answer is affirmative (see below). Third, there
are the four categories of contribution, by nature, location, use, or
purpose. These are illustrations of effective contributions. The list is
not exhaustive. Fourth, "nature" refers to military material and buildings. Thus, these items are never *"hors de combat"*, even if not used
at a certain moment. The relevant point is that they could be used
again. This does not mean that such items are military objectives in a
single case; the military advantage remains to be checked anew in every
situation. Fifth, "location" refers to places having a strategic value, for
example bridges. A future military use, now still in its preparation
phase, is sufficient here. Conversely, the strategic value of the place is
not in itself considered enough. Thus, a simple possible future use does
not suffice. The contribution would here not be effective. The future
use must be planned. This raises issues of intelligence and knowledge
of such planning. Sixth, "use" refers to the effective use of an object,
which is not in itself a military asset. The former example of the tree
garnished with ammunition would fall in this category, as would a
military use of a university building or a military use of a civilian car.
Seventh, "purpose" is the destination given to an object which is not in
nature military. Thus, if the intended use of an electricity production
plant is to serve the army at least partly, this intended use warrants a
military contribution. The use can here be future, if only it is a concrete
and certain destination (the matter may again raise difficult evidentiary
issues). A merely conditional intended use is not enough, for example,
the intended military use of an object. But this use can only be envisaged if another object is no longer functioning or available. The Eritrea/
Ethiopia arbitral Tribunal found, in the *Western Front* case (2005), that
the Hirgigo electricity production plant was a military objective even if
the production of electricity had not yet started, since it was intended
that the army should benefit from a fraction of the electricity produced
there and the works on the plant were about to be completed.[8] Eighth,
the element "to military action" makes clear that the contribution

---

8 *RIAA*, vol. 26, pp. 332ff.

cannot simply be to the general war effort, which would encompass an endless list of possible items, such as State finances. It must be limited to military action, in other words, the conduct of offensive or defensive military operations. No indirect link to such operations is sufficient, since otherwise the contribution criterion would lose any contour.

Seventh, what is a "*military advantage*"? First, an "advantage" may be defined as everything which facilitates the military operations, in other words, the destruction or weakening of adverse military facilities or personnel. An advantage also exists when a support is given to one's own forces. Thus, a belligerent has an advantage in bombarding a prisoner of war camp in adverse territory, in order to allow its own forces to escape (a bombardment which, we may assume, will be crafted in such a way as to avoid casualties amongst its own forces). The advantage is thus a relative notion: weakening of the enemy or strengthening of own forces. Second, the advantage must be "military". It must therefore possess a direct link with the military operations. A purely psychological advantage (trying to induce the enemy to surrender), a financial advantage, or a political advantage (attack on symbols of the adversary), is not enough (compare many authors from the Anglo-Saxon world). These are not military advantages. If any advantage, which could speculatively and indirectly lead to a military advantage, were enough, the domain of what could be attacked would be far too broad. Take the example of the psychological advantage: bombing a television station or water supplies for attacking the morale of the population, so that they constrain their rulers to surrender. Such an advantage is indirect, speculative and not military. In many cases the effect will be exactly the reverse: the attack will exacerbate the fierceness of resistance. Moreover, since IHL applies reciprocally, such a course would have to be allowed to both belligerents. CNN or Fox TV as military targets? Third, the military advantage must be "definite" (French: "*précis*"). This rules out potential or hypothetical advantages, as well as highly indirect ones (in other words, advantages with a speculative chain of causality). The advantage may, however, be indirect when there is a sufficiently certain causal link; for example, there is an advantage in attacks for the defence of one's own troops, where the effect on the adverse party is only a reverberation of the strengthening of one's own men. The advantage must be sufficiently proximate in time; otherwise it fades away into the speculative. Fourth, the military advantage must exist "in the circumstances ruling at the time" (French: "*en l'occurrence*"). What counts is therefore the concrete perspective prevailing at the moment of the attack. At that very moment, the military advantage must exist. Consequently, military objectives do not exist once and for all time, but fluctuate in time. An object may be a military objective at certain moments and not at others. The assessment must always be made in the circumstances, since the military advantage requires such a renewed contextual assessment. Fifth, a difficult question has arisen with regard to the measuring rod of the advantage: is it the single object attacked, or is it a series of objects linked together in the complexion of an overall attack? The problem is that for manifest practical reasons the advantage cannot be limited to the single object (where it could, however, be most easily assessed) but must be extended to the whole of an integrated military operation (where it may, on some account, be more difficult to limit, since it is more difficult to determine what is a "single military operation"). A simple example may make clear that a limitation to a single object is not sensible. Assume there are in a town 13 radio stations, able to transmit military messages. If only one of these stations is attacked, the military advantage may not appear at all. If the overall capabilities of the adverse party to transmit messages are not reduced, there is no military advantage, and the station is not a military objective in the circumstances. However, if a single military operation (even if the timing of the several attacks is not simultaneous) hits, say, ten of these stations, the military advantage appears. The belligerent will here have weakened the military transmission capacity of the adverse party. The relevant advantage appears only in the perspective of the full context, not with regard to a single attack. It is thus unavoidable to assess the whole of a military operation, unified by a common military aim (in regard to which the advantage will appear). On the other hand, this approach is fraught with dangers.[9] The broader the definition of the military operation, the easier it will be to find some advantage – at the extreme, the whole armed conflict is one interrelated military effort. If it is thus necessary to concede some cumulative-effects doctrine, the exact limit of the relevant military operation remains a matter of some difficulty. The interpretation should remain rather strict, lest the restrictions of AP I be circumvented.

Eighth, some particular problems may now be mentioned. First, there are so-called *dual-use objects*. These are objects serving at once civilian and military purposes. Thus, for example, a railway may transport civilians as well as military assets. From the point of view of article 52,

---

9 L. Vierucci, "Sulla nozione di obiettivo militare nella guerra aerea: recenti sviluppi della giurisprudenza internazionale", *Rivista di diritto internazionale*, vol. 89, 2006, pp. 704–5.

§ 2, of AP I, it will be a military objective if the two conditions (contribution/advantage) are fulfilled. However, as there is also a civilian use here, the proportionality issue arises.[10] The military advantage must be assessed in the sense that the collateral civilian damage must not be excessive with regard to it. Thus, if an electricity plant produces 98 per cent civilian energy, and many hospitals are vitally affected by its destruction, and the military contribution is only marginal (and so also the advantage), the attack on it would not be allowed. Second, there is the question of useless destruction. Such destruction is always prohibited under the two-pronged test of article 52. Legally, destruction is "useless" even if it has a non-recognized purpose; for example, revenge, instead of a military advantage. Third, we must notice the legal (and rebuttable) presumption contained in article 52, § 3, of AP I. If an object normally has a civilian use, it is presumed that it is used according to its designation. Thus, a university building is presumed to be a civilian object. The belligerent wishing to attack it must show that this building has become a military objective in accordance with the criteria of article 52, § 2. Difficulties in such a proof cannot relax the presumption, contrary to what has been claimed by the US during the Kuwait liberation war.[11] Any other position would allow a belligerent to shoot first and ask questions thereafter, in other words, would produce a great number of attacks on civilian objects. Fourth, the criteria contained in article 52, § 2, are exhaustive for the purposes of IHL. Objects to be attacked can further be designated under a relevant Security Council Resolution under Chapter VII of the UN Charter. But this would then pertain to the *jus ad bellum* limb and escapes from the orbit of article 52 of AP I. We will come back to this point.

Ninth, and lastly, an example may be given in order to concretely assess the preceding developments. Take a radio-television station, broadcasting civilian sequences and also military messages. Is that a military objective? If there is a transmission of military messages, there is a contribution to military action. The military advantage of an attack must then be assessed. It depends on many factors, such as: Were other available stations also attacked, so that the overall result is to effectively weaken the channels of transmission of the adverse party (see above)? Or, was the station attacked the one with the greatest territorial reach

---

10 See correctly the Sep. Op. of Arbitrator H. Van Houtte, *Western Front* Award, Eritrea/ Ethiopia Claims Commission, *RIAA*, vol. 26, p. 348.

11 US Department of Defense Report to Congress on the Conduct of the Persian Gulf War – Appendix on the Role of the Law of the War, 10 April 1992, in *ILM*, vol. 31, 1992, p. 627.

for messaging, so that the advantage could be admitted even in isolation? Or, was it the only station which could code the messages, so that again the advantage only materialises in isolation? For how much time could the transmission of messages be expected to be interrupted by a specific attack? If the time-span were short, was the advantage sufficient? Was there, for example, an important military operation under way at that very moment, so that even a short-term interruption could garner a significant advantage? And so on. Since our station is a dual-use object, we should also consider proportionality issues (see the discussion of proportionality below). If the interruption of messaging could be expected to last roughly three hours before the adverse party reconstructs the broadcasting capacity, could approximately twenty casualties and twenty injured persons be considered proportionate? Again, if an important military operation was under way at that very moment, the proportionality requirement will certainly be satisfied. If there is no operation at all under way, the equation could appear in a different light. The question also turns on the timing of the attack. Was the building attacked at 2 a.m., when there is almost nobody in the building, so that collateral civilian losses could be minimized? Does a belligerent have the technical capacity to attack at night? Or was the attack flown at 10 a.m., when there is maximum affluence in the building and thus a maximum risk of collateral damage? What weapon was used? A precision weapon, where the collateral damage could be expected to be minimized? Or was a much less precise weapon used? And so on.

What can be elicited from all the proceeding developments is a certain sense for the context-relatedness of the assessment. It is also evident that the whole operation of assessment is heavily dependent upon proper information and intelligence. From this latter point of view, there is an inherent advantage for the armies of developed States, with good staffing and proper intelligence services. Before the Libyan military operation pursuant to UNSC Resolution 1973 (2011) was started, NATO airplanes flew over the territory of the target State for weeks in order to determine the location of military objectives. This was only made possible by reason of a significant technical and logistical capacity. Context and information are thus key assets for modern targeting procedures.

7.2   Precautions in attack: article 57 of AP I

Article 57, AP I is among the most important provisions in the Protocol. It aims at minimizing at all times, as much as feasible, the collateral civilian losses, by forcing a belligerent carefully to prepare and plan its attacks. Thus, article 57 is a direct complement to the principle of distinction, which it seeks to reinforce on the planning and execution level. The wording of this important provision is as follows:

Article 57. Precautions in attack

1. In the conduct of military operations, constant care shall be taken to spare the civilian population, civilians and civilian objects.
2. With respect to attacks, the following precautions shall be taken:
   (a) those who plan or decide upon an attack shall:
      (i) do everything feasible to verify that the objectives to be attacked are neither civilians nor civilian objects and are not subject to special protection but are military objectives within the meaning of paragraph 2 of Article 52 and that it is not prohibited by the provisions of this Protocol to attack them;
      (ii) take all feasible precautions in the choice of means and methods of attack with a view to avoiding, and in any event to minimizing, incidental loss or civilian life, injury to civilians and damage to civilian objects;
      (iii) refrain from deciding to launch any attack which may be expected to cause incidental loss of civilian life, injury to civilians, damage to civilian objects, or a combination thereof, which would be excessive in relation to the concrete and direct military advantage anticipated;
   (b) an attack shall be cancelled or suspended if it becomes apparent that the objective is not a military one or is subject to special protection or that the attack may be expected to cause incidental loss of civilian life, injury to civilians, damage to civilian objects, or a combination thereof, which would be excessive in relation to the concrete and direct military advantage anticipated;
   (c) effective advance warning shall be given of attacks which may affect the civilian population, unless circumstances do not permit.
3. When a choice is possible between several military objectives for obtaining a similar military advantage, the objective to be selected shall be that the attack on which may be expected to cause the least danger to civilian lives and to civilian objects.
4. In the conduct of military operations at sea or in the air, each Party to the conflict shall, in conformity with its rights and duties under the rules of international law applicable in armed conflict, take all reasonable precautions to avoid losses of civilian lives and damage to civilian objects.
5. No provision of this article may be construed as authorizing any attacks against the civilian population, civilians or civilian objects.

Notice that there is no equivalent provision in AP II (NIAC). This does not mean that a tribunal cannot apply by analogy some of the provisions of article 57 in a NIAC, as the ECtHR has shown in the *Issaieva* case discussed above.

7.2.1   Scope of application

Article 57 is geared towards all military personnel effectively having the power to influence the decisions or the execution of an attack. It is not limited to the level of the commander.[12] The responsibility follows the effective attributions and thus varies according to the level of command or power. The duties posed in article 57 encompass the soldier executing a mission. Thus, if the pilot flies out to hit the target according to his or her mission, there remains, for example, the obligation to cancel or suspend an attack, or even to deflect a missile, if it appears at the last moment that the equation of proportionality has dramatically changed with regard to expectations (for example, if a school-class is by accident just near the target). The same pilot must also make an article 57 assessment if during his flight he or she encounters a target of opportunity and decides to hit it. The evaluation must then go as to its character as a military objective, as to possible collateral damages, and so on. Article 57 covers all forms of attacks, as defined in article 49 of AP I, in other words, offensive but also defensive military actions.

7.2.2   Article 57, § 2, letter a, (i): verification of the objectives

The first thing to notice is that the obligation is qualified and to some extent of a soft nature, or better, of a contextual complexion: "do everything feasible". What is feasible in a particular set of circumstances is essentially a question of fact. However, it is necessary to organize the army as well as possible with the resources available, so that the feasibility does not fall beneath a minimum level of due diligence. A belligerent cannot argue that something is not feasible simply because it failed to organize its armed forces properly: nobody can reap advantages from his or her own tort. Of course, what is feasible depends quite heavily on the resources and technical possibilities at disposal. The necessary means to reasonably comply with IHL obligations are, however, always due. If there is a slight doubt on the nature of the objective, must further inquiries be made? This is suggested by the

---

12 In this regard, the text of article 57 is too narrow when it refers to "those who plan or decide upon an attack"; it also encompasses those who execute an attack, as § 2, letter b, shows.

ICRC Commentary.[13] The question depends essentially on context. Such an obligation certainly exists if the object is dual use and if the danger of significant collateral damage looms large. Thus, the standard of care must vary according to the gravity of expected and expectable collateral damage.

The verification will bear on the objective as such and also on its immediate environment. It will be relevant to know whether civilian objects or persons are in the vicinity of that objective. An attack launched on the basis of simple suspicions and without prior verification automatically entails a violation of this rule. This is true even if the attack has not led to any collateral damage. In such a case, putting a civilian object into jeopardy is the legal reason for holding that the rule has been breached. As already suggested, the obligation also exists when a pilot attacks a target of opportunity (in other words, a target discovered by chance and while flying). An assessment has to be made by the pilot, even if the verification will perhaps be more rudimentary than if prepared by the commanding group. In the *Central Front* award, Ethiopia's Claim No. 2 (2004) of the Eritrea/Ethiopia Claims Commission,[14] the arbitrators found that article 57 had been breached by a bombardment without any adequate preparation, carried out by inexpert pilots, and without any assessment after the fact. It held that what was practically feasible in the circumstances had not been done.

7.2.3   Article 57, § 2, letter a, (ii): minimizing the collateral damage

This obligation is supplementary to the one expressed in article 51, § 5, letter b, of AP I. There, the collateral damage must not be "excessive" with regard to the expected military advantage. Here, there is the stricter obligation to try to minimize the collateral damage. This latter obligation tightens the duties of a belligerent in the context of an attack. There are different devices by which the minimizing of collateral damage can be obtained; for example, using laser-guided precision weapons, previous area-scanning for sensitive targets, such as hospitals, choosing the best time-window of the day or night for attacking, choosing the best angle to launch a missile (so that behind the target

---

13 Y. Sandoz, C. Swinarski and B. Zimmermann (eds), *Commentary on the Additional Protocols of 8 June 1977 to the Geneva Conventions of 12 August 1949*, Geneva, 1987, p. 680.
14 *RIAA*, vol. 26, pp. 189–90, § 110.

there are no civilian objects), taking measures to limit the blasting or fragmentation effect of the weapons used, and so on. The fact that the adverse party does not respect its obligations under article 58 of AP I (avoiding, as far as feasible, locating military objectives within densely populated areas, and so on), does not justify the other belligerent ridding itself of the present obligation. There is no *tu quoque* argument in IHL. However, such a violation by the adverse party can influence what is practically feasible in the circumstances. The question as to how high flying or low flying interacts with the present obligation has been much discussed. High flying may reduce the accuracy of the targeting and maximize collateral damage, especially if low-precision weapons are used. On the other hand, it will tend to preserve the pilot from being shot down. Low flying may increase this accuracy, but potentially also increase the risk of being shot down. However, low flying also entails a greater nervous stress on the pilot, and thus increases the risk of inaccurate bombing. Thus, no general answer can be given to this question. The collateral damage flowing from such a tactical choice is context-related, and hinges on factors such as the type of weapon used, the military capabilities of the adverse party, the type of targets to be attacked, the natural configuration of the territory where the mission is flown, and so on.

7.2.4   Article 57, § 2, letter a, (iii): refraining from launching an attack

This duty exists whenever an attack appears to be disproportionate in the sense of article 51, § 5, letter b, of AP I, or if the objective turns out not to be a military objective, either at all or at a specific moment. The duty applies to the command level and to the executing military personnel, for example, the pilot. There is thus an obligation constantly to take account of all military information, notably new information, which progressively completes the picture of the target and its surroundings.[15] Conversely, to rely only on what was originally known is not sufficient. The process must be ongoing, up to the concrete moment of the attack, but always only according to what is practically feasible. This is a matter of due diligence.

---

15 A good example of a last minute verification during the Kosovo military campaign (1999), is to be found in J. F. Quéguiner, *Le principe de distinction dans la conduite des hostilités*, Ph.D., Geneva, 2006, p. 380.

7.2.5   Article 57, § 2, letter b: cancelling or suspending an attack

Again, this obligation applies to situations where it turns out at the last moment that an objective is not military or that the collateral damage is excessive in the circumstances. The obligation at stake is the natural prolongation of the one under the previous paragraph, applied to the phase of execution. Thus, for example, in the Kosovo conflict (1999), a NATO missile launched against a radar station was deflected into a nearby forest when it appeared, at the last moment, that there was a church in the immediate vicinity.[16] A problem arises when it comes to judging the proportionality of an attack in its aggregate, in other words, when the military operation is a complex one and implies a series of interrelated attacks on a series of military objectives considered as a whole. The person executing one attack cannot assess the proportionality with regard to the aggregate of the operation. However, even in such a case there are clear-cut situations, especially when there are unexpected events, such as the presence of a school-class in the vicinity of an objective.

7.2.6   Article 57, § 2, letter c: effective advance warning

This is a traditional obligation. It has been heeded in many armed conflicts, ranging from World War II to the Kosovo War.[17] The obligation was already contained in article 19 of the Lieber Code of 1863.[18] The obligation is a relative one: it is stated under the saving clause "unless the circumstances do not permit". Some attacks can be successful only if launched by surprise. Moreover, a belligerent is not bound to jeopardize his pilot, taking the risk of a shooting down, by warning in advance. It is in most cases impossible to warn in advance when the target is a moving one. It has to be noticed that the obligation exists only if civilian persons or objects risk suffering losses. Article 57 has to do only with the protection of civilians, in other words, with the principle of distinction. The warning can be either general (that a certain target will be attacked) or special (that there is a concrete military operation under way). The warning must be "effective"; it is thus not sufficient to warn the adverse military authorities, notably if they will not have time in turn to warn the civilian population. The warning is

---

16 I. Henderson, *The Contemporary Law of Targeting*, Leiden/Boston, 2009, p. 182.

17 J. F. Quéguiner, *Le principe de distinction dans la conduite des hostilités*, Ph.D., Geneva, 2006, p. 385.

18 See D. Schindler and J. Toman, *The Laws of Armed Conflicts*, Leiden/Boston, 2004, p. 6.

only effective if it reaches the relevant civilian population. It must be as concrete and precise as the circumstances permit. Timing is a matter of context: the warning must be given with sufficient advance to permit evacuation, but it can be given on the expectation of an expeditious evacuation.

7.2.7   Article 57, § 3: choice of the military objective causing the least collateral damage[19]

This is an application of the principles of necessity and proportionality as they are typical for HRL and for administrative law in general. The principle stated is that of *civiliter uti*. The rule can be applied only in a particular set of circumstances. There must be a precise military aim pursued and a plurality of military objectives, each one allowing the full realization of that aim. Example: a line of supply is to be cut off.[20] We are in a mountain region. There are three bridges over large precipices. Bridge one is situated in a village; bridge two is used for military and civilian purposes, such as transporting medical stuff; bridge 3 is situated in an uninhabited region. The choice here should be to attack bridge 3. However, it may appear that an attack on two or all three bridges ensures a more lasting cutting-off of supplies to the adverse military. It is thus not prohibited to attack all three bridges, if that is necessary to obtain the pursued military advantage. Conversely, if the cutting-off of the line of supply is militarily relevant only during a certain time-span, say during the conduct of a particular military operation in the region, only the attack on bridge 3 would be warranted under the provision at stake here. Once again, all turns on a contextual assessment. Paragraph 3 certainly contains a useful criterion for the planning phase. It should not, however, be understood too strictly, but as a hint as to what is proportionate in the circumstances. A difficult situation arises if lives of civilians and the protection of objects are concurrent. What weight must be given to each of these in view of minimizing collateral damage? Is it possible to hold that life always has precedence, even if the object is a cultural object of greatest value? The Protocol contains no specification on such issues.

---

19 See also the same principle in article 6 of Protocol II (1999) to the Hague Convention on the protection of cultural property in times of armed conflict (1954).

20 The Commentary of the Protocol gives as an example the attack of a railway line, either in the railway station or in the countryside, expecting that the latter should prevail: Y. Sandoz, C. Swinarski and B. Zimmermann (eds), *Commentary on the Additional Protocols of 8 June 1977 to the Geneva Conventions of 12 August 1949*, Geneva, 1987, p. 687.

7.2.8 One example

During the NATO operation "Unified Protector" in Libya (2011), different measures of precaution were taken under article 57 of AP I:[21] an attentive choice of weapons (laser- or GPS-guided); renunciation of weapons of dubious legality, such as cluster bombs; use of light weapons in order to avoid or limit the range of the blast; use of ammunitions programmed to explode after the impact, so as to avoid damage to persons or objects external to the object hit, and so on. It also seems that some operations have been suspended or cancelled in view of getting better information or in view of sparing civilians.

7.3 Proportionality[22]

The principle of proportionality in the context of IHL is stated mainly in article 51, § 5, letter b, of AP I. That provision reads: "[An attack is indiscriminate and thus prohibited if it] may be expected to cause incidental loss of civilian life, injury to civilians, damage to civilian objects, or a combination thereof, which would be excessive in relation to the concrete and direct military advantage anticipated". Proportionality in IHL thus concerns first of all the equation between a military advantage and the civilian losses caused by pursuing the advantage. The rationale behind this rule is that a belligerent must be authorized as a matter of principle to attack a military objective. It may attack only such objectives; but, then, it must be able to do so, lest the belligerent is prohibited from attacking anything. This is the reason why only "excessive", in other words, disproportionate, civilian losses brush away the general faculty to launch an attack on a military objective. The point is not that a belligerent must insure a certain balance (positive proportionality), but that it must avoid a manifest imbalance (negative proportionality, excess). The ICRC Commentary suggests that any extensive or massive collateral civilian damage must always be considered as legally excessive.[23] This position is grounded in articles 48 and 51 of AP I. However, this idea is not accepted in State practice. If the military advantage

---

21 See G. Bartolini, "L'operazione 'Unified Protector' e la condotta delle ostilità in Libia", *Rivista di diritto internazionale*, vol. 95, 2012, pp. 1050–53.

22 On this principle, see: I. Henderson, *The Contemporary Law of Targeting*, Leiden/Boston, 2009, p. 197ff. See also: E. Cannizzaro, *Il principio della proporzionalità nell'ordinamento internazionale*, Milan, 2000, pp. 305ff.

23 Y. Sandoz, C. Swinarski and B. Zimmermann (eds), *Commentary on the Additional Protocols of 8 June 1977 to the Geneva Conventions of 12 August 1949*, Geneva, 1987, p. 626.

pursued is sufficiently important (for example, a decisive attack, allowing, in all probability, the war to be won), acceptable collateral damage may rise into the somewhat extensive. It remains true, on the other hand, that extensive damage to civilians is difficult to justify under a military advantage, especially in an era where belligerents fear to wreak great havoc in the civilian sphere. Modern war is also fought through the hearts of people and the reports of journalists. A belligerent will do everything to avoid being accused of massive civilian slaughter.

The proportionality test is grounded in a hypothesis of a future result. Nobody knows what civilian losses an attack will concretely produce. With some chance, contrary to expectations, there might be no casualty at all, or no civilian object damaged. With some misfortune, the opposite may be true, and the collateral damage turns out to be much greater than could be reasonably expected. The law does not require a belligerent to know what it could not foresee: *ad impossibile nemo tenetur*. The point is rather that there must be a reasonable assessment of what can be expected. Conversely, once the operation has been conducted, the proportionality test is not to assess the effective number of victims or damaged objects against the military advantage, but rather to compare the figures of losses which could be reasonably expected with the pursued military advantage. There is thus no *ex post facto* responsibility for the actual losses, as compared with the foreseeable ones. This aspect is sometimes forgotten. It may be added that the rule we are discussing shows how wrong the usual reflex of the journalists is, when they conclude from the death of a number of civilian persons that there is a violation of IHL. IHL may in such a case be violated; for example, if there is a direct attack on civilians, or if collateral loss of civilians is excessive with regard to the pursued military advantage. But otherwise it is not.

The most significant problem with the proportionality test is its openness. How can one compare a military advantage with civilian losses, the two sides of the balance sheet being filled with objects essentially different from one another? It would be the same comparing two different currencies without defining an exchange rate, or comparing two fruits without defining the criterion of comparison (weight, colour, and so on). The task is rendered slightly easier by the fact that the comparison is not as to equilibrium or proportion, but rather as to manifest non-equilibrium or disproportion. But the problem of the currency rate remains. It may be considered disquieting in this regard that many States have always resisted the idea of trying to codify in a stricter way the criteria which are relevant to carrying out the assessment.

The military powers manifestly wish to maintain a certain room for manoeuvre, and also to avoid potential charges of war crimes with regard to stricter criteria leaving less room for contextual arguments. At the end of the day, the assessment must be made intuitively and in good faith. It must be made in view of all the concrete information at one's disposal. This also entails that it is in most cases impossible to judge from the outside if the equation has been respected, since that would suppose having at one's disposal the relevant files and decisional information. A judge may have this information after the fact; an external observer will not possess such sensitive and undisclosed information. The decision-making here ultimately relies on good faith efforts by each belligerent. There are some norms of the law which must essentially rest and rely on such an assumption. The belligerent must make an honest effort to put into balance the interests at stake, trying not to exaggerate its own. True, this is very difficult, especially in times of armed conflict, where tempers may rise high and some excessive indulgence for one's own party may dominate the floor. But the law has no alternative. The assessment has to be made at the level of high military command, consulting legal advisors of the army; or alternatively on a ministerial level. The so-called LegAd (legal advisor) has a most prominent role to play here. The decision-making supposes, moreover, a good state of information and intelligence. The law relies in this context on external conditions which it cannot create itself.

What are the objects and persons covered by the principle? First, we may notice that there is no rule of proportionality in the sense that a military objective must be attacked with the minimum amount of force; for example, the lightest bomb possible leading to its destruction. A military objective may be attacked by a device which produces an excessive amount of kinetic energy with respect to what would be necessary to destroy that object. This choice is left to the tactical plane of the attacker. If the object is dual use, however, proportionality issues arise with regard to its civilian functions. Second, the principle covers civilian persons (article 51, § 2, of AP I) and civilian objects (article 52, § 1, of AP I). It covers all civilian objects, not only adverse objects. Are objects belonging to persons of nationality of a belligerent and those of co-belligerents therefore also covered?

Contrary to what is sometimes affirmed,[24] the proportionality rule also applies to protected persons and objects, for example, injured

---

24 I. Henderson, *The Contemporary Law of Targeting*, Leiden/Boston, 2009, pp. 206–7.

or sick military personnel in sanitary installations. If these installations are attacked after a warning, for the reason that they are being used for prohibited military purposes,[25] the attacker must assess the losses in the protected personnel, even if the equation may here be somewhat more lenient than for civilian persons. Moreover, there will almost always be some civilians in such sanitary areas as well, so that the proportionality test must in any case be undertaken. This is certainly a blind spot in the proportionality rule, which is largely under-explored. HRL might also make important contributions here, with its own principles of necessity and proportionality (unless IHL applies as derogatory *lex specialis* on these issues). What about civilian human shields? The existence of involuntary human shields does not release a belligerent from assessing proportionality.[26] Conversely, voluntary human shields could be classified as civilians directly participating in hostilities and thus not be counted in the proportionality assessment. This aspect of the question is debated. Civilian workers in factories contributing to the war effort remain civilians and are counted in the proportionality equation.

There remains the thorny question as to the extent of allowable modulations in the equation on account of the technical capabilities of the belligerents. A State like the US could avoid much collateral damage by always using precision weapons (which are, however, much more expensive). Third World States in most cases could not. This can put into jeopardy the principle of equality of belligerents and the reciprocity of obligations. However, States do not easily accept an obligation under IHL to use necessarily the most precise weapon at their disposal. They intend to keep a tactical choice. Hence, it is not possible to find a strict obligation on this account in IHL. However, under article 57 of AP I, each belligerent is required to take account of the duty to minimize civilian losses, and also to assess its tactical choices in that regard, according to what is reasonably feasible. If necessary, this choice should be able to be objectively argued in front of an arbitration tribunal or a criminal judge.

Let us now turn to an atypical example and consider how the principles contained in article 52, § 2, and article 57 of AP I can apply.

---

25 This is allowed under article 21, Geneva Convention I.
26 See article 51, § 8, AP I.

7.4 Excursus: bombardments for humanitarian reasons and article 52, § 2, of AP I

Let us assume that there is an IAC between State A and State B. In the context of that conflict, some military operations take place according to the traditional belligerent practices, consisting in the weakening of the military assets of the adverse party. However, State B also commits various war crimes and crimes against humanity. Thus, for example, State B's forces deport civilians to extermination camps, as did the German forces during World War II. Auschwitz-like camps are erected in the country. The deportation, we may assume, is performed by train. The railway lines lead directly to the camps. The question may now arise as to whether the aviation of State A may bombard these railway lines in order to disrupt or at least to slow down the deportation and extermination process. We here assume that there is no definite "military advantage" to bombing the railway lines. In other terms, these lines do not serve any other purpose than the one of deportation. They do not make any contribution to the military action of State B's armed forces. We also assume that the bombardment of the railway lines has a distinctive effect on the deportation process. Clearly it is possible to argue, in a specific context, that the forces of State B could simply revert to buses in order to transport the persons to the extermination camp, so that the bombardment of the lines would appear to be useless, or deprived of sufficient efficacy. In other words, a distinctive advantage (a "humanitarian advantage" rather than a "military advantage") could often be open to discussion and subject to doubt. However, we shall here assume that the bombardment of the lines does provide a distinctive humanitarian advantage. It may be noticed that this question is today retroactively debated in the context of events of World War II. President F. D. Roosevelt is criticized, in certain circles, for not having bombed the railway lines leading to Auschwitz, despite the information the US forces had on what was happening there.[27]

It stands to reason that according to the assumptions we made, the bombardment of the mentioned railway lines is not compatible with the conditions under article 52, § 2, of AP I. The point need not be argued at length. It is apparent that an object becomes a military objective (and may thus be targeted) only if it makes a *military* contribution

---

27 See for example, S. G. Erdheim, "Could the Allies have Bombed Auschwitz-Birkenau?", *Holocaust and Genocide Studies*, 1997, pp. 129ff; R. H. Levy, "The Bombing of Auschwitz Revisited", *Holocaust and Genocide Studies*, 1996, pp. 267ff.

and if there is a *military* advantage in destroying or neutralizing it by an attack. As is rightly stressed by the ICRC,[28] the interpretation of the military contribution and advantage should be strict: if political, economic, social or psychological advantages become relevant, the assessment becomes speculative and the objects attacked are virtually unlimited. What military forces would attack an objective without *some* advantage? A military contribution and a military advantage suppose an impact on the war-fighting capacity of the enemy. But that impact cannot be designed in general terms or obtained by indirect chains of causality: what must be hit is the war-fighting capacity by a weakening of military forces and assents. In other words, the attack bears directly on the capacity of the enemy to conduct offensive or defensive military action. If an object participated in that context and if its destruction or neutralization weakens the capacity of the enemy armed forces, it is a military objective.

In our case, the bombardment has a humanitarian purpose. It does not weaken the armed forces of the enemy; nor do the railway lines contribute to any extent to the adverse military action. Under article 52, § 2, of AP I, they do not, therefore, constitute a military objective. Hence, under modern IHL, they may not be attacked. Is that necessarily condemnable? Let us notice that article 52, § 2, provides clear and limiting criteria for targeting, and thereby assures some legal certainly and the overall containment of destructive forces. In most contexts, this restriction works with satisfactory results. That a general and abstract rule cannot fit all highly particular circumstances is evident. The acid test has to be the overall performance. If we weaken the degree of prohibition in the provision to take account of highly exceptional contexts, such as the one of "humanitarian bombardments", how much do we gain by the new flexibility, but how much do we also lose on other destructive attacks which might become arguable and possibly lawful?

Are there elements of State practice that could soften this conclusion? The question arose first in the context of the situation in Rwanda during the genocide of 1994 (there was at that time a NIAC there). There were some media (notably Radio Mille Collines) heavily inciting hatred and calling for the commission of genocidal acts

---

28 International Humanitarian Law and the Challenges of Contemporary Armed Conflicts, Doc. 03/IC/09, Report by the ICRC to the 28th International Conference of the Red Cross and Red Crescent, 2003, p. 11.

and war crimes. A similar situation arose some years later with the RTS (Serbian Radio-Television) during the Kosovo conflict of 1999 (which was an IAC). Can the media become a lawful target if it is used to instigate war crimes? The Final Report to the Prosecutor by the Committee established to review the NATO bombing campaign against the Federal Republic of Yugoslavia (13 June 2000)[29] suggests that if media is used to instigate international crimes, "then it is a legitimate target". This may be true under *jus ad bellum*, in other words, under mandates by the UNSC, calling to neutralize "by all necessary means" such a broadcasting station. Conversely, it manifestly cannot hold true under IHL, since it ignores the conditions of article 52, § 2. Moreover, the terminology of the Report is vague and quite revealing: it speaks of "legitimate" target, which places the accent on the plane of moral and political considerations, and not of a "lawful" target under *jus in bello* requirements. The impression is that the Report is not based on expertise or on a thorough analysis of IHL.

If some authors concurred with the view of the Committee,[30] many legal writings rejected this approach as incompatible with the rules of IHL.[31] A different response would suppose that article 52, § 2, is either not exhaustive (which is untrue); or that it can be derogated from by contrary agreements (but that would not allow a unilateral violation); or that it can be set aside by a mandate of the UNSC, necessity, belligerent reprisals or other norms (see below). The net result of these two precedents is that there are voices for such an enlargement of the lawful (or legitimate?) targets, but that in the literature the doubts and the negative attitude prevail. It also stands to reason that the NATO-led experts take liberal positions when the targets are situated in Rwanda and in Yugoslavia – the "other" is always the bad one, and exceptional rules against that "other" are thus acceptable. However, if the rule as proposed by these experts

---

29 See www.un.org/icty/pressreal/nato061300.htm.

30 See N. Ronzitti, "Is the Non Liquet of the Final Report by the Committee Established to Review the NATO Bombing Campaign against the Federal Republic of Yugoslavia Acceptable?", *International Review of the Red Cross*, vol. 82, 2000, pp. 1017ff.

31 See A. Laursen, "NATO, the War over Kosovo, and the ICTY Investigation", *American University International Law Review*, vol. 17, 2002, pp. 785–6; M. Sassoli and L. Cameron, "The Protection of Civilian Objects – Current State of the Law and Issues de lege ferenda", in N. Ronzitti and G. Venturini (eds), *Current Issues in the International Humanitarian Law of Air Warfare*, Utrecht, 2006, pp. 56–7, note 83; G. Bartolini, "L'operazione 'Unified Protector' e la condotta delle ostilità in Libia", *Rivista di diritto internazionale*, vol. 95, 2012, pp. 1044–5, 1048.

were accepted, it would become generally applicable. If Yugoslavian or Rwandan forces bombarded US media, during a supposed armed conflict, for making the apology of Guantanamo or inciting some aggressive war (as was Iraq in 2003), it is hardly imaginable that those experts would find the rule very commendable or indeed applicable. There are thus many reasons to remain circumspect with regard to "exceptional" reasoning, when it is hardly to be squared with the general rules of IHL.

Overall, there are currently insufficient elements in State practice in order to accept a customary evolution of the criteria of article 52, § 2, towards a more relaxed standard of targeting, notably in order to prevent or punish the commission of international crimes. A rule of universal CIL would need to be based on the assent of a significant number of States of the different regional groupings of the world. There is no evidence for such a development. It is even highly improbable that most States (especially in the Group of 77) would accept such a construction of the military objective.

What legal arguments could then be tried, in order to allow exceptionally such a "humanitarian bombardment" in Auschwitz-like situations? The following avenues may be tested.

7.4.1   Argument 1: can a "state of necessity" under article 25 of the Articles on the Responsibility of States for Internationally Wrongful Acts be raised?

As is known, article 25 of the ILC Articles on the Responsibility of States for Internationally Wrongful Acts (2001) allows the "state of necessity" as a circumstance precluding wrongfulness under general international law. The actual conduct of the State must be the "only way for the State to safeguard an essential interest against a grave and imminent peril". However, the successful invocation of a state of necessity supposes the fulfilment of a series of conditions, specified in the various paragraphs of the quoted provision. It is not necessary to dwell on the matter further here, since the argument of necessity under general international law cannot be invoked in order not to apply obligations under IHL. Indeed, the exception clause of § 2, letter a, applies: "In any case, necessity may not be invoked by a State as a ground for precluding wrongfulness if: a) the international obligation in question excludes the possibility of invoking necessity. . .". As the Commentary of the ILC rightly states, this is the case namely for IHL provisions.[32] The law of armed conflicts is already designed for a highly exceptional situation of "necessity", namely warfare. It therefore has its own concept of "military necessity"; and it is accepted in the primary law of IHL that military necessity to suspend the application of a rule of IHL can be invoked only if the concrete IHL rule makes explicit allowance for it. A plea of necessity under general international law could not therefore legally serve to displace the injunction of article 52, § 2, of AP I (or related customary law), since that provision itself contains no military necessity exception. It may perhaps be added that the circumstances precluding wrongfulness are designed to guide the law of State responsibility, in other words, to determine when a State owes reparation to another or when certain consequences (such as countermeasures) may ensue. The aim of these secondary rules is not to alter the primary bodies of law by introducing new lawful conduct by the backdoor. On all of those accounts, the argument of necessity fails in our context.

7.4.2 Argument 2: the Security Council could provide a mandate, under Chapter VII of the UN Charter, to bombard such railway lines

The argument is that the UNSC could issue a binding resolution under Chapter VII of the Charter and allow such a bombardment. This resolution would be binding (article 25 of the Charter) and take precedence over contrary conventional law (article 103 of the Charter) and over non-peremptory CIL (*lex specialis* principle). The UNSC could in this context found itself on the notion of the "responsibility to protect".[33] This legal analysis is basically sound. The targeting of the lines would here be based on a *jus ad bellum*-mandate. The UNSC may consider that in order to maintain or restore international peace, some egregious IHL violations must be stopped, even by using force. The attacks flown against the lines must then comply with the other IHL requirements, namely proportionality (article 51, § 5, letter b, of AP I) and precautions (article 57 of AP I). It stands to be stressed that this legal argument does not wrongfully confuse *jus ad bellum* and *jus in bello* issues, contrary

32 See J. Crawford, *The International Law Commission's Articles on State Responsibility*, Cambridge, 2002, p. 185.

33 On this concept, see I. Winkelmann, "Responsibility to Protect", *The Max Planck Encyclopaedia of Public International Law*, vol. VIII, Oxford, 2012, pp. 965ff, with many references. See also the contribution of a former UN under-secretary-general of legal affairs, N. Michel, "La responsabilité de protéger – Une vue d'ensemble assortie d'une perspective suisse", *Revue de droit suisse*, vol. 131, 2012, pp. 5ff.

to the well-settled principle of separation of both. Objects may have to be neutralized by military force under *jus ad bellum*-considerations, for which the UNSC is the sole master. IHL is not intended to limit the powers of the UNSC to indicate which objects must be neutralized under "maintenance or restoration of peace" considerations. In other words, article 52, § 2, is certainly exhaustive concerning IHL targeting; but it is not exhaustive in the sense that the UNSC, under its Chapter VII powers, could indicate according to that provision only military objectives for destruction or neutralization. The two sets of norms run parallel and do not limit each other. The question could be raised as to what extent this position would amount to an unlawful derogation from IHL. This body of the law is often qualified as peremptory law from which no derogation is permitted.[34] But even assuming that article 52, § 2, of AP I were a peremptory norm in dealings between States, it would not necessarily be one with regard to the competence of the UNSC. This is not as surprising as it may seem at first sight: article 2, § 4, of the UN Charter is often styled as a norm of peremptory law for States;[35] and yet it is uncontroversial that the UNSC may use force in a quite discretional way (article 42 of the UN Charter). The better view is in any case that there is no derogation at all. The two sets of provisions work each one *in ordine suo*. The UNSC does not interfere in an armed conflict between States by allowing one or the other of them to take liberties with the targeting provision applicable *in bello*. It rather has its own agenda and asks for the destruction of an object under the "maintenance and restoration of peace" logic. *Jus ad bellum* and *jus in bello* therefore remain perfectly separated, each one pursuing its own aims.

7.4.3   Argument 3: HRL and responsibility to protect without the Security Council; article 1 of the Geneva Conventions of 1949?

An attempt could be made to read some other norms of international law as allowing action which article 52, § 2, of AP I would otherwise prohibit. A first potential argument is that HRL may carry an obligation to act. The argument would rest, for example, on the positive duties a State incurs under the "right to life" guarantee, enshrined in all the relevant human rights instruments as one, if not the most

---

34 E. David has argued in this sense in the first editions of his monograph on IHL; cf. for example, E. David, *Principes de droit des conflits armés*, 2nd edn, Brussels, 1999, pp. 86ff.

35 See the precise argument in O. Corten, *Le droit contre la guerre*, Paris, 2008, pp. 295ff.

basic, right.[36] A second potential argument would be to use the already mentioned concept of the "responsibility to protect" in order to postulate some duty of action, even aloof from a Security Council authorization. A third potential avenue would be to rely on common article 1 of the Geneva Conventions I–IV. This provision stipulates that the "High Contracting Parties undertake to respect and ensure respect for the present Convention in all circumstances".[37] However, none of these arguments is solid from the legal point of view. The first two rights mentioned may imply positive obligations, but not obligations which would violate the non-use of force rule under article 2, § 4 of the UN Charter or IHL provisions. It would be hard indeed to claim that the right to life under HRL is *lex specialis* with regard to the relevant IHL provisions for the protection of life during warfare, when the ICJ has emphasized exactly the opposite.[38] As to article 1 of the Geneva Conventions I–IV, it stands to reason that the aim of this article is to prevent a belligerent selectively putting to rest an applicable provision of the body of IHL. The aim of the provision is to strengthen the application of IHL, not to be taken as a basis for circumventing other provisions of IHL. It is thus legally impossible to justify the bombardment of the railway lines on such bases. There being a clear prohibition to attack – under IHL – other objects than military objectives, there is also no room for a balancing process, for example, as to the relative importance of the prevention of international crimes and the sacrifice of the targeting provision under article 52, § 2.

7.4.4   Argument 4: subsequent practice modifying article 52, § 2, of AP I?

A belligerent might try to argue for some elements of State practice showing a customary law modification of article 52, § 2, of AP I. A treaty can indeed be modified by concordant subsequent practice of the treaty parties. However, the threshold for admitting such a modification binding all parties to a convention (or all States under CIL) is quite high. There must be a significant practice and a shared *opinio juris* (in principle of all the parties to the convention, or at

---

36 D. Korff, *Le droit à la vie – une guide sur la mise en oeuvre de l'article 2 de la Convention européenne des droits de l'homme*, Strasbourg, 2007.

37 For a thorough analysis, see A. Frutig, *Die Pflicht von Drittsaaten zur Durchsetzung des humanitären Völkerrechts nach Art. 1 der Genfer Konventionen von 1949*, Basel, 2009.

38 *Nuclear Weapons* advisory opinion, ICJ, *Reports*, 1996-I, pp. 240, § 25.

least almost all), expressed either by doing or by not opposing the new practice. In view of the Rwandan and Kosovo precedents discussed above, it would be completely adventurous to claim that such a modification of article 52, § 2, has taken place. Thus, subsequent practice may modify that provision in the future, but for the time being a modification on the lines of an allowance for "humanitarian bombardments" has not taken place.

7.4.5   Argument 5: countermeasures (armed reprisals) *in bello?*

It might be attempted to argue that the deportations and exterminations are a "grave breach" of IHL and that therefore an armed reprisal *in bello* is allowable. There are a series of conditions before the belligerent reprisal can be taken,[39] such as a prior warning, a decision at the highest command/government level, respect for necessity and proportionality, means of last resort, and so on. But these conditions could be fulfilled. It is not impossible to satisfy them in the context of our railway lines bombardment. Article 52, § 2, of AP I does not belong to the provisions which cannot be set aside under the law of reprisals. This is true at least as long as protected persons are not attacked.[40] As has been said, in our case only the railway line is attacked. The difficulty flowing from the fact that the initial violation of the law does not relate to the legal rights of the State bombarding the railway lines can possibly be overcome if the violation, because of its object and its gravity, is seen as a violation of *erga omnes* rights.[41] It would then also be a violation of the rights of the attacking State, amongst all the other States. A forcible answer would be possible here because the non-use of force rule does not apply *in bello* between the belligerents. Thus, the fact that the reprisals are "armed" would not pose any particular problem here. It is true that in peacetime, armed reprisals are prohibited under article 2, § 4, of the UN Charter. However, in times of armed conflict, there is already a basic licence to use force. The armed reprisals fit into this general legal scheme, which they do not subvert. There remains, however, the unpalatable fact that belligerent reprisals are meant to set aside rules of IHL and that they have a dark historical record. Taking liberties with IHL rules under reprisals law is opening

---

39 See J. M. Henckaerts and L. Doswald-Beck, *Customary International Humanitarian Law*, vol. I, Cambridge, 2005, pp. 513ff.

40 See article 51, § 6, AP I.

41 Article 48 of the ILC Articles on the Responsibility of States for Internationally Wrongful Acts (2001).

the gates to dangerous precedents and to a constant spiralling down. In World War I, the whole law of maritime warfare collapsed under the weight of reprisals and counter-reprisals.[42] This is not to say that the argument could not be tried in the extreme circumstances we are envisaging here. But it is fraught with its own dangers of multiple "loaded guns", and must be at least mistrusted from that point of view. One knows where one starts; one never knows where one ends.

7.4.6   Argument 6: a teleological expansion of article 52, § 2, of AP I?

Another potential argument runs as follows. The object and purpose of article 52, § 2, of AP I is to protect the target State, its civil society and the civilians from excessive belligerent destruction. However, in the present case, the normative injunction of article 52, § 2, has the opposite effect. It heavily harms civilians, who are deported and massacred. Hence, in order to realize the main aim of the provision, which is protective of civilians, the limitation could be dropped in our specific context. This teleological argument has sometimes been applied for setting aside contextually inequitable IHL provisions. The most famous example is the transfer of prisoners of war aboard ships in the Falkland/ Malvinas war of 1982. The ships were the safest and warmest place to hold these prisoners in the circumstances occurring at the time. But article 22 of Geneva Convention III prohibits the transfer of prisoners of war on ships.[43] This provision was finally set aside under a teleological argument (effective maximum protection), with the agreement of the ICRC.[44] The dangers and difficulties of such an argument are quite clear: under the guise of interpretation, a provision is to some extent "refashioned". It may not always be as obvious as it was in the Falkland/ Malvinas case what is the more protective regime for the concerned persons and what is thus compatible with the gist of articles 6/6/6/7 and 7/7/7/8 of the Geneva Conventions I–IV (no diminution of the rights of protected persons by special agreements among the belligerents; no renunciation of protections by the protected persons themselves). However, *in extremis*, even such an argument – problematic

---

42 E. G. Trimble, "Possible Restatement of the Law Governing the Conduct of War at Sea", *Proceedings of the ASIL*, 1930, pp. 119ff. See also J. A. Hall, *The Law of Naval Warfare*, 2nd edn, London, 1921.

43 The reason is that ships are considered less safe places than land locations. Moreover, in the past, since the Napoleonic Wars, prisoners transferred on ships disappeared.

44 F. Bugnion, *Le Comité international de la Croix-Rouge et la protection des victimes de la guerre*, Geneva, 1994, p. 754.

as it is – could be tried. The danger is to damage the whole system of IHL by taking liberties in single situations. A very careful and cautious assessment has therefore to take place.

7.4.7   Argument 7: a violation of article 52, § 2, to be accepted?

Respect for the law is essential if a complex society is called to function and to prosper. But respect of the law is not an absolute duty. There are highly exceptional circumstances when the putting aside of a legal injunction may be necessary or legitimate. The legal philosophers discuss this issue in the loaded context of radically unjust laws. However, the question has a more general reach. It stands to reason that if I find an injured person, I would be entitled to rush to hospital by car (if I had learned to drive, indeed) without respecting the traffic limitation signs. This remains true notwithstanding the fact that a plea of necessity was or was not available to me, since I would probably not even think of this issue in the situation. In such cases, a subject has to make a careful assessment and take a position which might carry moral risk. The other members of society may then accept the highly exceptional conduct breaching the law. They may condone it in the circumstances; for example, by not attaching to it the consequences of unlawful behaviour. However, the other members of society might not share the arguments of the actor and condemn its conduct as being illegal. Such a choice of conduct under moral risk should be made only in the most highly exceptional circumstances of life, lest the legal order becomes a sort of pick and choose option. At the end of the day, in our example of deportation and mass destruction, such a highly exceptional situation might occur. A general and abstract rule is workable in the greatest amount of factual situations. But it cannot perform equitably in every single and perhaps highly atypical set of circumstances. The general prohibition must continue to stand, since it is convenient for the bulk of real circumstances. An exceptional liberty under moral risk can be attempted in the most extreme fringes of circumstances – but to remain "just", such behaviour has to test itself against the strictest standards, and to check in particular any self-serving or self-righteous deviations.

Each legal rule of some clarity has its own blind spot in which it does not operate satisfactorily. The question as to what to do in such situations is as old as the law itself and quite difficult to solve. In our present context, it is certainly better to keep the restrictive rule under article 52, § 2, and to exclude "humanitarian" or "criminal-prevention" bombardments. The gaps opened by an exception would be more harmful than the good concurrently gained. As we have seen, there are, however, two ways by which the problem can be pragmatically approached, without damaging the system too heavily.

First, there may be a mandate of the UNSC under *jus ad bellum*, in other words, Chapter VII of the UN Charter. The Security Council could ask willing member States, carrying out an operation under its mandate, to take all necessary measures to stop a broadcasting station or a deportation, including by using force. Second, failing such a Security Council mandate, a State could weigh up the stakes and decide to give prevalence to a moral duty over the legal one. It will then violate article 52, § 2, of AP I. At the same time, it might state the precise reasons and dilemmas it faced. Confronted with such a concrete situation and its related discourse, the rest of the community of States will have to take a position. Either they condone the violation, finding that the circumstances of the individual case warranted such a course. Or they condemn the violation, finding that the arguments put forward in its defence were not convincing in the circumstances.

8 Implementation of international humanitarian law: the Achilles heel of the system

8.1 General features of the implementation system

The system of implementation of IHL[1] has three main characteristics, which in turn produce one main result.

First, the system is based on voluntary and normative means of implementation. Hence, spontaneous compliance plays a greater role than external control and sanctions. The term "voluntary" connotes the idea that the belligerent is in most cases largely responsible for the implementation of the law itself. The means of implementation are based on the concept that some goodwill and cooperation by the single belligerent is needed in order for them to work. The term "normative" signifies that most means of implementation are based on the statement of a duty in some primary or secondary rule of IHL. Conversely, there are few actions of fact which could be imposed if the legal duties are breached. Both elements, the voluntary and the normative, converge in the concept of a consensual law on implementation. The system is subjective rather than objective. It largely depends on will rather than on coercion; it is self-centred rather than other-centred, in other words, autonomous rather than heteronomous.

Second, there is only a very feeble degree of direct sanction of IHL. Most means of sanctioning the breach of IHL rules are indirect. Thus, there is no institution which would have as a mission to control and enforce IHL rules. The ICRC displays such a function of control, and it is the sole international body specialized therein. But its functioning is particular, in the sense that it works under the guise of a quite strict confidentiality. Conversely, there is no IHL court, no IHL High Commissioner, no IHL Commission on the model of the human

---

1 On this system, see the literature indicated in M. Sassòli, A. Bouvier and A. Quintin, *How Does Law Protect in War?*, vol. I, 3rd edn, Geneva, 2011, pp. 353ff, in the various contexts.

rights bodies. The result of this state of affairs is that IHL is most often enforced indirectly, if at all. It will be enforced through human rights courts and international criminal courts. But the enforcement is here not strictly speaking one of IHL. It is enforcement of human rights or of international criminal law, whose autonomy is not interrupted by their relationships with IHL. IHL can here serve only as inspiration for interpretation of some provisions. Take as an example criminal international law. It is based on criminal offences. War crimes differ to some extent from the corresponding IHL provisions, if only on account of the whole *mens rea* side (irrelevant in IHL), and sometimes also on account of the fact that provisions are more tightly formulated in criminal law in order to satisfy the particularly strict requirements of that branch of the law with regard to legal certainty (*Bestimmtheitsgrundsatz*).

Third, there is very little judicial implementation of IHL. There are some rare cases or series of cases on the issue, such as the *Nicaragua* case (1986)[2] and the *Armed Activities* case (2005)[3] of the ICJ, or the Eritrea/Ethiopia arbitrations by a Claims Commission of the PCA.[4] The consequence of this "judicial absence" is that the whole implementation issue remains ordinarily embedded in political processes of reprisals, negotiation and agreement. Problems are settled mostly not through the application of existing law, but through bilateral agreements or dealings creating new law *inter partes*.

The net result of these common features is that the means of implementation of IHL remain characterized by a distinctive weakness. This is the reason why the ICRC and many States have put the issue on the agenda and are currently looking for ways to strengthen this branch of IHL.

The general vision of implementation of IHL is negative. Most people do not believe that IHL is respected at all. Newspapers report only the violations; and the actors always complain of violations, since that suits their war propaganda. In reality, most violations occur in NIAC, where one belligerent is qualified as a "criminal" by the other, and where the principle of equality of belligerents has little room. In NIAC, the humanitarian aspiration has always had precedence over the realistic

---

2 ICJ, *Reports*, 1986, pp. 14ff.

3 ICJ, *Reports*, 2005, pp. 168ff.

4 *RIAA*, vol. 26.

assessment of the record of compliance. But after all, if IHL in NIAC allows some persons to be saved from death and torture, it may already be worth the effort. In IAC, the record is much better. Modern armies have huge staffs of legal advisors. The fear of criminal prosecution has added a pull for respect. The problems arise mainly in contexts of ideological hatred (for example, Iran/Iraq, 1981–1988) or where there is a lack of resources (for example, Eritrea/Ethiopia).

The necessity to implement IHL has come into the limelight only progressively. In 1864, at the time of the first Geneva Convention, the optimistic outlook prevailed that a State having ratified a certain convention would obviously do the necessary to implement it. The Franco–Prussian War of 1870–1871, if only with the thorny *franc tireurs* issue,[5] showed that this view was too simplistic and that some new rules for implementation had to be devised. However, the growth of that branch of IHL has always been slow and belated. It is not easy to provide means of sanction in a social context where there is violence.

The implementation of IHL turns around three legal categories: prevention, control and suppression. We may discuss these categories in that order.

8.2 Prevention

Preventive duties exist on many planes, and are really of the essence. The majority of violations of IHL rules occur not because of bad will, but because of lack of information, training and resources. Thus, the preventive stage can help a great deal in improving the situation on the spot. There are many preventive duties. Some examples include:

- the duty to disseminate IHL[6] to the circles that have to have some knowledge of it, mainly the army, but to some extent also civilians at large;
- the duty to train the armed forces adequately;[7]
- the provision of translations of the texts of the applicable conventions into the local language(s);

---

5 See for example, C. Calvo, *Le droit international théorique et pratique*, vol. IV, 5th edn, Paris, 1896, pp. 131ff; J. S. Risley, *The Law of War*, London, 1897, pp. 110–11.
6 Articles 47/48/127/144 of the Geneva Conventions I–IV.
7 *Ibid.*

- the passing of implementing legislation, where necessary (for example, in dualist countries like the United Kingdom);
- the adoption of criminal offences in the criminal code or in some other legislation for the enforcement of IHL violations, the protection of emblems, and so on;
- the marking of the protected objects, for example, cultural property. Charts with the location of that property have to be prepared and the protective emblem to be disposed in a way so as to be ready in case of conflict;
- the hiring of legal advisors for the army, essential, for example, for the assessment of targeting issues;
- the consultation of National IHL (or Red Cross) Committees, with advisory functions;
- there are also more idiosyncratic ways of insuring preventive aims: for example, the passing on the radio of popular series, where famous singers tell stories in which there is some IHL education. This was done in Somalia under the aegis of the ICRC.

In most cases, the ICRC will be the main actor trying to carry forward the necessary activities. It will insist that a State adopts an implementing legislation; prepare model implementing legislation for facilitating the task; disseminate the law as far as it can in NIAC, and so on. It is hardly possible to over-estimate the practical importance of preventive measures. These may not be visible, as are the suppressive ones, but have a much greater impact for the proper working of IHL than the latter, which by definition are always "belated".

8.3   Control

There are three main aspects of control: protecting powers, the ICRC and fact-finding. It can immediately be stated that this remains the feeblest branch in the implementation system. Moreover, some means apply only to IHL in IAC, and not to IHL in NIAC. This is the case of the protecting power.

8.3.1   Protecting powers

The first mechanism is that of *protecting powers*. The protecting power is a neutral State or a State not party to an IAC, which is nominated in order to safeguard the interests of one or more States parties to that armed conflict when direct diplomatic relations are severed, in order to contribute to the control of implementation and respect for the applicable IHL.[8] This system has worked only five times since 1949 and has fallen into disuse since the Falkland/Malvinas War (1982).[9] Protecting powers have in most cases not been nominated. There are many reasons for this state of affairs. First, it has been proven difficult to find States considered to be sufficiently neutral and acceptable to the belligerents, in a world dominated by grave ideological dissonance and dissention. Second, few States were ready to accept the task, since it is expensive, constitutes a heavy burden and risks tainting the relations with the belligerent against which the function is exercised. This is not a glorious perspective for a neutral State. Thus, in most cases, there has been a substitute to the protecting power, which has ultimately been the ICRC.[10] The ICRC exercises in union the functions of a *de facto* protecting power and its own functions of control in the context of implementation of IHL. Moreover, the ICRC exercises as a third basis of power its right of humanitarian initiative, proposing its services to the parties subject to their consent.[11]

8.3.2   The ICRC

This leads naturally to the second limb of activities, the ones of the *ICRC*.[12] The ICRC does a host of things: visits to the prisoners, establishment of family links, organization of humanitarian aid, organization of repatriations, and so on. Let us look to these activities in slightly greater detail. Not all of these activities are geared exclusively towards the control of implementation. Many activities are directly protective.

First, the ICRC aims at protecting civilians. Civilians often endure horrific ordeals in today's conflicts: they serve as direct targets, they face massacres, hostage-taking, sexual violence, harassment, expulsion and forced transfer, looting, denial of access to water, food and health care, terror practices, and so on. Persons displaced because of the conflict need a particular assistance. They often end up as refugees or internally displaced persons (IDP). As part of the civilian population the IDPs are protected under Geneva Convention IV. They benefit from

---

8 Articles 8/8/8/9 of the Geneva Conventions I–IV.

9 F. Bugnion, *Le Comité international de la Croix-Rouge et la protection des victimes de la guerre*, Geneva, 1994, pp. 1008ff.

10 See articles 10/10/10/11 of the Geneva Conventions I–IV.

11 Article 3 (common) and articles 9/9/9/10 of the Geneva Conventions I–IV.

12 M. Sassoli, A. Bouvier and A. Quintin, *How Does Law Protect in War?*, vol. I, 3rd edn, Geneva, 2011, pp. 481ff.

ICRC protection and assistance programmes. For the refugees, the primary responsibility rests with the Office of the United Nations High Commissioner of Refugees. The ICRC here also controls the application of the duties of belligerents towards civilians, mainly under Geneva Convention IV.

Another important branch of ICRC activities relates to the *protection of detainees*. In IACs, the Geneva Conventions recognize the right of ICRC delegates to visit prisoners of war and civilians deprived of their liberty, including civilian internees. In NIAC, the ICRC may just offer its services to visit the detainees. States are not obliged to accept such visits, but they often accept in practice. Through these visits, the ICRC aims to:

- control the proper application of the Geneva Conventions and prevent, by repeated presence, tendencies towards violations of these texts;
- prevent or put an end to disappearances and summary executions;
- restore family links where they have been disrupted and inform the families on the current state of their members in foreign captivity;
- improve conditions of detention when necessary by making proposals to the detaining power.

A further important task of the ICRC is to *restore family links*. The ICRC's Central Tracing Agency works to establish family links in situations of armed conflict. In such situations, thousands of persons are missing because of flight, displacement, captivity, and so on. Individual inquiries are opened. The persons traced are given the opportunity to send and to receive Red Cross messages, being thus put in contact with their families. In IACs, the ICRC's Central Tracing Agency fulfils the task assigned to it under IHL of gathering, processing and passing on information on protected persons, notably prisoners of war and civilian internees. For detainees and their families receiving news of their loved ones is always of huge importance. Sometimes it is necessary to issue a travel document in order to allow a person to be repatriated or to leave for a third country (for example, a neutral state where he will be interned). Such documents have been issued by the ICRC and recognized by States.

In all these tasks, issues of control and of implementation of IHL mix with the broader category of humanitarian action.

8.3.3   Fact-finding

Finally, the Geneva Conventions provide for a system of *fact-finding* or inquiry.[13] The rationale behind this institution is that in armed conflict the truth is the first casualty. There is a significant potential for breaches of the law, retaliation and escalation if allegations of atrocities or breaches of the law are not investigated and if no light is brought on the matter. Investigation, it was thought, might diminish mistrust and alleviate hatred. This system of inquiry has again not worked as was hoped for. There are several reasons for the failure. First, the belligerents use the untruth as a means of propaganda. They are interested in pitching their troops and followers against the adversary by wholesale exaggerations. Since an inquiry supposes the consent of the concerned belligerent, it is understandable that they refrain from giving it. Second, an inquiry is a sensitive intrusion into domestic affairs. Some international fact-finders will come into the territory and "put their nose" in the sensitive affairs of a State. This is already difficult to accept in peacetime, but is all the more unacceptable to a belligerent in the highly sensitive situation of warfare, where it struggles for survival. Third, the fact-finder is not designed in the Geneva Conventions, so that an agreement remains necessary on the person, the procedure, and so on. Such an agreement is difficult to obtain from parties who are in armed conflict. This last disadvantage has been eliminated by the Fact-Finding Commission under article 90 of AP I,[14] but the first two reasons for State's mistrust against inquiry explain why the AP I Commission has not been seized for a single inquiry up to this date. Fourth, since there now exist various international criminal courts, belligerents will often resist any inquiry even more strenuously, since they may feel that the finding of facts is the first step before seizing the ICC or some other criminal court.[15] This is not to say that no inquiries will ever take place. The point is only that inquiries will be situated outside the system of IHL. Thus, the UNSC has established fact-finding missions since the time of the Greek Civil War (1946–1949) to the

---

13 Articles 52/53/132/149 of the Geneva Conventions I–IV. On the system of inquiry, see for example, S. Vité, *Les procédures internationales d'établissement des faits dans la mise en oeuvre du droit international humanitaire*, Brussels, 1999.

14 On this Commission, see the literature indicated in M. Sassoli, A. Bouvier and A. Quintin, *How Does Law Protect in War?*, vol. I, 3rd edn, Geneva, 2011, p. 389.

15 M. Sassoli and J. Grignon, "Les limites du droit international pénal et de la justice pénale international dans la mise en œuvre du droit international humanitaire", in A. Biad and P. Tavernier (eds), *Le droit international humanitaire face aux défis du XXe siècle*, Brussels, 2012, pp. 141–3.

famous Darfur Commission in 2005. The UN Human Rights Council does the same; for example, in the flotilla affair near the coast of Gaza (2008). As of now there is no patented means by which it would be possible to insufflate new life into the limb of IHL fact-finding.

8.4   Suppression

Suppression comes after the fact. It seeks to secure reparation for the tort inflicted and sanctions on the persons who have committed violations.

First, there is a distinction to make between simple violations of IHL and grave violations of IHL (war crimes). The sanctions are not the same. The slight delay in filling out the capture card under article 70 of Geneva Convention III will not lead to any sanction at all in most cases (or only to some administrative sanction). Conversely, the killing of prisoners of war will constitute a war crime and a "grave breach" under the Geneva Conventions system.[16]

Second, the judicial sanctions, if any, will not necessarily be criminal, in other words, directed against a natural person. They can also be placed under the limb of State responsibility, be it at the ICJ or in some arbitration. The two types of judicial procedures remain neatly separated: the first concerns individuals and their criminal responsibility, the second concerns States and their "civil" responsibility.

Third, on the criminal plane, there is first of all national suppression under the recognized headings of jurisdiction (territoriality, personality, universal jurisdiction if applicable). The complexion of such prosecutions depends on municipal law. In Switzerland, there are currently 14 prosecutions, mostly based on universal jurisdiction, against persons accused of having committed, among other international crimes, war crimes, mainly in NIAC. Such prosecution by States has not been frequent. However, it now becomes of more common use. There are also the international criminal tribunals, such as the ICTY, the ICTR, the Special Court for Sierra Leone, or the ICC. These tribunals have a conspicuous jurisdiction over war crimes. They have developed a dense case-law, whose main shortcoming is that it is limited to some specific

---

16 For the grave breaches, see articles 50/51/130/147 of the Geneva Conventions I–IV.

armed conflict: Yugoslavia, Rwanda, Sierra Leone, and so on. The ICC is the only "universal" international criminal court, but universality is limited by the ratification mechanism and the law on the seizing of the Court. The ICTY has notably established the notion that war crimes can also be committed in NIAC. This was, to a large extent, a novelty in 1995.[17] The bulk of the cases, however, are handled at a national level. In that sense, international criminal justice can only be subsidiary even if some tribunals, like the ICTY, have a power of *evocando* (in other words, they have a primary jurisdiction). There is no personal or functional immunity at the international criminal tribunals created by the UNSC, and there is no such immunity for the States parties to the ICC.[18]

Fourth, on the level of State responsibility, there may be suits brought by one State against another on issues of IHL. We have already mentioned the *Nicaragua* and *Armed Activities* cases at the ICJ and the Eritrea/Ethiopia arbitrations. There were further cases, such as the *Pakistani Prisoners of War* case[19] at the ICJ (concerning repatriation of prisoners of war) or the *Wall* opinion of 2004,[20] both at the ICJ. Civil complaints by individuals for reparation of losses flowing from war crimes or other breaches of IHL are possible at international human rights courts, like the ECtHR, or in front of international tribunals such as the ICJ by the device of diplomatic protection (in other words, a State has to espouse the claim of the individual possessing its nationality and bring it in its name to the international court). Individuals cannot successfully channel such cases through municipal courts, since the foreign State will enjoy sovereign immunity (unless there is waiver of immunity by treaty or *ad hoc*).[21] Conversely, there are sometimes international schemes for the individual reparation of damages due to violations of IHL, such as the UN Compensation Commission for Iraq following the Gulf War of 1991 (created by Resolution 692, 1991).[22]

Fifth, there can be action under the lead of the UNSC. The UNSC takes regular action for the sanction of IHL. The establishment of the ICTY and the ICTR may be seen as conspicuous examples in that

---

17 See the *Tadic* case (Appeals Chamber, 1995), §§ 89, 96ff, 128ff.

18 Under article 27 of the ICC Statute (1998).

19 ICJ, *Reports*, 1973, pp. 328ff, the case being then discontinued, *ibid.*, pp. 347–8.

20 ICJ, *Reports*, 2004-I, pp. 136ff, a non-binding opinion.

21 *Jurisdictional Immunities* case (*Germany v. Italy*), ICJ, *Reports*, 2012.

22 On this Commission, which handled millions of claims see for example, R. B. Lillich (ed.), *The United Nations Compensation Commission*, New York, 1995.

direction. The UNSC also passes many non-binding resolutions concerned with the protection of war victims.[23] In this context, article 89
of AP I must be recalled. It reads: "In situations of serious violations
of the Conventions or of this Protocol, the High Contracting Parties
undertake to act jointly or individually, in co-operation with the United
Nations and in conformity with the United Nations Charter". The provision is far from clearly worded. But it may be noticed that the UNSC
has undertaken a series of fact-finding missions and/or of sanctions in
situations involving armed conflict; in recent times, we may recall Iraq
(1991), Somalia (1992), former Yugoslavia (1991–1995), East Timor
(1999), Kosovo (1999), Afghanistan (2000–2002), Sierra Leone (2003),
Liberia (2003), Haiti (2004), Sudan (2005), and so on.[24] The many resolutions where the Security Council deals with issues of protection of
civilians (or certain groups of civilians, women, children, and so on);
the establishment of criminal tribunals under Chapter VII of the UN
Charter or by agreement with the concerned State; and further action
must be seen in the light of article 89 of AP I.

Overall, there is thus a wide array of possible suppressive actions,
which must, however, be effectively exercised. Most often, it is not
legal obstacles but the lack of political will which accounts for the
insufficient use of suppressive techniques.

8.5 Possible reforms

The point is not at this juncture to canvass all possible blueprints for
a reform and a strengthening of IHL implementation. The possibilities
are too many to be discussed here. Nor are they all promising or even
realistic. There is a natural limit to what can be achieved when one
comes to the "vanishing point" of the law,[25] as IHL has been called with
some grudging humour. The environment of IHL is that social order
has to some extent crumbled and fighting has taken its place. If it is
certainly untrue that "necessity knows of no laws" (*inter armas silent
leges*, as said the poet), the effective devices of enforcement, rare and
stony already under the international law of peace because of State

---

23 G. Gaggioli and R. Kolb, "Le Conseil de sécurité face à la protection des civils dans les
conflits armés", in W. Kälin, R. Kolb, C. Spenlé and M. D. Voyame (eds), *International Law,
Conflict and Development, Essays in Honour of M. Voyame*, Leiden/Boston, 2010, pp. 49ff.

24 See D. Fleck (ed.), *The Handbook of International Humanitarian Law*, Oxford, 2008, p. 713.

25 In the famous terms of H. Lauterpacht, "The Problem of the Revision of the Law of War",
BYIL, vol. 29, 1952/1953, p. 382.

sovereignty, are here even more arduous. But there is at least one proposal for reform and development which should be keenly considered
and which is currently under discussion. The gist of it is to establish a
regular, and as strong as possible, "Conference of the Members States
to the Geneva Conventions". This Conference would convene regularly
(much more than it does today), and have as a regular item of discussion issues of implementation of IHL. A system of State reports on
IHL implementation, as is known and practised in the HRL system,
could then be introduced, putting into focus issues of implementation
and control, and ensuring that States develop the necessary sensitiv-
ity for these matters. If such a regular scrutiny takes place, States will
pay more attention to the matter; at least those with some degree of
goodwill may receive a positive stimulus for identifying problems as
well as for improvements and solutions. Moreover, this Conference
would also be the centralized basis for discussing how to improve the
different mechanisms of implementation; for example, the question
of inquiry. An idea which has been ventilated in that area is to confer
upon the Fact-Finding Commission under article 90 of AP I further
powers, stemming from other legal instruments than AP I. Legally, this
would pose no problem, since the Commission is not bound to apply
only the provisions of article 90 of AP I, under which it was established.
Every international organization or organ can assume further powers,
if these powers are not incompatible with its constitutive instrument.
Thus, in 1950 UNGA could lawfully agree to arbitrate on the fate of the
territory of Eritrea, under an agreement of the Allies of World War II
conferring on it that power (which it exercised).[26]

As can be seen, there are promising avenues for a betterment of the
unhappy situation in which the law of implementation of IHL finds
itself today. Certainly, there is no reason to be overly optimistic, but the
establishment of a body with centralized, institutional, public and precise control powers in the area of implementation would fill a great gap
in IHL – relieving its Achilles heel from a sort of chronic inflammation.

---

26 See V. Coussirat-Coustère and P. M. Eisemann, *Repertory of International Arbitral
Jurisprudence*, vol. III/1, Dordrecht/Boston/London, 1991, pp. 196–9.

9 Conclusion: the challenges ahead

The time has come to conclude this short journey into the lands of IHL. It ventured, at once, into some aspects of general interest and hopefully also opened some less-known perspectives. At this ultimate juncture, the question may be asked what great issues remain ahead of this branch of the law, as far as is foreseeable? The following points may be made:

1. There will remain the question of asymmetric warfare (now the "War on Terror") and its impact on the applicability of IHL rules, as well as on reciprocity. Question of status of the belligerents may also surface, as too will the question of the geographical scope of the battlefield.

2. In the area of belligerent occupation, there will be problems with regard to prolonged occupation, transformational occupation and occupation *longa manu* through proxies.

3. Private contractors will continue to feature importantly, raising problems of regulation and of distinction (combatants/civilians).

4. Weapons law will raise questions, not only regarding the atomic bomb, on which progress has been awaited a long time. There is also the problem of different conceptions between the continental Europeans and the Anglo-Saxons in this area of the law, the latter often being significantly more permissive.

5. NIAC will continue to puzzle, with the question as to what rules apply to it under CIL and what is the true state of its gaps. Conversely, it is hardly imaginable that much progress will be made for offering some status of "combatants" to the non-State fighters and to increase the scope of the principle of equality of belligerents.

6. There will be significant questions relating to the relationship between IHL and HRL. The issue is relevant to many areas and rights. There remain many doubts as to the fine-tuning between both branches of the law. Derogatory *lex specialis*? Parallel application? One law complement to the other? Such issues have to be

canvassed for every single area and possibly every single right.

7. New areas of IHL will render necessary some effort of adaptation of the traditional rules and put into operation the principles of IHL. This is now the case, for example, in the context of cyber warfare.

8. Lastly, there remains the great and troublesome issue of implementation and sanction of IHL. Implementation is often rendered difficult by lack of adequate means, training, resources, knowledge, and in other cases by bad will. The responses of IHL to this day are not fully adequate for ensuring an honourable degree of execution of the rules, even if IHL may not be truly the vanishing point of international law – or at least not the only one!

If some progress is to be made, we must probably hope and act for more than we can ultimately get; however, this action must be grounded in solid craftsmanship, devoid of any illusion or empty pathos, if it is to be taken seriously at all. That is not a dilemma. It is an ultimate expression of the genius of IHL, constantly balanced between humanitarian aspirations and military sobriety.

Select bibliography

This bibliography is limited to some important general tools for deepening the knowledge on IHL. Further bibliographical indications can be found in the quoted monographs, for example, in the Sassoli/Bouvier/Quintin Digest.

Documents

Schindler, D. and J. Toman (eds), *Droit des conflits armés: recueil des conventions, résolutions et autres documents*, 4th edn, Geneva: ICRC/Institut Henri Dunant, 1996.

Schindler, D. and J. Toman (eds), *The Laws of Armed Conflicts: A Collection of Conventions, Resolutions and Other Documents*, 4th edn, Dordrecht: Martinus Nijhoff, 2004.

Digests

Sassoli, M., A. Bouvier and A. Quintin, *How Does Law Protect in War? Cases, Documents and Teaching Materials on Contemporary Practice in International Humanitarian Law*, 3rd edn, Geneva: ICRC, 2011.

Sassoli, M., A. Bouvier and A. Quintin, *Un droit dans la guerre?: vol. 1: Présentation du droit international humanitaire; vols. 2–3: Cas et documents*, Geneva: ICRC, 2012.

Commentaries

Bothe, M., K. J. Partsch and W. A. Solf, *New Rules for Victims of Armed Conflicts*, The Hague/Boston/London: Martinus Nijhoff, 1982.

Henckaerts, J.-M. and L. Doswald-Beck (eds), *Customary International Humanitarian Law* (ICRC): *vol. 1: Rules; vols. II and III: Practice*, Cambridge: Cambridge University Press, 2005 (updates on the site of the ICRC).

Pictet, J. (ed.), *Commentary I, Geneva Convention for the Amelioration of the Condition of the Wounded and Sick in Armed Forces in the Field*, Geneva: ICRC, 1952.

Pictet, J. (ed.), *Commentary II, Geneva Convention for the Amelioration of the Condition of Wounded, Sick and Shipwrecked Members of Armed Forces at Sea*, Geneva: ICRC, 1960.

Pictet, J. (ed.), *Commentary III, Geneva Convention relative to the Treatment of Prisoners of War*, Geneva: ICRC, 1960.

Pictet, J. (ed.), *Commentary IV, Geneva Convention relative to the Protection of Civilian Persons in Time of War*, Geneva: ICRC, 1958.

Sandoz, Y., C. Swinarski and B. Zimmermann (eds), *Commentary on the Additional Protocols of 8 June 1977 to the Geneva Conventions of 12 August 1949*, Geneva: ICRC/ Martinus Nijhoff, 1987.

Manuals

Bouchet-Saulnier, F., *The Practical Guide to Humanitarian Law*, 2nd edn, Lanham, MD: Rowman & Littlefield, 2007.

Corn, G., V. Hansen, R.B. Jackson, C. Jenks, E. Talbot Jensen and J. A. Schoettler (eds), *The Law of Armed Conflict: An Operational Approach*, New York: Wolters Kluwer Law and Business, 2012.

Crowe, J. and K. Weston-Scheuber, *Principles of International Humanitarian Law*, Cheltenham, UK and Northampton, MA, USA: Edward Elgar, 2013.

David, E., *Principes de droit des conflits armés*, 5th edn, Brussels: Bruylant, 2012.

Detter, I., *The Law of War*, 3rd edn, Ashgate: Farnham, 2013.

Deyra, M., *Le droit dans la guerre*, Paris: Gualino, 2009.

Dinstein, Y., *The Conduct of Hostilities under the Law of International Armed Conflict*, 2nd edn, Cambridge: Cambridge University Press, 2010.

Fleck, D. (ed.), *The Handbook of International Humanitarian Law*, 3rd edn, Oxford: Oxford University Press, 2013.

Gasser, H. P. and N. Melzer, *Humanitäres Völkerrecht, Eine Einführung*, 2nd edn, Baden-Baden: Nomos, 2012.

Green, L. C., *The Contemporary Law of Armed Conflict*, 3rd edn, Manchester: Manchester University Press, 2008.

Hasse, J., E. Müller and P. Schneider (eds), *Humanitäres Völkerrecht*, Baden-Baden: Nomos, 2001.

Kalshoven, F. and L. Zegveld, *Constraints on the Waging of War*, 4th edn, Cambridge/ New York: Cambridge University Press, 2011.

Kolb, R., *Ius in bello, Le droit international des conflits armés*, 2nd edn, Basel/Genf/ Munich: Helbing & Lichtenstein, 2009.

Kolb, R. and R. Hyde, *An Introduction to the International Law of Armed Conflicts*, Oxford/Portland: Hart Publishing, 2008.

Ronzitti, N., *Diritto internazionale dei conflitti armati*, 4th edn, Turin: Giappichelli, 2011.

Solis, G., *The Law of Armed Conflict*, New York: Cambridge University Press, 2010.

Monographs on the history of modern international humanitarian law

Best, G., *War and Law since 1945*, Oxford: Clarendon Press, 1994.

Bugnion, F., *Le Comité international de la Croix-Rouge et la protection des victimes de la guerre*, Geneva: ICRC, 1994.

Gillespie, E., *History of the Laws of War*, vols I–III, Oxford: Hart Publishers, 2011.

Harouel, V., *Genève – Paris, 1863–1918, Le droit humanitaire en construction*, Geneva: Société Henry Dunant, 2003.

Mattei, J. M., *Histoire du droit de la guerre (1700–1819)*, two volumes, Aix-en-Provence: Presses Universitaires d'Aix-Marseille, 2006.

See also the histories of the ICRC: P. Boissier, *Histoire du Comité international de la Croix Rouge, De Solférino à Tsoushima*, Geneva: Institut Henry Dunant, 1963; A. Durand, *Histoire du Comité international de la Croix-Rouge, De Sarajevo à Hiroshima*, Geneva: Institut Henry Dunant, 1978; C. Rey-Schyrr, *Histoire du Comité international de la Croix-Rouge, 1954–1955, De Yalta à Dien Bien Phu*, Geneva: Georg, 2007; F. Perret and F. Bugnion, *Histoire du Comité international de la Croix-Rouge, 1956–1965, De Budapest à Saigon*, Geneva: Georg, 2009.

Websites

Texts of Conventions and Commentaries	www.icrc.org/ihl
IHL sites	www.icrc.org
Some Courts and Tribunals:	
ICC	www.icc-cpi.int
ICJ	www.icj-cij.org
ICTR	www.unictr.org
ICTY	www.icty.org

Index

Abella (La Tablada) (1997) 110
Additional Protocols to Geneva
    Conventions (1977)
Additional Protocol I on Protection of
    Victims of International Armed
    Conflicts (AP I, 1977)
    applicability issues 120, 123
    background, effects and uses 59
    bombardments for humanitarian
        reasons (Article 52) 176–86
    civilians and combatants
        divide between 127, 139, 140–42
        reform regarding 134–42
    countries not party to 73
    customary international law,
        importance 65
    distinction in targeting 150
    environmental modification
        techniques 62
    fact-finding 193
    non-international armed conflict
        32–3
    pouring formulations into AP II 32
    precautions in attack (Article 57)
        165–72
    principles of IHL 80–82
    proportionality principle 152
    protection of civilians 58
    reforms 197
Additional Protocol II on Protection
    of Victims of Non-International
    Armed Conflicts (AP II, 1977) 29,
    31–2
    applicability issues 112, 114–15,
        120
    articles 39
    background, effects and uses 59

customary international law,
    importance 65
    distinction in targeting 150
    pouring AP I formulations into 32
    Preamble 44
    principles of IHL 86
    proportionality principle 152
    protection of civilians 58
    provisions for NIAC 114–15
    war crimes 60
    written law 39
    applicability of rules 34–5
    articles 16
        reasons for 15–16
    see also Geneva Conventions (1949)
advance warning, precautions in attack
    170–71
aerial warfare 73
Al-Qaeda 150
anti-personnel mines 64
applicability issues 93–123
    material applicability of international
        armed conflict 94–104
    material applicability of non-
        international armed conflict
        104–15
    mixed armed conflicts 105, 116–20
    problem stated 93–4
    recommended actions 120–23
    uncertainty 120
    Wall opinion (2004) 45, 89, 102–3, 195
    see also armed conflict; international
        armed conflict (IAC); non-
        international armed conflict
        (NIAC)
armed conflict
    applicability issues 96–100

basic types 22–3
defined as issue of fact 93
existence of 147–9
humanization of law 12–13, 34
international *see* international armed
    conflict (IAC)
legal principles applicable to all law
    of 76
mixed 105, 116–20
non-international *see* non-
    international armed conflict
    (NIAC)
see also applicability issues
armed reprisals 40, 42–3
armies
    armed forces of States 98
    modern missions 13
asymmetric warfare (War on Terror) 15,
    125, 198
    civilians and combatants, divide
        between 134–6, 140, 143, 147–55
attribution-of-rights approach, legal
    difficulties 18–19
Auschwitz extermination camp 176, 179
avant la lettre (HRL paradigm) 46

belligerency
    adverse belligerent 128, 133
    areas of law exclusive to IAC 37
    definition of belligerents 105
    equality of belligerents principle 30
    intention 99
    recognition of 10–11, 25–6
    reprisals, belligerent 40, 42–3
    rules of belligerent occupation 101
    situations of 13, 149
Biological and Toxic Weapons
    Convention (London, Moscow and
    Washington), 1972 39, 61
Bohemia, German "protectorate" over
    101
bombardments for humanitarian reasons
    (AP I, Article 52) 176–86
    countermeasures (armed reprisals) *in
        bello* 183–4
    responsibility to protect without
        Security Council 181–2

Security Council possible mandate to
    bombard railway lines 180–81
subsequent practice modifying Article
    52 182–3
teleological expansion of Article 52
    184–5
whether a "state of necessity" on State
    responsibility for intentionally
    wrongful act can be raised 179–80
whether violation of Article 52
    accepted 185–6
border incidents, international armed
    conflict 98
Boskoski (2008) 111–13
Bosnian War (1992–1995) 120, 122
Brussels Conference (1874) 56, 125

Central Tracing Agency, ICRC 192
chaoticness, non-international armed
    conflict 32–3
Charter of United Nations 183, 186, 196
    Security Council mandate to bombard
        railway lines 180–81
chemical weapons 61
    Paris Convention (1993) 63–4
CIL *see* customary international law
    (CIL)
civil wars
    classical laws of war 25–6
    foreign military intervention in 117–19
    and modern IHL 14–15
    as non-international armed conflicts
        10–11
    reasons for regulating NIACs 26–7
    Russian Civil War (early 1920s) 24,
        26–7
    Spanish Civil War (1936–39) 24–7, 38
    Sri Lankan civil war (1983) 37
    Syria (since 2011) 64, 104, 120
    see also non-international armed
        conflict (NIAC)
civilian objects
    defined 156–7
    dual-use 163–4
    example 164–5
    prohibition of attack on 156–65
        list approach, shortcomings 158–9

military advantage 159–60, 162–3
military contribution 159–62
and military objectives 156, 158–60
civilians
absence in classical IHL 5–6, 14
aim of ICRC to protect 191–2
aircraft, civilian members 128
categories directly participating in
hostilities 143–4
combatants distinguished 124–55
Additional Protocol I, reform
through 134–42
asymmetric warfare 134–6, 140
civilians directly participating in
hostilities 142–7
enjoyment of privilege/status,
entitlement of combatants to
126–34, 148
general aspects 124–6
mutually exclusive legal categories of
persons 126–7
open carrying of arms 131, 133,
136–7
War on Terror and IHL 147–55
defined 127
direct participation in hostilities
142–7, 155
belligerent nexus requirement 146
direct causation requirement
145–6
persons covered 143–4
subject matter 145–7
temporal beginning and end 146
threshold of harm requirement 145
peaceful 127
prohibition of attack on civilian objects
156–65
see also civilian objects; combatants;
Convention IV relative to the
Protection of Civilian Persons in
Time of War (Geneva Convention
IV, 1949)
civiliter uti principle, choice of military
objective 171
classical international humanitarian law
(1864–1949) 2–12
absence of civilian in 5–6, 14

doubts on possibility of a law on war
11–12
few efforts devoted to international
implementation mechanisms 8–9
gaps in application, increasing 9–11
incomplete character 3–5
inter-war period 11–12
military character 3
military necessity principle,
predominance 7–8
municipal law, predominant weight
8–9
subjective triggers for applicability of
the law 9–11, 93
see also international humanitarian
law (IHL)
classical laws of war 23–6
codification of laws/rules 106, 173
armed conflict 33, 39
phases of IHL 6, 8–9, 20
principles of IHL 77, 82
sources of IHL 49, 57–8, 70–73
collateral damage 91
minimizing, when targeting 168–9, 171
combatants
areas of law exclusive to IAC 37
civilians distinguished
asymmetric warfare 125, 134–6, 140
enjoyment of privilege/status,
entitlement of combatants to
126–34
general aspects 124–6
mutually exclusive legal categories of
persons 126–7
open carrying of arms 131, 133,
136–7
reform through Additional Protocol
I 134–42
War on Terror and IHL 147–55
continuous combat function 37, 144,
152
defined 15–16
enjoyment of privilege/status,
entitlement to 31, 126–34, 148
categories of persons entitled 129
combatant immunity 126
levy in mass (levée en masse) 130–31

members of armed forces of a State
129–30
militas, volunteer corps and
resistance movements 132–4
as prisoners of war 126–9
unlawful 127
see also civilians
conduct of hostilities (IHL) 44, 47
Congo, armed conflict in (1960–1963) 67
Congress of Paris (1856) 9
constitutional principle, military
necessity principle as 83
Convention for the Protection of Cultural
Property in the Event of Armed
Conflict (Hague Convention of
1954) 58
Convention I for the Amelioration of
the Condition of the Wounded and
Sick in Armed Forces in the Field
(Geneva Convention I, 1949) 56, 69,
98, 124
see also Additional Protocols to
Geneva Conventions (1977);
Geneva Conventions (I–IV, 1949)
Convention II for the Amelioration of the
Condition of the Wounded, Sick and
Shipwrecked Members of Armed
Forces at Sea (Geneva Convention
II, 1949) 56, 124
see also Additional Protocols to
Geneva Conventions (1977);
Geneva Conventions (I–IV, 1949)
Convention III relative to the Treatment
of Prisoners of War (Geneva
Convention III, 1949) 56, 60, 68–9,
79, 194
civilians and combatants, divide
between 124, 126–8, 130, 136,
140–41
non-international armed conflict
117–18
see also Additional Protocols to
Geneva Conventions (1977);
Geneva Conventions (I–IV, 1949)
Convention IV relative to the Protection
of Civilian Persons in Time of War
(Geneva Convention IV, 1949) 57

applicability issues 96, 120
civilian protection 191–2
civilians and combatants, divide
between 124, 127
principles of IHL 87, 90
see also Additional Protocols to
Geneva Conventions (1977);
Geneva Conventions (I–IV, 1949)
Convention on Hospital Ships (1904) 2
Convention on Prohibitions or
Restrictions on the Use of Certain
Conventional Weapons Which
May Be Deemed to Be Excessively
Injurious or to Have Indiscriminate
Effects (Geneva, 1980) 62–3
Convention on the Prohibition of
Development, Production and
Stockpiling of Bacteriological
(Biological) and Toxic Weapons
and on their Destruction (London,
Moscow, Washington, 1972) see
Biological and Toxic Weapons
Convention (London, Moscow and
Washington), 1972
Convention on the Prohibition of
Development, Production and
Stockpiling of Bacteriological
and Toxic Weapons and on their
Destruction (1972) see Biological
and Toxic Weapons Convention
(London, Moscow and Washington),
1972
Convention on the Prohibition of
Military or Other Hostile Use
of Environmental Modification
Techniques (New York, 1976) see
New York Convention (1976)
Convention on the Prohibition of
the Development, Production,
Stockpiling and Use of Chemical
Weapons and on their Destruction
(1993) see Paris Convention
(Convention on the Prohibition
of the Development, Production,
Stockpiling and Use of Chemical
Weapons and on Their Destruction),
1993

Convention on the Prohibition of the Use, Stockpiling, Production and Transfer of Anti-Personnel Mines and on Their Destruction (Oslo, 1997) 64
counter-insurgency operations 46
criminal international law
  military necessity principle operating in 91–2
  Rome Statute of International Criminal Court (1998) 60
  war crimes 34, 60, 177
cultural property, protection 58
customary international law (CIL) 23, 25, 50, 69, 115
  content with regard to IHL 70–74
  importance 65–70
  ratione personarum 68
  as subsidiary source of IHL 68
Customary Law Study, ICRC 33–4, 41–2, 151

damages, rules as to reparation 75
Darfur Commission (2005) 194
declared war/declaration of war
  applicability issues 95, 97, 100–101
  declaration in nineteenth century 9
detention, rules on 35
direct participation in hostilities (DPH) 142–7, 155
  belligerent nexus requirement 146
  direct causation requirement 145–6
  persons covered 143–4
  subject matter 145–7
  temporal beginning and end 146
  threshold of harm requirement 145
discretionary jurisdiction principle, military necessity principle as 83
distinction principle 39, 80–81, 141
DPH *see* direct participation in hostilities (DPH)
drones
  human rights law 154–5
  in Pakistan 148–50, 153
  "signature strikes" 150
  US, use by 150

environmental modification techniques 62
equality of belligerents principle, in NIACs 30
erga omnes rights, violation 183
Ergi v. Turkey (1998) 47
Eritrea/Ethiopia Claims Commission 168
Eritrea/Ethiopia War (1998–2000) 66
Eritrea/Ethiopia *Western Front, Aerial Bombardment and Related Claims* case (2005) 70, 72, 195
Ethiopian War (1935) 61
European Convention on Human Rights (ECHR)
  Article 2 32, 47
European Court of Human Rights (ECtHR) 32
extermination camps 176, 179

fact-finding 193–4
  Fact-Finding Commission 193, 197
Falklands War (1982) 184
First World War *see* World War I
Former Yugoslav Republic of Macedonia (FYROM) 111, 113, 148
fragmentation of international law 18
franc tireurs issue, Franco–Prussian War (1870–71) 189
FYROM (Former Yugoslav Republic of Macedonia) 111, 113, 148

Gas Protocol, Geneva (1925) 12, 61
General Assembly of United Nations *see* United Nations General Assembly (UNGA)
general principles of law (GPL) 49
  examples, in relation to IHL 78–92
    distinction principle 39, 80–81, 141
    humanity/humane treatment 44
    humanity/humane treatment principle 78–80
    limitation principle 80
    military necessity principle 82–92
    precaution principle 81–2
    proportionality principle 81, 152–3
  role in international law 75–6
  role in relation to IHL 76–8
Geneva Committee 51

Geneva Conference (1977) 29
Geneva Convention 1864 (Convention
    for the Amelioration of the
    Condition of the Wounded in
    Armies in the Field) 2–3, 6, 189
Geneva Convention 1906 (Convention
    for the Amelioration of the
    Condition of Wounded, Sick and
    Shipwrecked Members of Armed
    Forces at Sea) 2, 12
Geneva Convention 1929 (Convention
    for the Injured or Sick Military
    Personnel) 2, 12
Geneva Convention 1929 (Convention
    relative to the Treatment of
    Prisoners of War) 12
Geneva Conventions (I–IV, 1949) 12, 14,
    20, 60, 100, 117, 149, 184, 191
    Additional Protocols see Additional
        Protocols to Geneva Conventions
        (1977)
    applicability issues 94–8, 102–3, 120,
        122–3
    articles 13, 17
        common Article 1 57, 87
        common Article 2 94–5, 98, 101
        common Article 3 see under non-
            international armed conflict
            (NIAC)
        modern IHL 14–15
    civilians and combatants, divide
        between 124, 126–8, 130
    and customary international law 68–9
    drafting 26–7
    international armed conflict 94–8,
        102–3
    parties to 15
    principles of IHL 79, 87, 90
    responsibility to protect under Article
        1 181–2
    as treaties of IHL 56–8
Geneva Convention (1980) (Convention
    on Prohibitions or Restrictions on
    the Use of Certain Conventional
    Weapons Which May Be Deemed to
    Be Excessively Injurious or to Have
    Indiscriminate Effects) 62–3

Protocol II on Prohibitions and
    Restrictions on the Use of Mines,
    Booby-Traps and Other Devices
    (1996) 64, 72
Geneva Law (relating to the protection
    and humane treatment of persons
    hors de combat) 20, 38, 100, 124
    principles of IHL 78, 87
    sources of international humanitarian
        law 57, 59
genocidal acts 177
Gentili, Alberico 51
GPL see general principles of law (GPL)
Greece
    civil war (1946–49) 193
    conflict with Turkey (1990s) 99
Grotius, Hugo 8
guerrilla warfare 15–16, 138

habeas corpus 35, 153
Hadzi-Vidanovic, V. 22
Hague Convention (1899) 6, 83, 125
Hague Conventions (I–XIV, 1907) 6,
    55–6, 58
    Preamble 7
Hague Convention (Convention for the
    Protection of Cultural Property in
    the Event of Armed Conflict) 1954
    83
    and Additional Protocols of 1954 and
        of 1999 58
Hague Law (relating to means and
    methods of warfare), 1907 124
    armed conflict 38–9
    declared war 100
    and phases of IHL 2–3, 20
    principles of IHL 78–80
    sources of IHL 57, 59
    targeting 156
Hague Peace Conference (1899) 56
Hague Regulations (1907)
    articles 4–5, 13
    civilians and combatants 135
    civilians and combatants, divide
        between 127, 129, 131–2
    international armed conflict 95, 101
    phases of IHL 13–14

principles of IHL 80, 85–8, 92
sources of IHL 56, 59, 70–71
targeting 156
Hamdan v. Rumsfeld (2006) 23
High Contracting Party
    territory of 102, 108
Hostages Trial (In re List) (1948) 86
hostilities
    civilians directly participating in
        142–7, 155
        belligerent nexus requirement 146
        direct causation requirement 145–6
        persons covered 143–4
        subject matter 145–7
        temporal beginning and end 146
        threshold of harm requirement 145
    conduct of 44, 47
    defined 99
    nature of 137
    termination 138
Human Rights Council, UN 194
human rights law (HRL) 13, 153–5, 198
    and Additional Protocols to Geneva
        Convention 16
    drones 154–5
    human rights covenants (1966) 13
    law enforcement 44, 47–8
humane treatment principle 44
humanitarianism
    and classical IHL 2–3
humanity/humane treatment principle
    78–80
humanization of IHL 12–13, 34

IAC *see* international armed conflict
    (IAC)
ICJ (International Court of Justice) 67
ICTR *see* International Criminal Tribunal
    for Rwanda (ICTR)
ICTY *see* International Criminal Tribunal
    for the former Yugoslavia (ICTY)
IDT (internal disturbances and tensions)
    106
IHL *see* international humanitarian law
    (IHL)
ILC *see* International Law Commission
    (ILC)

implementation of international
    humanitarian law (IHL)
classical international humanitarian
    law (1864–1949) 8–9
control
    fact-finding 193–4
    ICRC 191–2
    protecting powers 190–91
general features of implementation
    system 187–9
judicial, limited degree of 188
negative vision of 188–9
normative means 187
possible reforms 196–7
prevention 189–90
suppression 194–6
voluntary means 187
India
    AP I, not party to 73
Institut de droit international
    Resolution on "The Application of
        International Humanitarian Law
        and Fundamental Human Rights
        in Armed Conflicts in Which
        Non-State Entities are Parties"
        (1999) 68
internal disturbances and tensions (IDT)
    106
internally displaced persons (IDP) 191
international armed conflict (IAC) 11,
    22–3, 26–7
areas of law exclusive to 36–8
armed forces of States 98
"attacks" launched by mistake
    99–100
civilians and combatants, divide
    between 124, 142
declared war 100–101
deinternationalized 116
distinction in targeting 150
High Contracting Party, territory of
    102
intensity, no criterion of 98–9
material applicability 94–104
military necessity principle 86–7
peacetime 95–6
proportionality principle 152

reform through Additional Protocol
I 135
territory occupied without armed
resistance 101–3
see also Additional Protocol I under
Additional Protocols to Geneva
Conventions (1977); non-
international armed conflict
(NIAC)
International Committee of the Red
Cross (ICRC) 6, 144
Central Tracing Agency 192
civilian protection 191–2
Commentary 168, 172
control 191–2
Customary Law Study 33–4, 41–2, 151
Draft 122
Final Report to the Prosecutor (2000)
178
Interpretive Guidance 146–7
right of humanitarian initiative 24–5
International Court of Justice (ICJ) 67
Legality of the Threat or Use of Nuclear
Weapons opinion (1996) 71–2
International Criminal Court (ICC)
Rome Statute (1998) 60
International Criminal Tribunal for
Rwanda (ICTR) 33
International Criminal Tribunal for the
former Yugoslavia (ICTY) 33–4,
36, 91
Tadic case (1995) 72
international humanitarian law (IHL)
challenges 198–9
classical (1864–1949) see classical
international humanitarian law
(1864–1949)
complexity and technical matters 51
conduct of hostilities 44, 47
content applicable to NIAC 33–48
applicable to both parties to the
conflict 35–6
and areas of law exclusive to
international armed conflict
36–8
interplay of IHL and HRL 44–8
limits of reasoning by analogy 40–44

similarities to IHL in international
armed conflict 34–5
two general principles 44
written law 38–40
conventional, rules of as CIL 71
and customary international law 68,
70–74
developmental phases 1–2
direct sanction, degree of 187–8
epochs 1–21
general norms 19
grave violations, as war crimes 34, 60
hierarchical construction 87–8
"human centred" approach 13
humanization 12–13, 34
implementation see implementation
of international humanitarian law
(IHL)
modern (1949 to the present) 1–2,
12–15, 93
civilians and combatants, divide
between 126–7
principles of IHL 83, 87
principles see principles of
international humanitarian law
sources 49–74
as system attributive of powers or
a system prohibitive of action
17–21
traditional ideal 134
treaty law, importance to 50–54
see also treaties and conventions
violations by Syria, relating to NIAC
31–2
and War on Terror 147–55
International Law Commission Articles
on the Responsibility of States for
Internationally Wrongful Acts
(2001) 85, 98, 129
whether "state of necessity" under
Article 25 can be raised 179–80
International Military Tribunal (IMT),
Nuremberg 71, 101
inter-war period 11–12, 26
Iraq
Iran–Iraq War (1981–88) 79
US intervention 116

Israel
  AP I, not party to 73
  Israel–Arab War (Yom Kippur War),
    1973 122
  Issaieva and Others v. Russia (2005) 32

jus ad bellum (law on use of force) 27, 30
  international armed conflict 101–2
  targeting 180–81, 186
  War on Terror 147
  whether military necessity principle
    under 89–91
jus cogens (peremptory norm) 15, 88
jus contra bellum (law on the prevention
  of war) 11
jus dispositivum (derogable norms) 88
jus in bello (law in war) 11, 27, 30
  international armed conflict 101–2
  military necessity principle 89–90
  targeting 178, 180–81
  War on Terror 147

Korean War (1950) 65–6, 69
Kosovo War (1999) 59, 170, 178
Kuwait, as occupied territory (1991)
  102
Kyoto regime (1997) 50

landmines 64
law enforcement, human rights law 44,
  47–8
laws of war 12, 26
  classical 23–6, 85, 93
  see also classical international
    humanitarian law (1864–1949)
League of Nations 11, 97
Lebanese conflict (2006) 111
levy in mass (*levée en masse*) 5, 130–31
lex ferenda principle 75
lex generalis principle 84
lex lata principle 75
lex posterior principle 15, 94
lex specialis principle 15, 18, 47
  civilians and combatants, divide
    between 153, 155
  sources of IHL 60, 70
  targeting 175, 180

Libya
  intervention of 2011 116, 165
  NATO warfare 32, 172
Lieber Code (1863)
  advance warning 170
  limitation principle 80

Macedonia *see* FYROM (Former
  Yugoslav Republic of Macedonia)
Mali, French troops in (2013) 13, 32
maritime warfare, areas of law exclusive
  to IAC 37
Martens Clause 7
  armed conflict 23, 39
  modern IHL 19–20
  principles of IHL 78
military advantage 172–3, 177
  civilian objects, prohibition of attack
    on 159–60, 162–3
military contribution 159–62, 177
military necessity principle 82–92, 180
  as a constitutional principle 83
  criminal international law, operating
    in 91–2
  and customary international law 70
  definitions 82
  as a discretionary jurisdiction principle
    83
  as a dual principle of limitation and
    extension 83–6
  as exemption from the respect for rules
    of IHL 84–5
  and humanitarian need 77
  as an operational principle 87–8
  predominance 7–8
  as a principle for both international
    and non-international armed
    conflict 86–7
  whether necessity principle under *jus
    ad bellum* 89–91
military objectives
  choice, causing least collateral damages
    171
  civilian objects, prohibition of attack
    on 156, 158
  distinction principle 81
mines 64

minimality
    non-international armed conflict 29
mistake, "attacks" launched by 99–100
mixed armed conflicts
    applicability issues 105, 116–20
Moravia,German "protectorate" over 101
municipal law 13
    and NIACs 27–8
    predominant weight, in classical IHL
        8–9

Namibia, territory occupied without
    armed resistance 101–2
NATO (North Atlantic Treaty
    Organization), actions by
    Federal Republic of Yugoslavia 178
    Libya 32, 172
necessity principle see military necessity
    principle
neutrality 10, 55
    applicability issues 97, 115
    armed conflict 25–6, 37
    inapplicable to NIAC 38
New York Convention (1976) 62
NGOs (non-governmental organizations)
    64
NIAC see non-international armed
    conflict (NIAC)
Nicaragua (1986) 74, 118, 195
non-international armed conflict (NIAC)
    Additional Protocols to Geneva
        Conventions (1977)
        Additional Protocol II (AP II) 15,
            114–15
        reasons for 11
    areas of IAC law not extended
        significantly to 37–8
    case-law
        Abella (La Tablada) (1997) 110
        Boskoski (2008) 111–13
        intensity and organization in 111–14
        Nicaragua case (1986) 74, 118, 195
        protractedness in 110–11
        Tadic case (1995) 72, 110
    civil war as 10–11
    civilian objects, prohibition of attack
        on 157

civilians and combatants, divide
    between 124, 142
common Article 3 of Geneva
    Conventions 15, 22, 28, 35
    applicability issues 108–14
    content of IHL applicable to NIAC
        40, 43, 46
    intensity and organization in case-
        law 111–14
    low-threshold NIACs 46
    minimum of intensity of armed
        conflict 109
    non-State armed groups, minimum
        organization requirement
        108–9
    protractedness in case-law 110–11
    protractedness of armed conflict 109
    written law 38–9
content of IHL applicable to 33–48
    applicable to both parties to the
        conflict 35–6
    and areas of law exclusive to
        international armed conflict
        36–8
    interplay of IHL and HRL 44–8
    limits of reasoning by analogy 40–44
    similarities to IHL in international
        armed conflict 34–5
    two general principles 44
    written law 38–40
counter-insurgency operations 46
defined 24
distinction in targeting 150–51
existence of 148
future challenges 198
gaps of IHL in 53
general state of IHL relating to 28–33
    chaoticness 32–3
    minimality 29
    unbalancedness 30–32
    versus internal disturbances 104
internationalized 105, 116–17
low-threshold 46
material applicability 104–15
    lower threshold of application 106–7
military necessity principle 86
neutrality law inapplicable to 38

proportionality principle 152
reasons for regulating 26–8
rebel forces 119
State forces 118–19
system of international humanitarian
    law with respect to armed conflict
    107
war crimes 34
see also Additional Protocol II under
    Additional Protocols to Geneva
    Conventions (1977); civil war;
    international armed conflict
    (IAC)
non-occupied territory
levy in mass (levée en masse) 131
North Sea Continental Shelf cases (1969)
    67
Nuremberg Laws, Germany 28

operational principle, military necessary
    principle as 87–8
opinio juris
sources of IHL 65, 71, 73
targeting 182–3
Oslo Convention (Convention on the
    Prohibition of the Use, Stockpiling,
    Production and Transfer of Anti-
    Personnel Mines and on Their
    Destruction), 1997 64
Oxford Manual (1880) 9

Pakistan
drones used in 148–50, 153
Pakistani Prisoners of War (1973) 195
Palestinian occupied territories 13
paramilitary movements
enjoyment of privilege/status,
    entitlement of combatants to
    132–4
Paris Convention (Convention on the
    Prohibition of the Development,
    Production, Stockpiling and Use of
    Chemical Weapons and on Their
    Destruction), 1993 39, 63–4
patriotic warfare 131
PCA (Permanent Court of Arbitration)
    66, 72

PCIJ see Permanent Court of
    International Justice (PCIJ)
peacetime
international armed conflict 95–6
perfidy 40–42
Permanent Court of Arbitration (PCA)
    66, 72
POWs see prisoners of war
precaution principle 81–2
precautions in attack (AP I, Article 57)
cancelling or suspending an attack
    170
choice of military objective causing
    least collateral damage 171
effective advance warning 170–71
example 172
minimizing collateral damage 168–9
refraining from launching an attack
    169
scope of application of Article 57 167
verification of objectives 167–8
wording of Article 57 170
principles of international humanitarian
    law
case-law
    High Command Trial (1949) 92
    Hostages Trial (In re List) (1948) 86
    Rauter case (1948) 86
    Von Lewiski case (1949) 86
general principles see general
    principles of law (GPL)
military necessity principle 82–92
    as a constitutional principle 83
    criminal international law, operating
        in 91–2
    as a discretionary jurisdiction
        principle 83
    as a dual principle of limitation and
        extension 83–6
    as an operational principle 87–8
    predominance 6–8
    as a principle for both international
        and non-international armed
        conflict 86–7
    whether necessity principle under
        jus ad bellum 89–91
unnecessary suffering, avoiding 21, 55

prisoners of war 15, 60
  civilians 139–40
  combatants, privilege and status
    126–9
  Geneva Conventions relating to 12, 56
proportionality principle 81
  civilians and combatants, divide
    between 152–3
  targeting 172–5
protected persons, "humane treatment"
  20
Protocol for the Prohibition of the Use in
  War of Asphyxiating, Poisonous or
  Other Gases, and of Bacteriological
  Methods of Warfare (Geneva, 1925)
  see Gas Protocol, Geneva (1925) 12
Protocol II on Prohibitions and
  Restrictions on the Use of Mines,
  Booby-Traps and Other Devices
  (1996) 64, 72

railway lines, Security Council possible
  mandate to bombard 180–81
Rauter case (1948) 86
realism 12
reprisals, belligerent 40, 42–3
resistance movements
  enjoyment of privilege/status,
    entitlement of combatants to
    132–4
revolving door principle
  distinction in targeting 151
ROE (Rules of Engagement) 67
Rome Statute of International Criminal
  Court (1998) 60
Roosevelt, President F.D. 176
Rousseau, Jean-Jacques 8
Rules of Engagement (ROE) 67
Russian Civil War (early 1920s) 24, 26–7

San Francisco Conference on
  International Organization (UN) 100
Sassoli, M. 23
Second World War *see* World War II
Security Council of United Nations *see*
  United Nations Security Council
  (UNSC)

self-defence principle 89
Solferino, battle of (1859) 5, 51
Somalia, ONUSOM II phase (1992) 67
sources of international humanitarian
  law 49–74
  case-law
    Eritrea/Ethiopia *Western Front,
      Aerial Bombardment and
      Related Claims* case (2005) 70,
      72, 195
    Nicaragua case (1986) 74, 118, 195
    North Sea Continental Shelf cases
      (1969) 67
    Tadic case (1995) 72
  customary international law *see*
    customary international law (CIL)
  definition of term "sources" 49
  opinio juris 65, 71, 73
  treaties *see* treaties and conventions
sovereignty concept, classical IHL 6, 8
Spanish Civil War (1936–39) 24–7, 38,
  122
Sri Lanka, civil war 37
St. Petersburg Declaration Renouncing
  the Use, in Time of War, of
  Explosive Projectiles under 400
  Grams Weight (1868) 6, 21, 54–5
"state of necessity", intentionally
  wrongful acts 179–80
States
  armed forces of 98
  foreign intervention, NIACs 118–19
  intentionally wrongful acts,
    responsibility for 179–80
  members of armed forces 129–30
  recognition of belligerency by 10–11,
    25–6
  "State practice" notion 74
suppression 194–6
Syria
  civil war (2011–present) 64, 104, 120
  violations of IHL 31–2

Taliban 150
targeting
  bombardments for humanitarian
    reasons (AP I, Article 52) 176–86

countermeasures (armed reprisals)
in bello 183–4
responsibility to protect without
Security Council 181–2
Security Council possible mandate
to bombard railway lines
180–81
subsequent practice modifying
Article 52 182–3
teleological expansion of Article 52
184–5
whether a "state of necessity"
on State responsibility for
intentionally wrongful act can
be raised 179–80
whether violation of Article 52
accepted 185–6
civilian objects, prohibition of attack
on 156–65
contemporary law 159
distinction in 150–52
precautions in attack (AP I, Article 57)
165–72
cancelling or suspending an attack
170
choice of military objective causing
least collateral damage 171
effective advance warning 170–71
example 172
minimizing collateral damage
168–9, 171
refraining from launching an attack
169
scope of application of Article 57
167
verification of objectives 167–8
wording of Article 57 166
proportionality 172–5
Third Draft Manual on Air and Missile
Warfare 73
total war 5, 80
treaties and conventions
Biological and Toxic Weapons
Convention (London, Moscow
and Washington), 1972 39, 61
Convention on Hospital Ships (1904) 2
Gas Protocol, Geneva (1925) 12, 61

Geneva Convention (1864) 2–3, 6, 189
Geneva Convention (1906) 2
Geneva Conventions (1929) 2, 12
Geneva Conventions (1949) *see* Geneva
Conventions (I–IV, 1949)
Geneva Convention (1980) 62–4
Hague Convention (1899) 6, 83, 125
Hague Conventions (I–XIV, 1907) 6–7,
55–6, 83
Hague Convention (1954), and
Additional Protocols 58
importance of treaty law 49–54
in general 50
to IHL 50–54
legal certainty 52
modification of the law 53
unification of the law 52–3
written rules, necessity for 51–2
New York Convention (1976) 62
Oslo Convention (1997) 64
pacta tertiis nec nocent nec prosunt
rule 23, 65
Paris Convention (1993) 39, 63–4
Rome Statute of International Criminal
Court (1998) 60
St. Petersburg Declaration (1868) 6,
21, 54–5
Vienna Convention on the Law of
Treaties (1969) 15
Turkey, conflict with Greece (1990s) 99

Ukraine situation (2014) 98
unbalancedness, non-international armed
conflict 30–32
"Unified Protector" operation (NATO)
Libya 172
United Nations (UN)
Commission of Inquiry 111
Committee on Disarmament 61
human rights covenants (1966) 13
peacekeeping forces 117
San Francisco Conference on
International Organization 100
United Nations General Assembly
(UNGA) 61, 73
United Nations Security Council (UNSC)
89, 186

applicability issues 112, 121
bombardment of railway lines, possible
    mandate for 180–81
responsibility to protect without 181–2
United States (US)
    AP I, not party to 73
    drones, use of 150
    and existence of armed conflict 148–9
unnecessary suffering, avoiding 21, 55
Upper Silesia, armed conflict (1921) 24

Vattel, E. de 8
Vienna Convention on the Law of
    Treaties (1969) 15
Vietnam War (1964–73) 16, 61–2, 120
volunteer corps
    enjoyment of privilege/status,
        entitlement of combatants to
        132–4
Von Lewiski case (1949) 86

Wall opinion (2004) 45, 89, 102–3, 195
war crimes 34, 60, 177
War on Terror (asymmetric warfare) 134,
    143, 147–55, 198
war(s)
    aim 83–4
    asymmetric 15, 125, 134–6, 140, 143,
        147–55, 198

avoidance of 11
civil *see* civil wars
concept of war 10
declared 9, 100–101
doubts on possibility of a law on 11–12
law relating to conduct of 16
as legal act 10
of national liberation 134
total war 5, 80
victims of 12
see also specific wars
Weapons Convention (1980) *see* Geneva
    Convention (1980) (Convention
    on Prohibitions or Restrictions on
    the Use of Certain Conventional
    Weapons Which May Be Deemed to
    Be Excessively Injurious or to Have
    Indiscriminate Effects)
weapons, law of 20–21
    400 grams of weight criterion 21, 54–5
    biological weapons 61
    chemical weapons 61, 63–4
Wolff, C. 8
World War II 92, 100, 176, 197
    armed conflict 24, 38
    civilians and combatants, divide
        between 127, 132, 141
    phases of IHL 2, 6–7, 12–15
    sources of IHL 57–8, 61

Printed by Printforce, United Kingdom